Governor Winthrop's Mill, 1650, New London, Conn.

OLD PATHS AND LEGENDS

OF THE

NEW ENGLAND BORDER

CONNECTICUT

DEERFIELD

BERKSHIRE

BY

KATHARINE M. ABBOTT

AUTHOR OF

"OLD PATHS AND LEGENDS OF NEW
ENGLAND—THE EASTERN COAST"

G. P. PUTNAM'S SONS
NEW YORK AND LONDON
The Knickerbocker Press
1907

The Knickerbocker Press, New York

Inscribed to
P. M. A.
and to
The Exiles from New England

PREFACE

In our new historical journey, we shall attempt to follow, as far as may be in a few pages, the ever-shifting border line of colonial settlement—the westward drift of the log-hut across the wilderness of New England in the days when we were still subject to kingly rule.

The story of border life in the North American colonies is more of a romance than an historical study, a vivid illustration of Daudet's aphorism—"Romance is the history of men, and history the romance of kings."

It was in the reign of King Charles that the inevitable course of empire swept on to the New England coast; the great Anglo-Saxon wave crept onward from river-valley to river-valley, the Indian kings retreating before it, ever westward, exiles from the hunting-grounds of their fathers; until, in the reign of "our sovereign Lord—George the Second," nought but the Taconic range of Berkshire stood between the homes of the English yeomanry on the Housatonic and the feudal manors of Dutch Patroons on the Hudson.

The experience of our colonists is unique in the history of nations: in part a peaceful tilling of the soil; in part a strife with a race of red-men, some amenable to friendly overture, others implacable fiends in human form, dreaded, even as allies, by both French and English. Yet the acts of these strange, primitive chiefs changed the history of the Courts of Europe.

It is a fascinating occupation to trace the westward path trodden by our ancestors. Perchance a fine old Norman name, a trifle Anglicized, appears on the passenger list of the good ship *Mary and John;* this shows that its possessor was unceremoniously deposited, plus goods and chattels, on Nantasket Point by Captain Squeb, who, fearing to face the intricacies of Boston Harbor, left the "godly families of Devonshire and Dorsetshire" to shift for themselves in the wilds. A year later, that same sturdy name is found attached to Dorchester land-grants, and shortly appears anew at Windsor on the Connecticut, or at palisadoed Northampton as of a freeman and proprietor. His eldest son elects to carry the name over the ragged Hoosacs, taking up his Province grant in the picturesque valley of the Housatonic. In turn, *his* son passes beyond the New England border to plant our Western Reserve. In the great Northwest to-day we discover four several towns endowed with that knightly Norman name, so marvellously far-travelled since first transplanted by William the Conqueror.

The marked and pretty contrast between the rich scenes of New England's border-land and her eastern coast has been interpreted for me by artists, each of whom has deeply breathed the air of this, his native heath. Likewise I am again indebted to publishers, English and American, and to Messrs. Houghton, Mifflin, and Company for permission to transcribe verses of the poets, who sprang full-armed from this rocky land spied out by their forefathers.

K. M. A.

Belvidere, Lowell,
    August, 1907.

CONTENTS

vi   Contents

ILLUSTRATIONS

Illustrations

Illustrations

Illustrations

Illustrations

OLD PATHS AND LEGENDS OF THE NEW
ENGLAND BORDER

Bash-Bish, Berkshire

The most remarkable cascade in Massachusetts; it plunges 200 feet in all, and leaps on through a gorge, between Alandar and Cedar Mountain, to join the mighty Hudson. Rare varieties of the fringed gentian have been found here by Professor Peck.

OLD PATHS AND LEGENDS OF THE NEW ENGLAND BORDER

THE FIRST VOYAGE OF THE *RESTLESS*

HOW A DUTCH YACHT, SAILING OUT OF MANHATTAN, DISCOVERED THE HOUSATONICK, CONNITTECOCK, AND PEQUOT RIVERS

> "*They goe abord
> And he eftsoone gan launche
> his barke forthright.*"
> THE FAERIE QUEENE.

IN the bright, inspiring days peculiar to spring on the Island of Manhattan, some six years before the *Mayflower* entered Plymouth harbor, and seven seasons after the romantic adventure of Captain John Smith with Powhatan, "Emperor of Virginia," and the Princess Pocohontas, it happened that the small Dutch yacht *Onrust*—"The Restless"—swiftly slipped her ways to search out the hitherto unexplored waters of our Long Island Sound. Unexplored? Yes, unless perhaps the castled galleons of Spain passed through in search of treasure, or a Viking's dragon prow chanced here on quest by sagas unrecorded.

The yacht's name—*Onrust*—indicates the poetic temperament of Adriaen Blok (Block), her builder and commander, who, with the relentless longings of a born explorer, had indeed become *restless*, having been forced by the burning of his ship *Tiger* [1] to spend an inert, impatient winter among the natives of Manhattan.

Friendly these savages were. but looked askance at the huge black dog of the *schipper*—"Sachem of dogs," the Indians called him. Tradition says of the first arrival of the Dutch at Manhattan Island (as communicated to the Rev. John Heckewelder by the Indians themselves) that they took every white man for a Mannitto, yet inferior to the Supreme Mannitto of the red and laced clothes. The whites asked them only for so much land as the hide of a bullock would cover, which hide was spread upon the ground. The Indians readily granted this request and the whites cut the hide up into a rope not thicker than the finger of a little child, and drawing it out this hide encompassed a large piece of ground. The Indians were surprised at the superior wit of the whites, but did not contend about a little land, as they had enough.

" The Delawares call New York island Mannahattanink, 'the island of general intoxication,' because here their chiefs first tasted fire-water offered them by Mannitto or the white-skins. "

---

[1] Possibly Blok's ship was that same famous *Tiger* commanded by "Pretty Lambert" when Holland's "pigmy menagerie" fleet gained a phenomenal victory over Spain's bulky squadron within the very horns of Gibraltar? What an incomparable chapter is Motley's picturing of that valorous day for the Dutch sea-conquerors! "It is difficult for Netherlanders not to conquer on salt water," said Admiral Heemskerk, standing in front of his mainmast on the *Æolus*, "clad in complete armor, with the orange plumes waving from his casque." And following his command the *Tiger*, *Sea Dog*, *Griffin*, *Golden Lion*, and *White Bear* grappled with Admiral Avila's ponderous galleons.—*United Netherlands*.

Now with winter's first relenting, these sea-conquering[1]
Hollanders and Zeelanders were seized with violent spring-

*The Housatonic River and Mount Everett from the Old Red
Bridge, Sheffield.*

*" Thither drifted the Mohican from the Hudson,
Housatonic signifying "over the mountain."*

fret and a burning fever to attain fame by exploration of
America—the magic Unknown.

[1] Toward the end of the great war the Netherlands were first in commerce and held supremacy on the seas.   Amsterdam is described by
Antonio Donato as the very image of Venice in its prime, the streets being
so thronged and bustling, *the scene looked to him like a fair to end in one
day.*—Motley's *United Netherlands.*

The Northern Provinces of the Netherlands scarcely exceeded two
million of souls, but were animated by a spirit which Sir Philip Sydney
said to Queen Elizabeth "is the spirit of God and is invincible."

The *Onrust* piloted her way along the river Hellegat between islands not yet white with flowering dogwood; she escaped unscathed out of the old vixen whirlpool where the waters of East River meet Long Island Sound in rampant swirl, rushing across the Gridiron and overflowing the Pot into the Frying-pan of Hell Gate,[1] as the sailor has it.

Giving a wide berth starboard to the sand bars and spits of Metonwacs or Sewanhacky, "land of the periwinkle" or the "country of the ear-shell" (Long Island), Block hugged the "Great Bay's" north shore, where shifted a panorama of serene meadows and low-lying hills, until was met the Housatonick's mouth.

Close at hand lay golden landholdings, for the *Onrust's* merchant owners in Amsterdam, a new Netherland. Therefore it behooved Adriaen Blok to hasten to surpass in the new West, the English, Holland's jealous rival in the East. America was the meaty bone now snatched at by three European mastiffs. The red flag of England waved over Virginia, the white banner of France in Canada, and the tri-color of a new nation now displayed itself in the region between.

EAST RIVER.

LANDMARKS: Fortified in '76 from the Battery to Hell Gate. Wallabout Bay—" Waal-booght in the bend of the inner harbor "—here during the Revolution anchored the terrible British prison ships; Fulton Ferry—at which point Wash-

The coming struggle for the American Continent was *foreshadowed* when *de Halve-Maan*, flying the orange, blue, and white flag of Holland, anchored within Sandy Hook and, with his mixed

---

[1] The entire East River was called "Hellegat" by Adriaen Blok, its first European pilot, in honor of a branch of the Scheldt. The whirlpool of Hell Gate is formed by the far long sweep of the waves from the Race in the east from Montauk (the first measure of the tide being from Montauk to Block Island) accumulating all the length of the Sound and meeting the lesser tides from Sandy Hook.

ington made his masterly retreat, outwitting General Howe. New York itself daily grows more picturesque, adding graceful bridges at dizzy heights. United States Marine Hospital stands on site of the house of the Catelyn's mother of Breucklyn. Beyond Hell Gate are Buchanan's and Montresor's, or Randall's and Ward's Islands, whence the British planned to attack Washington at Harlem. Opposite Port Morris and Astoria you run between North Brother and South Brother, "who never spoke to each other"; a Lorillard house near Old Ferry Point; College and Whitestone Points with Vliessingen or Flushing; Westchester, the "Neutral Ground"; Fort Schuyler and Willett's Point; Stepping Stone Light; in Cow Bay Shelter stormbound boats await smooth water; Hart, City, and Glen Islands; East Chester Bay; Pelham Manor, named for Dr. Thomas Pell of Saybrook and Fairfield who settled in Westchester; Ann Hutchinson murdered by the Indians; New Rochelle, founded by the Huguenots. All vessels in the Sound run for Execution Light. Outside East River is Hempstead harbor, Long Island, Eaton's Neck Light, the beautiful land-locked harbor of Port Jefferson, Mt. Sinai and Crane Neck, the General Spinola estate.

crew of Dutch and English, Henry Hudson climbed the River of the Mountains, named by the Dutch "Mauritius" in honor of Prince Maurice of Nassau. Saluting the frowning Dunderberg at sunset the *Half-Moon* awoke near West Point amid sublimest scenery in the Matteawan mountains. At future Fort Nassau (Albany) the Dutch vessel was met by her Eldorado—the Indians, laden with countless rich beaver skins,[1] to say nothing of grapes and pumpkins.

Foreshadowed also was the coming contest at the same moment in Canada; there one perceives the noble, striking figure of the Father of New France, Sieur de Champlain, raising the citadel of Quebec with martial form and Catholic faith, "in one hand the crucifix, the other the sword."

Foreshadowed when the words *America* and *Virginia* became the topic of fashion in England. Lords of the Admiralty and Commoners alike gossiped over Captain John Smith's bold expeditions up the Chesepeak, and each placed a venture in some ship bound for Virginia, all Britain

---

[1] Thenceforth the Dutch assiduously cultivated commercial acquaintance with the tribes of the Hudson who "go further than twenty days' journey into the interior to catch beaver for us" writes Miles Van Der Donck, Doctor of Laws, to the merchants at home. The beaver, he says, resembles "the shape of a cucumber which has a short stem, or

had gone mad over a shipload of gold dust, or "fool's gold," (iron pyrites) just imported from the precious sands of the James. What applause, when Britons of "brave heroic minds" set sail, bathed in the molten light of Raleigh's glory and adventure, while Michael Drayton wafted down the Thames a Godspeed in twelve stanzas:

> "*And cheerfully at sea,*
> *Success you still entice*
> *To get the pearls and gold,*
> *And ours to hold*
> VIRGINIA
> *Earth's only paradise.*"

How different the scene on the Thames, on the exodus to settle "North Virginia" (New England). Nonconformists of high degree, Pilgrim and Puritan, stole away as secretly as possible, dreading even the creaking of an anchor-chain lest it betray them and an order of detention be served by the King's Council. Among these were Thomas Hooker and John Davenport, the founders of Hartford and New Haven.

Half a score of miles east of the Housatonick the *Onrust* entered a deep bay—New Haven harbor. Conspicuous above the coast line rose sharply serrated iron-rusted cliffs, a fair valley between. The Netherlanders were vastly interested in the unique topography of this spot and described it in their scenic log as Roodenberg—"the Red Mount Place." These two Red Hills are now famous.

---

a duck that has the neck and head cut off." In those days beaver skins were currency in New Netherland and covered men's heads not women's shoulders. The Indians called the whites "men with hats on" and pictured in beads on their wampum the warrior of the scalp-lock and the Dutch trader wearing a beaver hat. "The Dutch crossed the Atlantic to trade for beaver even as the Puritans came to catch fish and the Cavaliers to cultivate tobacco."—*The American in Holland*, Griffis.

East Rock is tipped by its shaft of Liberty and West Rock
holds the Judges' Cave which willingly concealed the
Regicides, fugitives from the wrath of the followers of

East Rock, New Haven.

Charles, who is yet spoken of as "the royal martyr [1]; a
remarkable episode this in the history of the Puritan town
with laws dipped in deepest indigo.

It has been misstated that East and West Rock are
terminals of that most ancient range, the Green Mountains,
made millions of years before these rocks were deposited:
they are of igneous origin turned into sandstone and the
sandstone worn away. The near-by wonderful Hanging

---

[1] The first Lord Holland used to relate, with some pleasantry, a usage
of his father, Sir Stephen Fox, which proves the superstitious veneration
in which the Tories held the memory of Charles I. On the 30th of January,
the wainscot of the house was hung with black, and no meal of any sort
was allowed till after midnight. This attempt at rendering the day

Hills of Meriden and Talcott Mountain, also Mt. Holyoke
and Mt. Tom are lava flows. Judges' Cave is a boulder
carried down from Meriden and dropped on the ice.

Adriaen Blok sailed on eastward toward the country of
the "Pekatoos" (Pequots). New Haven's West and East

At Sachem's Head, Guilford, in 1907.

The Thomas Leete house of 1730.

Rocks, "with summits finely figured," faded from view,
whilst Mount Carmel, the sleeping giant of the Quinnipiacs,
lay a deep purple cloud on the horizon. Skirting the shore

---

melancholy by fasting had a directly contrary effect on the children;
for the housekeeper, apprehensive that they might suffer for food, gave
the little folks clandestinely confits and sweetmeats, and Sir Stephen's
intended fast was looked upon by the younger part of the family as a
holiday diversion.—*Correspondence of C. J. Fox*, edited by Earl Russell.

of Menunkatuck (Guilford)—to be colonized by men of
Kent under the leadership of Henry Whitfield and Samuel
Desborough—the *Onrust* entered "Connittecock" River;
astonished at the strong current moving downward and the
unusual freshness of the waters near the mouth, Blok named
it Verch or "Fresh-Water River."

Blok entered the Connecticut highlands (at present
Haddam), where the broad stream is compressed to thirty-
five rods in a remarkable gorge of crystalline rocks, the
Strait Hills. Near Mount Tom the Hollanders may have
heard strange earth rumblings like the roaring of cannon
or cracking of small shot; the "Moodus noises" occur
spasmodically at Mackimoodus near the mouth of Salmon
River, where an early writer says the Indians "held pow-
wows with the devil." These subterranean thunderings
have been heard as far as New London. An old Indian
being asked the reason of the noises replied, "the Indians'
God very angry, Englishman's God come here."

Blok saw wigwams of the Sequins at Folly Point, just
below Hartford; had he chosen to land on the east side
(Glastonbury, to-day covered with orchards of pink peach
blossoms) and mounted the hill, he might have had a glorious view from Connecticut's Mt. Tom to Mt. Tom of
Massachusetts.

> On this hill was a fortified eyrie of the plucky Red Hills
> tribe, between whom and the Mohawks was deadly hatred,
> and the legend goes that the Mohawks thrice attempted to
> climb the hill, but the Red Hills rolled logs and stones down
> upon them; then they determined on stratagem. One day
> a "runner" brought news that the Mohawks were coming, and
> the Red Hills gathered the squaws within the fort. After
> long waiting the Red Hills dispatched scouts, who struck
> the trail near Enfield running to Roaring Brook. There
> the scent was lost; the Mohawks entered the stream, waded

down to the mouth, surprised and butchered the Red Hills from the rear. This happened about the period when the first settlers migrated to Connecticut, and Barber says that "the froward child was often subdued by the terrific exclamation, 'the Mohawks are coming!' "

Blok was able to navigate as far as Windsor Locks, then visited Siccanemos, or river of the Sachem, now Mystic; and Little Fresh River, or the Thames, skirting the site of New London. Blok's map, beautifully executed on parchment, in the Archives of the Hague (a copy is at Albany) was our first map of Southern New England. How joyously the Amsterdam merchants placed it before the Directors and obtained a trading charter, with exclusive rights "to visit and navigate" from New France to Virginia, "now named New Netherland."

Blok's map shows that he coasted to Montauk Point, naming it appropriately *Visscher's Hoeck*, touched Martha's Vineyard and the Indians' beautiful *Manisses*, with its great lake and ninety-nine small ones, and extraordinary Mohegan cliffs, to which he gave his name; we call it Block Island, the Dutch, *Adrian's Eyland*; the Rhode Island Assembly christened it *New Shoreham*, and Whittier revived *Manisses*, or the "Little God," the charming musical appellation of the cruel tribe who drove the Mohegans to the cliffs' edge, and watched them perish, penned between the sea and a more unmerciful enemy. To-day Block Island has two guardians:

> *"Point Judith watches with eyes of hawk,*
> *Leagues south by beacon flames Montauk!"*

UNCAS AND THE CHASE OF THE PEQUOTS

"Where erst the red brow'd hunter stray'd
And marks those streamlets sheen and blue
Where gliding sped thy slight canoe."

"Hark, hark, from yonder darksome field
Methought their thundering war-shout pealed—
Methought I saw in flickering spires
The lightning of their council fires."

Mrs. Sigourney on visiting the last of the Mohegans at Montville on the Pequot (Thames) River, Connecticut.

BECAUSE of a quarrel between two mighty Sagamores, Sassacus, the merciless, and Uncas the brave, came about the first sight of the beautiful shore of Long Island Sound by Englishmen, and an instant resolve to barter with the Indians for this fertile coast west of the Connecticut River. It was by guiding the white forces in their thrilling pursuit of the Pequots, who had been driven out of their stronghold by Captain John Mason, that Uncas gained a stern revenge over Sassacus in the midsummer of sixteen hundred and thirty-seven, and caused New Haven Colony to be added to King James's colonial possessions.

The glory of the Pequot tribe was approaching its meridian when the Dutch on the *Onrust* discovered their wide hunting-grounds, which by conquest the tribe had extended, from where their Prince held his court on the Mystick River (Groton, Conn.) quite beyond Quinnipiac to the Housatonic and even farther north into the "Whetstone" country of the Nipmucks (the Oxford lakes, south of Worcester).

These Pequots and also the Mohegans are both believed

to be branches of the Mohican nation who roamed the Upper Hudson, drifting eastward, some attaching themselves to the Berkshire Hills, others establishing themselves about the Thames. Prince Sassacus and Uncas, at first the lesser Sachem, were both of royal blood and entitled to wear the wolf-badge emblem of the Mohegans; *Les Loups*

Shantic Falls, Mohegan, Conn.

"*Not by her sunbeams only, summer's known,*
But by her deepening shadows, fern-flecked stone."

was the name by which the French distinguished them, being the nation of the wolf's-head totem, the enchanted wolf of supernatural power. Captain John Smith, so quick to observe distinctions, describes a savage as wearing "a wolf's head hanging in a charm for a jewell."

"And they painted on the grave posts
On the graves yet unforgotten,
Each his own ancestral Totem,
Each the symbol of his household;
Figures of the Bear and Reindeer,
Of the Turtle, Crane, and Beaver."

The tomahawk of the great Prince of the Pequots, fierce Sassacus, was against every hut and wigwam. He had never been known to bury the hatchet until now, in 1636, he sought alliance with the powerful Narragansetts, in order to wipe out forever these pale-faced Europeans who, the astute aborigine perceived, would presently cover his royal hunting grounds as the saplings of the forest, and become rooted like the kingly oak, yea, even as the tangled underbrush which hinders the red deer from roaming until scorched by the hunter's torch.

The blood-red star of the fierce Pequot fell, soon after the redoubtable Lion Gardiner, serving a company of patentees, built a fort at Saybrook, in the very midst of the haughty, warlike nation of the "Pequttoogs" or "Destroyers" as their rivals the Narragansetts called them.

Driven from their forts at Mystic by Captain John Mason and Narragansett allies, the Indians concealed themselves in swamps near Saybrook. Reluctantly they turned their faces toward the setting sun, the land of their enemy, the great Mohawk. Swiftly fleeing through the wilderness by the great water, the night silence held no terrors for these children of the forest. But the hated Uncas, friend of the white man, following close on their trail, led the *Owanux* (English) with fearful powder and shot.

"How fled what moonshine faintly shewed!
How fled what darkness hid!

How fled the earth beneath their feet,
The heaven above their head!"

SCOTT.

Three hundred men led by Captain Stoughton pursued, some by water, some by

The Medicine Man

A North American Indian from life, by G. Catlin. The Pequots doubtless wore similar feather decorations, although no portraits of the tribe are known to be extant.

land. The troops pursued through Menunkatuck, Quinnipiac, Wapowagee, to Unquowa (now Fairfield), and surrounded the tribe in Sasqua swamp. It was the last battle of the Pequots. Sassacus escaped only to be beheaded by the Mohawks, who, fearing the English, sent his head to the Great Counsellors at Hartford.

This tragedy was the first cause of the settlement of a fair village. Roger Ludlow, haunted by its beautiful fields on his return to Hartford, turned again with wampum to buy Fairfield and Norwalk, leaving forever the Connecticut Valley.

One of the prisoners of war, the clever young Indian, *Cockenoe-de-Long Island* (as his biographer, Wm. Wallace Tooker, phrases him), was carried off to Dorchester by Sergeant Richard Caldicott. The Indian servant's unusual wit was discovered by John Eliot, who first learned of him Indian words, and armed with the savages' musical metaphors, preached to Waban's tribe at Watertown and from his leafy pulpit on Brook Farm, and the Indians answered "with multitude of voyces that they all of them did understand." [1] This showed that "the identity between these two dialects [of Eastern Long Island and Massachusetts] is closer than exists between either of them and the Narragansetts of Roger Williams." Cockenoe returned to Long Island and became a famous intermediary between the Sachems and the leaders of the New Haven Colony.

To the Fringed Gentian.
" *Thou blossom bright with autumn dew,*
And colored with the heaven's own blue."—BRYANT.

[1] Valuable notes of the apostle Eliot's meetings have been contributed by Mr. Wilberforce Eames of the Lenox Library to Pilling's Algonquian Bibliography.

SAYBROOK (PASHESHAUKE), 1635

"We be situated at the mouth of a beautiful river which meeteth the Sea."—Diary of Peace Apsley in *A Lady of the Olden Time*.

THE future of Saybrook (at the blue Connecticut's mouth) once hung on the fate of a small craft, *The Bachelor*, bound from London to the little town of Boston, and scarcely more fit to face old Ocean's frown than a Dutch cradle. She carried as passengers Lion Gardiner, his young Dutch wife, her maid-servant and one other.

A few short weeks before, Gardiner was "Engineer and Master of Fortifications in the legers of the Prince of Orange," and now, through the persuasion of Mr. John Davenport and Mr. Hugh Peters at Rotterdam, he had made an agreement "for $100 per annum for four years in the making of a city or forts of defence" in New England for certain Englishmen of high degree and republican opinions. They were a small but powerful company of patentees, including some distinguished Commoners, with two daring and popular men as leaders,—Lord Say and Sele and Richard Greville, Lord Brooke,[1] later of "rusty Warwick founded by King Cymbeline in the twilight ages."

These noblemen had sternly resolved to brook no longer the despotism of Kings and Courts, but to place the wide Atlantic between themselves and the erring throne of the faithless Charles; therefore, they had purchased of a lover

---

[1] The portrait of Richard Greville, second Lord Brooke, hangs in the collection of Warwick Castle, the seat of his lineal descendant, the present Right Honorable, the Earl of Warwick. This portrait and that of Robert, Earl of Warwick, are contained in Lodge's *Portraits of Illustrious Personages of Great Britain*.

of the Puritans, Robert, Earl of Warwick,[1] his splendid American domain (being the old patent of Connecticut), extending from Narragansett Bay to the South Sea. The distinguished engineer, Lieutenant Lion Gardiner, retainer of the " Fighting Veres " and officer under Sir Thomas Fairfax in the wars of France with the Low Countries, was engaged to build a fort and a city of solid grandeur at Connecticut River, whose rich meadows were already celebrated in England. In this Dream City, their *Carcassonne*, where one day peace, freedom, and wealth should meet together, they saw visions of yonder serene green fields of Saybrook crowded with jostling drays loaded with robes of beaver, otter, mink, and fox, shipped by successful merchants in many-masted ships from Saybrook's creaking wharves.

Lion Gardiner's birthplace was unknown until recently, when his name was found among the retainers of the " Fighting Veres. " Gardiner's fortunes were thus indirectly linked with the fortunes of the Fairfaxes of Yorkshire and Virginia, as he received his training in the camp of an illustrious Fairfax, whose family helped turn the American Revolution in our favor, by association with the Washingtons, so that the lustre of the Fairfaxes has become an American inheritance. Lion Gardiner's superior officer, Sir Thomas Fairfax, became Baron Fairfax of Cameron of the Peerage of Scotland. When being instructed in fencing, dancing, and mathematics in the camp of Lord Vere of Tilbury in Holland, the third and "great" Lord Fairfax—"fiery young Tom"—married Catherine, heiress of Thomas, Lord Culpeper, acquiring title to the northern neck of Virginia. Anne, daughter of Sir William Fairfax,

---

[1] Robert of Warwick was accused of loving our pilgrim Nonconformists too well and not only his house but his pockets were searched for treasonable papers by Sir William Beacham, Clerk of the Privy Council. On the other hand, Parliament created Warwick Lord High Admiral of England, and Governor-in-chief of all English plantations in America.

Collector of Customs on the Potomac, whose home, Belvoir, was immediately below Mount Vernon, married Lawrence Washington, and his half-brother George was much influenced by Thomas Fairfax, a commissioned officer and contributor to the *Spectator*, who, jilted by his lady-love, sought seclusion on his American estate.[1]

It was while engaged on the battlements of the quaint fortress-town of Woerden on the old Rhine that Gardiner met his consort, the sweet Mary Wilemsen of gentle birth, being a sister of Prince Garretson "old Burgomeister."[2] Verily proud was the plighted one of her sweetheart's silver button with the motto, "Long live the Prince of Orange."[3] Especially when they strolled among their acquaintance in the flower-market, where Lion would offer her a pot of Bloomendaal's rarest tulips, that turban flower over which all Holland had gone mad. (You may still find to-day Woerden's flower-market a mass of color in crisp head-dresses and sweet-scented blooms, while Gardiner's defiant, picturesque ramparts stand but as shells of a past glory. Woerden has been twice sacked by the French and little Woerden's surrender to Louis XIV. was so pathetic that the Master Voltaire wrote it down.)

[1] The story of charming Sally Fairfax of Virginia is contained in *Belhaven Tales*, by Constance Cary Harrison. Mrs. Burton Harrison is one of the Fairfaxes and in her New York house are many memorials of them. A picture of the Alexandria town-house of Lord Thomas Fairfax of Virginia is included in *Fascinating Washington*. J. F. Jarvis, Washington, D. C.

[2] Upon the blank leaf of one of Lion Gardiner's Bibles is written cf Mary Wilemsen, "her mother's name was Hachir, and her aunt, sister of her mother, was the wife of Wouter Leanerdson, old Berger Muster dwelling in the hostrade, over against the Bruser in the Unicorne's head: her brother's name was Prince Garretson, also old Berger Muster."

[3] This silver button is reproduced in Mrs. Lamb's delightful sketch, "The Manor of Gardiner's Island," in the *American Magazine of History*, Vol. 13.

One day, when the hyacinths, anemonies, and tulips of all Holland were calling softly in a thousand tones to sweethearts to wander over perfumed, beckoning garden paths, came imperative summons to Gardiner to hasten the new undertaking "at Pequot river or Conectecutt." The honeymoon was passed on the voyage to London. Then followed trials by sea, for these brave and loving souls were storm-tossed three months and seven days, ere *The Bachelor* sighted Hull's rocky head rising above Nantasco's beacon sands, and tacked into the haven of Boston harbor late in November, 1635. Governor John Winthrop the Elder wrote in his Diary: "Her passengers and goods [1] are here all safe through the Lord's great Providence." John Winthrop the Younger, appointed agent of the patentees, impatiently awaited Gardiner at the wharf, having arrived some weeks previous from England with his commission as Governor of "the places at Connecticut river."

A warm welcome was meted out to the celebrated engineer newly arrived from the Low Countries by the many worthies of the little town of Boston. Governor Thomas Dudley, Mr. Haynes, Mr. Ludlow, Sir Henry Vane, Mr. Bellingham, Mr. Coddington, and more entreated him to advise about fortifications on Fort Hill and at Salem. Gardiner's impregnable fort-to-be[1] in the Connecticut Colony was a Godsend to these men whose friends had just gone out with Hooker from Newtown (Cambridge) into the Connecticut wilderness. The magistrates were much concerned for their safety, having received ill-news from an Indian runner concerning plots against the English, who as yet possessed no stout garrisons at Hartford, Windsor, or Wethersfield.

---

[1] Gardiner's freight for the fort included two drawbridges, staple hooks for a portcullis, and a wheelbarrow without handles.

Winthrop had previously sent Lieutenant Gibbons and Sergeant Willard "to take possession of the River's mouth"; they tore down the arms of the States-General which the Dutch had fastened on a tree at Kievit's Hook, changed the name to Point Saybrooke, and began "to build houses against the spring." Grateful shelters these were, for

Old Mill-Stone, Saybrook Point
Said to have been brought over from Holland by Lion Gardiner.

Mistress Gardiner caught her first glimpse of the new home at Saybrook Point, hedged in by drifting snow. ("The weather this morning is cold enough for an Esquimaux purgatory—terrible. What did the old Pilgrims mean by coming here?" once said Whittier.)

The unusual bitter cold seemed particularly vexatious when their first Saturday's baking would not rise above the pans; the young housekeeper often left her shining kitchen to watch the men hurriedly completing the palisade, now and then beating their frost-bitten hands; a sentinel pacing before the gate was ready to challenge with his snaphance red man or Dutch, who had planted a trading station on the river north, their "House of Hope"[1] (Dutch Point, Hartford).

April stripped the lovely peninsula of her ornaments of ice crystals and Saybrook Point put on a necklace of blue water. In early morning's soft air on the green cliff above white sands, Shelley might have found inspiration for his *Triumph of Life*, or Charles d'Orleans for a Spring Carol:

> "*Old Time has cast his robe away,*
> *Of wind and icy cold and rain,*
> *And is in raiment clad again*
> *Of warmest sun and brightest day.*
> *There is no beast but is at play,*
> *No bird but sings the joyous strain;*
> *Old Time has cast his robe away,*
> *Of wind and icy cold and rain.*"[2]

When the trailing arbutus wove its pink carpet of blossoms in Saybrook, Mistress Gardiner looked eagerly across the ramparts for vessels with news from home, and for one flying the English flag, with the promised "300 able men" on board to fortify, till the soil, and build houses, ere the "men of quality" should arrive to occupy the great squares of the future city.

"But," Gardiner says, "Our great expectation at the

---

[1] Whereby the Dutch lay claim to all Connecticut. A message of the Director-General from present New York, dated May, 1638, outlines the Dutch claims. "I, Wm. Kieft, Director General of New Netherland, residing in the Island of Manhattan, in the Fort Amsterdam under the Government that appertains to the High and Mighty States-General of the United Netherlands and of the West India Company, privileged in the Senate Chamber of Amsterdam, make known: That the Connecticut has been our property for years; occupied by our Fort [Fort of Good Hope], and sealed with our blood."

[2] From *Le Temps a laisse son Manteau* by Charles d'Orleans (15th century). Translated by Clara Linforth West and Edward Oliphant.

River's mouth came to only two men, viz: Mr. Fenwick
[one of the patentees] and his man, who came with Mr.
Hugh Peters, and Mr. Oldham and Thomas Stanton [1] the
Indian interpreter."

Gardiner, the diplomat,—as remarkable in solving the
problems of pioneers and savages as the rare Winthrop, who
mediated successfully with kings,[2]—would have postponed
war with the Pequots until the whites were stronger, by
accepting their presents of wampum and skin-coats, for
killing Captain Stone, a Virginian, on the Connecticut,
but the blundering shortsightedness of the rulers at "The
Bay" had "raised the wind" by sending Endicott with
troops thither.   Unhappily, his Indian interpreter, Kitchi-
makin, forwarded boastfully a Pequot scalp to Canonicus,
the Narragansett Chief, who passed the trophy derisively
from Sachem to Sachem, enraging the Pequots to frenzy:
this was the prime cause of the Pequot war.

The maddened Pequots pestered Saybrook Fort like
wasps.   No one dared venture outside the garden pales
to fish, or hunt the plentiful ducks, geese, and turkeys,

---

[1] Thomas Stanton became a famous interpreter for the Colonies and
made purchases from the Indians, notably of East Hampton from the
four Sachems of Eastern Long Island, as intermediary "for Theophilus
Eaton, Esq., Governor of the Colony of New Haven, and Edward Hopkins
Esq., Governor of the Colony of Connecticut."

[2] John Winthrop, Jr., in whom Bancroft says, "the elements of human
excellence were mingled in happiest union," obtained the Charter of
Connecticut from Charles II.   Winthrop was Governor for one year of
the plantation of Saybrook and his granddaughter married Judge Samuel
Lynde of that town.   Winthrop first met Gardiner in an official capacity;
they became warm friends and a brisk correspondence was carried
on between the two island proprietors—Winthrop on Fisher's Island and
Gardiner on his lordship of the Isle of Wight (Gardiner's Island).   Their
letters are among the *Winthrop Papers*, preserved first on Fisher's Island
where the Winthrop homestead held six generations, then by the New
London Winthrops, then by Robert G. Winthrop of Boston, and published by the Massachusetts Historical Society.

because of murders by Pequots. Lieutenant Gardiner dreads "Capt. Hunger"[1] more than foreign potent enemy and expects daily to lose that precious three acres of bread at Cornfield Point, "two miles from home"; the lives of all Connecticut actually hung on those ripening ears. The traveller visiting historic Cornfield Point is reminded of that cornfield in Plymouth grown by the aid of Squanto's fish which saved the Pilgrims from starvation that first winter. Plymouth and Saybrook had good cause to celebrate a Thanksgiving feast at green earing and harvest, after the custom of the tribes who believe Indian corn to be a gift direct from the Great Spirit.

It was at this juncture that Gardiner returned a messenger to the Bay bearing "as a token" the rib of one of his men pierced half through by an arrow to convince incredulous magistrates at Boston that Indian arrows were deadly,— indisputable, gruesome testimony indeed!

> Gardiner had placed five lusty men with long guns to guard the corn. Three foolhardy men disobeyed orders, left the Strong House, and went "a fowling" to their undoing. The savages lying low let the soldiers pass, and on their return loaded with game, shot all three. One

---

[1] Gardiner, in forcible, piquant language warns slumbering government concerning predicaments of new settlements, some being as helpless as babes in swaddling clothes: "War is like a three-footed stool, want one foot and down comes all; and these three feet are men, victuals, and munition, therefore, seeing in peace you are likely to be famished, what will or can be done if war?"

He concludes his relation of necessary stratagems in the blind contest of savage warfare with these lines: "And thus I wrote, that young men may learn if they should meet with such trials as we met with these [at Saybrook Fort] and have not opportunity to cut off their enemies, yet they may, with such pretty pranks, preserve themselves from danger, . . . for policy is needful in wars as well as strength."—Gardiner's *Pequot Warres.*

Polishing Gran'ther's Powder-Horn

escaped," two they tormented" as fiends invent torture. The survivors rowed hastily back across the South Cove with the ill news: the troops rescued a part of the corn before the Pequots razed all buildings outside the palisade.

Gardiner himself was attacked, but saved by his buff coat with a steel corselet and steel cap, a part of an English soldier's armor: it was worn also by Gardiner's contemporary, Captain Miles Standish, the hero of the first and only encounter of the Pilgrims with the Indians. Gardiner scented danger and called to his men firing reeds to come away, but they would not till they had burnt all their brimstone matches. Four Indians started out of the fiery reeds and Sentinel Robert Chapman cried out, "Indians in the marsh on the other side!" Gardiner and his men, almost surrounded, retreated in a half-moon, exchanging shots. Later the Pequots, approaching on pretence of a parley, were startled to see Gardiner unhurt, and believed he had a charmed life, not understanding the efficacy of a white man's coat as a fender of arrows, though they knew well the bark of his musket.

That summer Mistress Gardiner rocked her young child, David,[1] with anxious brow, because treacherous Pequots ever lurked in the long salt grass outside the garden pales. Even the soft lapping of waves on the short sands failed to soothe in the night stillness. Silence seemed ever to warn, to be a forerunner of attack.

The Pequots attempted again and again to use the torch, and then, if ever, Gardiner knew dismay when he thought of little David; he tells us of "pretty pranks" to prevent the savages "from firing our redoubt and battery." Three great doors were placed outside the fort, "being bored full

---

[1] David Gardiner was the first white child born in Connecticut, and, like his father, became Worshipful Lord of the Isle of Wight (Gardiner's Isle). David's youngest sister, Elizabeth, born on Gardiner's Island, was the first English child born in the State of New York.

of holes and driven full of long nails as sharp as awl blades, sharpened by Thomas Hurlburt . . . in a dry time and a dark night" the Pequots came as before, and found the way a little too sharp for them,—as they skipped from one, they trod upon another, and left the nails and doors dyed with their blood.

This episode of the "Pequot warres" is of the color of the old ballad of *Lilliput Town*, in which little Harold's harrow upsets the Giant's calculations: that cruel, crafty fox who, having devoured "the sheep with the wool on their backs—the fowls and the cock-turkey," vowed next to eat the babes "so plump and small."

> "*And every father took his sword,*
> *And sharpened it on a stone;*
> *But little Harold said never a word,*
> *Having a plan of his own.*
>
> *He laid six harrows outside the stile*
> *That led to the village green;*
> *Then on them a little hay did pile,*
> *For the prongs not to be seen.*
>
> *A toothsome sucking-pig he slew,*
> *And thereby did it lay;*
> *For why? Because young Harold knew*
> *The Giant would pass that way.*
>
> *The horses were being buckled in,*
> *The little ones looked for a ride,—*
> *When on came the Giant, as ugly as Sin,*
> *With a terrible six-yard stride.*
>
> *Now, left foot, right foot, step it again,*
> *He trod on—the harrow spikes—*
> *And how he raged and roared with pain,*
> *He may describe who likes!*"

The savage cloud was about to disperse. In April, 1637, the fort was relieved by Captain John Underhill, and May 10th another famous warrior, Captain John Mason, and Lieutenant Seely fell down the river to Saybrook on board a pink and a pinnace.

We take leave for the moment of Saybrook Fort watching daily for English ships, that we may enter the Court of Charles Stuart, in "Our Old Home," out of whose civil quarrels and cruel tyrannies many a sweet and peaceful village in New England came into being. Affairs approached boiling point between King and disaffected nobles. The date of sailing of Saybrook's patentees was postponed again and again, for the god-fathers of the plantation, Viscount Say and Sele and Lord Brooke precipitated open rebellion by refusing in the King's presence to sign his required pledge of obedience. Charles dismissed the two refractory courtiers to their houses, and soon after the Scottish rebellion began. Lord Brooke was appointed general of the rebel forces of Warwick and Strafford, and distinguished himself at Edgehill. Yet our two ambitious colonizers did not forget their god-child over seas, and many a night in the English camp they built castles[1] of independence on Connecticut River,—air castles indeed for them, but realities to later generations. Saybrook garrison watched in vain for its noble patrons detained by embroilments in England.

Reports came that a ship had weighed anchor in the Thames for New England with three of the patentees

[1] Sir Richard Saltonstall had returned from founding Watertown with enthusiastic accounts, and fitted out a ship to feed the infant Connecticut. The Connecticut River was then believed to be the best channel to command the free trade of Canada, a Northern Eldorado, and they counted on Iroquois and Abenakis to paddle in fur-laden canoes down the St. Lawrence, over lake (Champlain) and river (Winooski or Onion River), and follow the Connecticut to the sea at Saybrook.

aboard—John Hampden, Pym, and Heslerigge—and Hampden's first cousin, Oliver Cromwell [1]—all marked men; yet before her sails caught a free wind, Destiny's messenger hailed them with the Council's royal decree, forbidding the fleet to leave England. Had these powerful enemies of royalty left the United Kingdom to embrace America's colonies at this crisis, what history might have written of two worlds, none may conjecture. To-day, at Saybrook Point, west of Black Horse Tavern and just north of where the old fort's "big guns" once swept the horizon, some one will point out to you "the Cromwell Place," reserved for Oliver Cromwell, a charming spot commanding both river and Long Island Sound, and set nigh to other great squares destined for his illustrious compatriots. Saybrook named her first ship of

On Long Island Sound, 1907

[1] At this date, so little was Cromwell known to some, that on listening to his speech in Commons, Lord Digby asked Hampden who the sloven was; and was answered that "if there should come a breach with the King, that sloven would be the greatest man in England."

twenty-four guns the *Oliver Cromwell;* Pettipaug's Point in the Borough of Essex where she was built by Mr. Uriah Hayden in 1775, was attacked during the War of 1812 by a part of the British squadron blockading New London; British launches carrying twelve-pound carronades brought away twenty-two of Saybrook's vessels from river and coves.

Gardiner, desiring independence, purchased the beautiful Island of Mackonake of the Indians and departed to his eminent domain, unhampered by colonial dissensions.

At Saybrook fort a new reign opened, that of Colonel Fenwick's stately young wife, the sunny-haired Lady Alice Apsley Bouteler. In the interval between serious colonial affairs, Fenwick, now Governor, fashioned for my lady's pleasure a walled garden rich in roses, daffodils, and poppies of England, and here she planted seeds and medicinal herbs given to her by hospitable acquaintance in Master Hooker's church at Hartford, where their little Elizabeth was baptized. Fenwick writes to Governor Winthrop of Massachusetts in 1639: "*I am lastly to thank you kindly on my wife's behalf for your great dainties; we both delight much in that primitive employment of dressing a garden, and the taste of good fruits in these parts, gives us good encouragement, we both tender our love and respect.*" Often my Lady Alice was seen with her favorite "shooting-gun" riding with mounted escort, beyond Gardiner's corn-mill and the outer palisade which then fenced off the Neck at its narrowest part from cove to cove, the waters being more nigh to each other than now. The path she followed was the present highway to Saybrook and in sight of "Obed's hammock," an Indian village. Pursuing the trail to Cornfield Point she gloated over hosts of pink marshmallows,[1] though never

---

[1] There are rare wild flowers about Saybrook, the *Spiranthes vernalis* and other orchids.—*Studies on the Family Orchidaceæ* by Oakes Ames, A.M.,

had she tasted the root in confection.   Again, the Fenwicks
paid passing gay visits by boat to Mrs. Anna Wolcott
Griswold at Blackhall, or to the Governor of Connecticut,

John Winthrop, Jr.,
at Fisher's Island,
off Pequot (New
London). The ladies
compared household
notes, for in the
wilderness, the fash-
ion of the latest far-
thingale or dinner
service mattered
little, whereas, in
this m o n s t r o u s
changeable N e w
England climate, it
was exceeding diffi-
cult to discreetly
clothe and feed their
babes.

*The Tomb of Lady Alice Fenwick in the Old
Burying Ground at Saybrook Point.*

Merry Lady Alice was most often seen amidst her flowers
singing blithely old madrigals, while Elizabeth and Dorothy played with her pet rabbits; even staid Dr. Thomas
Peters [1] (who succeeded Master John Higginson as Fort
Chaplain) amused himself in feeding the rabbits as he
took counsel with my lady on church affairs, for the
Fenwicks were staunch Puritans.

---

illustrated in the Ames Botanical Laboratory by Blanche Ames.   Houghton, Mifflin, and Company.

[1] Dr. Thomas Peters, a brother of Hugh Peters (or Peter), was driven
out of England by the royalist forces, and after a short stay at Saybrook
preached at Pequot, now New London.   He acted as physician also.
Noted clerical physicians were Rev. Jared Eliot of Killingworth, Rev.

Colonel Fenwick gave over to Connecticut Colony in 1644 the rights of the old Warwick patent, to pay for which, Connecticut imposed tolls on all exports of grain and skins passing Saybrook Fort to sea: this caused the first controversy between Massachusetts and Connecticut: being carried to the General Court, Plymouth and New Haven representatives decided in Connecticut's favor, whereupon the Massachusetts Court determined to collect tolls from all other colonies for the maintenance of the fort at Boston. Fenwick returned to England to become Governor of Leith and Edinburgh Castle.

Colonel Fenwick left behind forever his sweet English lady sleeping within the ramparts of the Connecticut stronghold; his friend Matthew Griswold, whose grant of land at Blackhall lay across the river's mouth at Lyme, watched over Lady Fenwick's tomb erected by Fenwick's nephew-in-law, Benjamin Batten of Boston.[1]

For more than two centuries after the burning of the fort in 1647 Lady Fenwick's rude yet beautiful monument of Connecticut sandstone stood alone in the wind-swept grassy bluff of "Tomb Hill," until the Valley Railroad intruded on this loveliest of peninsulas the hideous and unsympathetic sheds of commerce; then it was removed with ceremony to the shadowy "yard" above. Sacred cypresses stand guard over the forefathers, and the waves "toll the knell of

LANDMARKS: At "The Point." Site of Lion Gardiner's Fort, burned 1647. Rebuilt on New Fort Hill. Old Burying Ground, Cypress Cemetery. Boulder on the first site of Yale College, begun at Saybrook. End of Water Street is the George Pratt house, residence of Mrs. Amelia Ingraham. Willoughby Lynde-Richard Dickinson house, residence Captain John Rankin. Black Horse Tavern (about 1700), built by John Burrows, property of Mrs. M. S. Potter. Plaster is of burnt oyster shells; old circular fireplace was 9 ft. 6 inches, chimney of English bricks. James Ingraham, Wickstroff House;

Gershom Bulkeley of New London and Wethersfield, Rev. Phineas Fisk of Haddam, and Rev. Stephen Holmes of Pautapaug. Rev. Hugh Peters succeeded Roger Williams at Salem. A step-daughter of the famous Hugh Peters was the second wife of Winthrop the Younger.

[1] *The Lady of the Olden Time*, by Emily Malbone Morgan.

Cromwell's lot, so-called, opposite the Union Chapel, which stands on site of Ayres Homestead. On old "Middle Lane," now Church Street, leading from Saybrook Village to Saybrook Point, stood the first church and house of Minister Buckingham, prominent in the Yale foundation. Several anniversary exercises probably held at this "Parsonage at the Point." Palisade built from cove to cove at narrowest part of Neck. Here from the "Point Road" is view, of "Obed's hammock" (hummock), one of Old Saybrook's three Indian vi.lages. Captain John Mason lived on Middle Lane and married daughter of Minister Fitch of Norwich. Old Buckingham house "at the bend" (about 1725). Property of Mrs. Amy Butler. Congregational Church, present building erected in 1835. Organized in the "great hall" of Saybrook fort in 1646. Humphrey Pratt Tavern (about 1785), property of Samuel Pratt. Major-General William Hart house (1767), property of Washington Berrian, Esq., and summer residence of Oliver Eaton Cromwell, Esq., a descendant of Governor Theophilus Eaton, the friend of Cromwell. Richard E. Pratt homestead (1800), opposite Post-office on Oyster River Road or road to Westbrook. Thomas Acton homestead (1801). Residence of the Misses Acton. Thomas Acton was Chairman of Police Commissioners in time of War Riots in New York, and head of the Sub-Treasury. Parson Hotchkiss house. Site of Captain Elisha Hart mansion, opposite. Rev. Azariah Mather house (1726). The second church building was erected on the Green during his pastorate. The mother of Azariah Mather was Hannah, daughter of Robert Treat, Governor of the

parting day" whilst lines from the great *Elegy* steal into the heart; our American sod would offer new and strange themes for the poet inspired by Stoke Pogis, for here at the Point burying-ground lies a son of Uncas, Sachem, who requested in his will that he be "buried like the white man."

Yonder is a memorial to John Whittlesey, the pioneer, who built his homestead at Saybrook Ferry (there is also the homestead of the Ayres family, who first resided at Saybrook Point, on the site of Union Chapel, opposite the Cromwell lot).

Here rise monuments to Priest Hart[1] and his successor Parson Hotchkiss; the curious, old-style biographical epitaph to Rev. Azariah Mather (a grand-nephew of Increase Mather and grandson of Robert Treat, 1685–1736) ends with these lines:

*"Haveing the Wings of earth
    and Love
And feathers of an holy Dove,
He bid this wretched world
    adieu*

---

[1] The interesting group of stones to the Harts were restored by Mrs. Samuel Colt of Hartford. The oldest stone in the yard decipherable is to Susanna Lynde, 1685, situated on the west side. At this point is a superb view looking across South Cove, to Light House Point at Fenwick;

Colony. Dr. Eliot house (1745) residence of Mrs. William Butterfield. Amos Sheffield house. Richard Tucker house, on road to Westbrook. Upper Cemetery founded 1787. Whittlesey and Richardson houses at Ferry Point. Indian Burying-Ground one mile above Ferry Point on the Connecticut. R. Kirtland - Nathan Southworth house (1799), Deep River Station, residence Mr. Horace S. Phelps. Lieutenant William Pratt sold lands in Hartford, removed to Potapaug quarter of Saybrook. Four of Indian settlements in Saybrook: at Oyster River, at Obed's hammock near mouth of the Pochaug, at Ayer's Point, and Chester.

*And swiftly up to heaven flew.
Disturb not then his precious Dust,
With censors that are most unjust."*

Neither are these all Puritans, as might be expected: yonder slab is dedicated to the fairest of the Hart sisters, who became a nun, and having been brought home from Rome, was buried with the service of the Church of England. Her sister in yonder enclosure was the betrothed of Bolivar, it was rumored, he having been hopelessly smitten with her beauty, as he saw her on the deck of the frigate *United States*, commanded by her brother-in-law, Commodore Hull.

When the Hart homestead was in its prime, Saybrook was celebrated as the home of the seven brilliant daughters of Captain Elisha Hart, their mother being the beautiful Jeannette McCurdy of Lyme. Two of the daughters, doubtless inherited an admiration for exploits on the sea, as they yielded their hearts, respectively, to Commodore Isaac Hull and his nephew, Commodore Joseph Hull. [His daughter Florence was widely admired for her beauty and charming hospitality in her native city, Philadelphia.] Two other sisters married, respectively, the Rev. Dr. Jarvis of St. Paul's Church, Boston, and the Hon. Heman Allen, our minister to South America.

The once merry house was bolted and barred after Captain Hart's death and believed to be haunted until it leaked out that the caretaker kept a calf in the cellar.

Vastly prominent in Yale's foundation was Saybrook's Minister Buckingham. In his parsonage were held Yale's

north is the historic Cornfield Point of Lion Gardiner.

earliest Commencements and the four days' discussion of
the Trustees in 1701. They opened the doors of the Collegiate School of Connecticut in "Back Lane"—now
"The Point" highway, in a one-story building donated by

The Tin-pedler's Cart en route to Westbrook.
On the left is the lean-to of the Lord homestead, residence of Dr. William
Kelsey, a descendant.

Saybrook's large landholder, Nathaniel Lynde, grandson
of the Earl of Digby. When the College was to be removed
to New Haven, Saybrook objected as spiritedly to giving
up her honors, as when Governor Edmund Andros at-

tempted to annex her to New York in 1675. Saybrook
citizens protested at yielding the library until forced by
the appearance of the Governor and entire Council. A
guard was set to protect the wagons provided to carry off
the books, but in the morning they were found broken and
the horses set loose; moreover the bridges on the New Haven
turnpike cut away, On surmounting these difficulties many
books were found missing, including some which cemented
the foundation ceremony in Branford.

"The Point," with its aforetime Wastoll's Inn facing the
training-green, was the busiest corner of Saybrook in old
boating days, when all traffic was by water, and turnpikes
unknown. On the river front Black Horse Tavern overflowed in the open season, for the coasting and up-river
trade obliged Landlord Burrows to crowd his long upper
room with mattresses, while huge logs crackled in the nine-
foot six-inch fireplaces upstairs and down. In the eighteenth century Blague's and Tully's wharves and Doty's
bake-shop swarmed with dark-browed sailors from the
West Indies. The picturesque Tavern is staunch to-day
in its hand-hewn beams, burnt oyster-shell plaster, and
chimney of English bricks, in spite of some two hundred
spring freshets tossing ice floes against its foundations,
propelled from the Crystal Hills of New Hampshire. The
sign of the Black Horse no longer swings to entreat the
traveller; nevertheless, the enchanting prospect across
the Great River's mouth, ruffled by a soft summer wind
from the sea beyond Montauk, compels him to linger
wistfully. Light crafts are passing over dangerous reefs
of sand, renewed ever by the drift of the tides from east
to west through the tunnel between Long Island and "the
main." Were not the Connecticut's mouth filled by sand,
preventing the entrance of heavy cargoes, Saybrook would
be an important seaport. Above Blackhall the spire of

Old Lyme shows itself among the trees. Alongshore are

"Old brown piers,
The haunt of seamen
Spent in years."

Hartford steamers "touched" just below the old Pratt house, the home of Mrs. Amelia Ingraham, who well remembers the Fenwick house burned long ago. At the Tully homestead, now "Heartsease," *The Lady of the Olden Time* (Lady Fenwick) was written by Emily Malbone Morgan.

Mostly deep-sea captains owned these gambrel roofs and bartered fish for corn, ground between the Holland stones of Gardiner's mill. One, Captain Mather, who possessed a just pride in his family tree, commanded the bark *Peace and Plenty*. She was hailed by a vessel, and asked the name of her captain; the answer came back, "Captain Rogers Selden Mather"—the other called out, "We don't want the names of the whole blasted crew, sir."

In the days of cottage prayer-meetings at "The Point" one hundred years ago, a lady directed her servant to go to each neighbor and say that Mrs. Bowles will have the prayer-meeting here to-night. She carried out instructions to the letter: "Mrs. Bowles says the prayer-meeting will be here to-night," and each lady put on her best gown, arranged her chairs, and made ready for the coming of the Parson; in consequence there was no meeting at all.

In the church built on the Green in 1680, a Connecticut Synod adopted the celebrated "Saybrook Platform" of 1708. Some years ago, a fisherman met a farmer driving a wagon-load of whitefish for his rye and potato fields: "Say, Cap., what is this 'Saybrook Platform' they talk about?" "Saybrook Platform, Squire?—why, I guess its that old platform down yonder, they used to clean fish on."

The name of Chapman is still rooted in Old Saybrook.

Robert Chapman, Gardiner's loving friend and Deputy to
the General Court for forty-three sessions, selected the
charming "Oyster River Quarter "for his homestead, having
received a land grant for public service in the Colony of
Saybrook; on a pane of glass he scratched:

> *"In 1636, I here appeared,*
> *In 1666, I this upreared."*

It was Captain Robert Chapman and the diplomatic
Captain Thomas Bull, commander of Saybrook Fort, who
circumvented the tyrant Andros without a blow.

The first minister of ye West Parish of Saybrook—at
a salary of £50 and fire-wood—was the Rev. William
Worthington [1] a grandson of Nicholas whose estates near
Liverpool had been confiscated because of his part in the
Cromwellian wars. The minister's slim salary at Westbrook appears to have been all sufficient as the pastorate
of Dr. Worthington and his successor the Rev. John Devotion covered together seventy-seven years.

The first corn-mill on Oyster River was built in 1662 by
Francis Bushnell, the ancestor of Horace Bushnell; David
Bushnell, born in Westbrook, was the inventor of the first
submarine boat, the *American Turtle*, built at Saybrook
Ferry. By mistake it blew up an American schooner instead of the British man-of-war *Cerberus*, successfully dem-
onstrating that gunpowder could be exploded under water.

A Valley Forge officer, a son of the Richard Lord lean-to

---

[1] The Rev. William Worthington married first a granddaughter of the
victorious Major John Mason, and second Temperance Gallup of Stonington whose wedding is described as being celebrated with "broad
spirit and good cheer" at Mr. Wm. Gallup's ample estate on the left
bank of the Mystic River—"White Hall Farm." The motto of the
Worthington arms borne in Lancashire, reads, "worthy by the virtues
of their ancestors." William Worthington of Hartford and Colchester
served in the (Turner's) Falk Fight. A member of this generation is
the Rt. Rev. George Worthington, Bishop of Nebraska.

(built 1771) on "Oyster River Road," sold his Saybrook
lands to provide shoes for his regiment: Lafayette is said
to have recognized him on the occasion of the festival made
for him at the Pratt Tavern, and embraced his comrade
in arms for *auld lang syne.*

The pleasant white homestead at the corner of Main
Street and Oyster River Road was the home of Captain
Morgan, that one of our winning masters of merchant
ships endowed with a "genial earnestness" which Dickens
says "does me good to think of." Captain Morgan was
introduced to Dickens by his intimate friend Leslie of the
Royal Academy.

> Dickens apprised Captain Morgan that he is the original
> of his hero *Captain Jorgan* in *A Message from the Sea:*
> "Here and there in the description of the sea-going hero,
> I have given a touch of somebody you know; very heartily
> desiring that thousands of people may have some faint
> reflection of the pleasure I have for years derived from the
> contemplation of a most amiable nature and most remark-
> able man."

> Young Mr. Morgan was a constant visitor at Gad's Hill.
> Miss Ruth Morgan is said to be the heroine of Mrs. Warner's
> *Say and Seal.*

North of the Congregational Church (the fourth building)
is the eighteenth-century home of gallant Major-General
William Hart, an original purchaser in the great Western
Reserve of Ohio; hospitable and fascinating it is, with two
huge ovens, one over the other, odd and innumerable
cupboards, ghost-like closets, yet remodelled in marvellous
manner to modern requirements, without losing the flavor
of its history or its original architecture.

The house built in 1785 by Parson Hotchkiss, who married
Miss Amelia Hart, faces also the wide street of Old Saybrook;
at the door opening into the garden, you remark some half-

circular stone steps hollowed by the feet of generations, and the same by which the worthy man entered his old "Church on the Green" for nigh sixty years. Four pews in its gallery troubled much the Ecclesiastical Society. The east pews were restricted to young women and the west to young men, yet the young men and maidens would get together for entertainment. Finally a division fence was built in the aisle, and a law made that "the females shall

e homestead of Captain Elisha Hart which stood on Old Saybrook's street. The home of the seven beautiful sisters.

not occupy the two westernmost pews, and the males shall not occupy the two easternmost pews, and every person guilty of a breach of same shall forfeit three dollars and thirty-four cents to the Society."

Saybrook's importance was early increased on becoming the "half-way stop" for the Boston "post." One morning in 1673, the ferryman of the lower Connecticut answered the horn from the Lyme shore, and welcomed the first regular postman between Boston and New York; he "drew rein" before Saybrook's tavern on Middle Lane and exchanged "portmantles" of few letters and many small parcels with the Haarlem post. Verily this was a red-letter day for every farmer, merchant, blacksmith, and cobbler between the Charles and Hudson rivers; mine host chuckled, for he "calk'lated" that the regular post would bring some patronage to his door.

No such thrill had swept from the village store to the Point wharves, since thirteen years before, when farewells had been exchanged on the Green with Parson Fitch and half his congregation who went out to Norwich to take up beautiful farm-lands bordering the Shetucket and Nyantic rivers; thereafter the postman once a month unlocked the mail-box (the beginning of the New York post-office) at the office of the Secretary of the Colony of New York, and rode to Saybrook, noted for its garrisoned fort, its courageous deep-sea captains, its excellent fish.   (Though in truth, at Saybrook Point that man was looked down upon who ate shad at his own table, just as on the Merrimack River, the hired man's contract with the farmer stated that he should not be obliged to eat despised salmon more than three times a week.)

In 1660, with Parson Fitch, the Saybrook families of Huntington, Larrabee, Hyde, Backus, Bliss, and Budd founded Norwich, Conn.   Saybrook's daring Ensign Leffingwell had won these Norwich lands by saving the besieged and starving Mohegans from the Narragansetts' clutches. Loading beef, corn, and peas into an open boat, Leffingwell secretly entered the Uncas fortress.   This rescue was of untold importance; had Uncas surrendered to Miantonomoh, the mighty plot hatched by the Narragansetts might have succeeded—first to destroy Uncas, and last to unite

Mohawk, Iroquois, and all the tribes against the English,
"the man with the beaver-hat" (Dutch), and the French,
and rid their sacred hunting-grounds of the white man's
moccasin.

Humphrey Pratt Tavern, 1785, Old Saybrook.
Washington stopped here. A ball was given to Marquis de Lafayette in the
ball room, which hangs on chains,

LYME (EAST SAYBROOK), 1645

"I and my forbears here did haunt
Three hundred years and more."
KING MALCOLM AND SIR COLVIN.

"Each man's chimney is his Golden Milestone."
LONGFELLOW.

IN Lyme on the *Great River* you will find the quality of
the picturesque from Whippoorwill to Blackhall, from
Ferry Road to the Neck and the old " North Quarter;" see
first of all that primitive feudal grant, extending wide
and long around her fascinating southeast corner, first
possessed by Matthew Griswold, Esquire, sometime Justice
of the Peace and Commissioner of Saybrook Plantation.
About the time of the sailing of his friend Governor Fenwick,
nigh three hundred years ago, he established on the east
side of the Connecticut, Blackhall, the earliest of Lyme's
family seats.   Sons of Griswold "dwelt here permanently"
on Lyme shore, their manes held sacred, undisturbed like
Latins of old.   As we have left behind us the custom of
entail, the long record of Blackhall as a family estate is
extraordinary and doubly precious.

"Happy he whom neither wealth or fashion
Nor the march of the encroaching city drives an exile
From the hearth of his ancestral homestead."

From the smooth beach of Blackhall, you look inland
into the southern face of a placid homestead of little
old-fashioned panes, built by Governor Roger Griswold.
"Young Roger" is swinging happily on the odd Dutch
half-door watching a cluster of butterfly sails on the far-off
horizon, and dreaming with the determination that when

The Elm Arch of Blackhall, planted by Charles Chandler Griswold. The House of Mrs. Elizabeth Diodati Griswold Lane near Matthew Griswold's Moss-lined Well.

43

he grows up he will be master of a ship and sail in search of Captain Kidd's treasure buried on Gardiner's Isle lying just over there between the prongs of Long Island, or fly over the sea and far away to visit the old wonders of the other Lyme on the English Channel (Lyme Regis of Dorset) which Aunt has read about in *Persuasion*.[1]   It is, however, far more probable that little Roger Griswold's cabin in life will be stacked with volumes in musty calf, and that he will guide some Ship of State as did his distinguished "forbears." Roger, enchained, listens to the true stories of the Manor of Gardiner's Island.   How splendid was the diamond dropped by Captain Kidd in the well-bucket at the Gardiner Manor-house, and the cloth of gold this roving buccaneer presented to Lady Gardiner in return for her unwilling mutton.   A scion of Gardiner Manor came courting at Blackhall in a splendid barge well-manned, and doubtless leaped out on the beach so impatiently to salute his lady-

---

[1] Lyme is said to have been named for Lyme Regis, the port from which the brothers Matthew and Edward Griswold probably sailed for the new World on leaving their native Kenilworth.   It is an interesting coincidence that Lord Lion Gardiner named his island in the Sound for the Isle of Wight, a neighbor of Lyme Regis on England's south coast.   In Jane Austen's description of the English town, one cannot but discover a flavor of the gentle and varied charms of seashore rocks and upland of our Lyme on the south coast of New England; evidently the colonists held in vivid remembrance the contour of the beautiful land of their old. love.   Of Lyme Regis, Jane Austen says:

"The remarkable situation of the town, the principal street hurrying into the water, its walks to the Cobb, skirting round the pleasant little bay, which in the season is animated with bathing machines and company; . . .   the woody varieties of the cheerful village of Up Lyme, and above all Pinny, with its green charms between romantic rocks . . .   more than equal to the resembling scenes of the far-famed Isle of Wight."

Other authorities believe it probable that Lyme, Conn. was named in honor of Lyme in Cheshire, England, the ancestral home of the Leigh family; one Thomas Lee being among the most influential of the settlers at "East Saybrook."

love, Mistress Sarah Griswold, that he stained his fine
top-boots in a salt ripple. .

Roger points out to you the fern-lined ghostly well of
Matthew Griswold close to the present spacious homestead
on the old site of Matthew Griswold's home to which the
Elm Lane leads.

On Sabbath mornings it must have been a charming sight

The Governor Roger Griswold Homestead, Blackhall, Lyme.

to see the many sons and daughters from the Griswold
homesteads and escorts with loaded muskets, standing on
the steps ready to mount pillion and saddle and follow
Indian file with due caution the Nehantic trail up to the
log meeting-house, to sit under the Rev. Moses Noyes [1]
who had led his little flock over from Saybrook [2] about 1666.

[1] The Rev. Moses Noyes was of a family of divines, "to all the
country dear." His father was the pioneer, Rev. James Noyes of Newburyport. His grandson, Judge William Noyes, was a Puritan autocrat. His four sons never presumed to ride by his side, but at a respectful
distance. He would allow no traveller to pass through Lyme on the
Sabbath.

[2] Saybrook and East Saybrook agreed on "a loving parting." The

Would that Hawthorne in his wonderful way had made us reverent guests in the Old Manse of ye venerable pastor of "Ye Prime Society of Lyme" as in that of Concord! and would that he might thus here immortalize the pure and rigorous atmosphere of The Street with its early homes of jurists and lawmakers, moulders of the Nation! There is no doubt that the outer shell of Lyme influenced the destiny of the pioneer, speaking to him everywhere of the Infinite and of good things provided for him who will but toil.

Standing on the sunny shore of the Connecticut's mouth looking east, the ancient Griswold domain spreads

Memorial Bridge across Black Hall River, erected by Mrs. William Lane to Charles Griswold Lane.

Soundward in sweet, shelving beaches cut by jagged rocks; green, tillable land runs down into the very sands, and Sowánshine, the South Wind, laughs long, because her

Lyme committee who signed the parting covenant were Matthew Griswold, Reinold Marvin, Richard Smith, William Waller, John Lay, Sen'r. The township patent was ratified unto Griswold, Mr. Wm. Ely and others.

On the Banks of Lieutenant River

"*Oh, father's gone to market-town, he was up before the day,*
And Jamie's after robins and the man is making hay,
And whistling down the hollow goes the boy that minds the mill,
While mother from the kitchen-door is calling with a will:
'*Polly!—Polly!—the cows are in the corn!*
Oh! where's Polly?'"—GILDER.

47

blustering rival Chékesu is barricaded on the northwest by the triangle of the River Range and of Meeting-House Hills which stretch away from the mouth of Duck River, one of Lyme's small tidal bayous, as the Southerner would call her little rivers; under Sowasáyeu's soft breath frosts melt rapidly in the Moon of Bright Nights and return tardily.

Half-way to New London Light, the Giant's Neck, like that of Alice in Wonderland, lengthens out remarkably and terminates in a natural flat rock wharf on three sides of which vessels of fair tonnage may ride. Giant's Neck is *The Golden Milestone*, so to speak, of the family of the "New York Griswolds," founded by the Rev. George Griswold. His grandsons, Nathaniel and George Griswold of New York, were distinguished merchants in the China trade.

Bride Brook or Sunkipaug, the original west bound of New London, was the scene of a pretty colonial wedding. In 1646 a young couple of Saybrook were to be married. The magistrate being absent, word was sent to Governor John Winthrop at New London who met the wedding party at Bride Brook on the boundary, dismayed at the breaking ice in the impassable stream. Winthrop pronounced them man and wife on his side, the twain promised to love, honor, and obey on the other, and sledded back to Saybrook rejoicing.

All the land between Bride Brook and Niantic Bay was in dispute for years: in 1671 Lyme and New London determined each to mow the grass on the debatable meadows: the swinging of scythes and sickles ended in blows and a warrant for Matthew Griswold. Tradition says that champions were selected and the stalwart son of Matthew Griswold won for Lyme. This was Matthew Griswold the second. The Griswolds were very tall, powerful men. The present Matthew Griswold, of the 7th generation, late member of Congress from Erie, Pennsylvania, and six of his sons are all some inches over six feet tall.

Along the Connecticut in upper Lyme, Richard and Thomas Lord, sons of the pioneer, reaped crop after crop and acquired wealth, exhausting the soil. (Now these charming fields are more picturesque than ever, if less edible, with their billowy crop of Indian posy so soothing in pillows.)

The family of Lord arrived in the *Elizabeth and Ann*, and being courageous, root and branch, journeyed with Thomas Hooker [1] to Hartford in the Connecticut Valley, compelling the wilderness to blossom like a rose on Lord's Hill, and from that day when the Lords and their neighbors, Governor Wyllys, Mr. Goodwin, and Mr. Matthew Allyn, planted the manorial farms of Hartford, the town has been noted for its glorious gardens.

William Lord was of the fibre of such pioneers as Winthrop, Higginson, Whittlesey, Griswold, and Kirtland and was loved by the aborigines as was Lion Gardiner: he became a large landholder in Saybrook and Lyme, the Chief Chapeto having consented to sell him large holdings because of his friendship for him. He also purchased the Indian's *Paugwonk*, the present town of Salem, for the

---

[1] This adventure was more remarkable, as many were persons of figure who in England had lived in affluence and delicacy, strangers to fatigue and danger.

Captain Richard Lord of Newtown (Cambridge), 1632, an original proprietor of Hartford, commanded the first Connecticut troop of horse and distinguished himself in Indian wars. Captain Lord was the richest man in the colony and with Captain Pyncheon was relied on to secure the regicides Whalley and Goffe for trial in England.

The heirs of Captain Richard Lord received by his will Holland linen, armor, " Salmon-nets, Dear Skins, a new damask Tabble-cloth," and land in London. His wife, Mrs. Sarah Lord, left her wearing apparel thus:

"I give my daughter Haynes my silk gown, my mohair petticoat and my red 'parrigon' petticoat.

" I give to my daughter Lord my best broad cloth gown and my red broad cloth petticoat.

" I do give to Hannah Ingersall (alias Kellsey) my dark cloth gown, my hay're coll'rd tammy petticoate and my green apron. "

government. Chapeto's deed to William Lord is one of the vivid documents of colonial history.[1]

Traverse the coast from Saybrook to New London and Watch Hill—over all is color, delicate, marvelous color: the sunlight has a brilliancy, the air a transparency, and at sun-setting, clouds, sea, and sky take on intimate, exquisite hues. Standing on Old Lyme's Watch Rock of the War of 1812 which commands the Connecticut, watch the violet and rosy tints make luminous the waters meeting dark rich foliage on strangely shaped hummocks—or "hammocks" as the old sea-dogs call these rounded landmarks.

Everywhere in sequestered nook or on the "King's Highway" of the colonial town sprout white umbrellas like huge mushrooms.

Miss Florence Griswold's house[2] on "The Street" possesses the rarest of door panels called into life by the brushes of those artists who have dwelt herein many a long, sweet summer. How curious to recall by contrast the "good old times" of the first century of our Republic when, if the grim Puritan thought of Art at all, it was as a vanity of a luxurious life: he believed the imaginative quality to be a wile of the devil, even to adorn the person was unpardonable, a waste of time which could much better be employed at

---

[1] A very old copy of Chapeto's deed is possessed by Mrs. Salisbury and included in the *Family Histories and Genealogies of Lyme* by Edward Elbridge Salisbury and Evelyn McCurdy Salisbury.

[2] This house in which Lyme's artist colony congregates has been rendered even more celebrated in 1907 in the painting by Metcalf, *May Night*, which received the first prize at the Corcoran Gallery exhibition. It hangs in the Pittsburg Art Gallery. Recent artists associated with the house include, Childe Hassam, William Howe, Gifford Beale, Henry R. Poore, Edward Rook, Alphonse Jongers. The discoverer of Lyme's possibilities for art was Henry W. Ranger and later Frank Vincent Du Mond brought his school here. Many others have established studios with homes, Louis Paul Dessar, Jules Turcas, Miss Saunders, Arthur Dawson, and the September exhibition is an event.

foddering the cows or building schoolhouses. Of some of
Lyme's rocky uplands,—adorable material for the artist—
the practical old-timer would remark: "Stone's got a pretty
heavy mortgage on thet ther land."

*e William Noyes House, built in 1818, Residence of Miss Florence Griswold.
e of "The Artists." Rendered even more celebrated in 1907 in the painting of
Metcalf—May Night.*

Connecticut's Colonel John Trumbull, artist particular
of the American Revolution, who has left to us in the famous
gallery of Yale the greatest military portrait of Washington,
whose aid-de-camp he was, bluntly said to an aspirant to
fame, "You had better learn to make shoes or dig potatoes

than become a painter in this country." On this question also Benjamin Franklin penetrated the future; he writes from London in 1771 to Peale; "*The arts have always*

Whitefield Rock, in the Garden of Charles H. Ludington, Esq.; earlier the Lot of the Rev. Jonathan Parsons. The preaching of his friend White- field caused dissension in the Lyme Church, and Dr. Parsons departed to Newburyport.

travelled westward: and there is no doubt of their flourishing hereafter on our side of the Atlantic, as the number of wealthy inhabitants shall increase who shall be able and willing suitably

*to reward them, since, from several instances, it appears that
our people are not deficient in genius."*

In one of the fascinating Art scrap-books, bequeathed
by W. H. Huntington to the Metropolitan Museum are
these lines under a Medallion of Franklin:

> *"Il a ravi le feu des Cieux*
> *Il fait fleuri les Arts en des clîmats sauvages*
> *L'Amérique le place à la tête des sages."*

Studio and House of Allen B. Talcott, Neck Road, overlooking the Connecticut River.

Franklin's prophecy is fulfilled throughout America; in
his beloved city stands the Philadelphia Academy; here in
Connecticut the Yale Gallery and the future Museum of Fine
Arts at Hartford, the gift to his native town of J. Pierpont
Morgan, Esq., are both established on Puritanical soil.

What an indisputable voucher for the fetching loveliness of Lyme is its ever-increasing colony of painters. In the lower Connecticut Valley the uplands are full of surprises and everywhere you may go, you will see about you pictures which would drive most artists wild with joy. Follow up the old "Street" from the church and McCurdy house, passing the Mather homestead, the old home of Chief Justice Henry M. Waite of Connecticut and his son, Chief Justice Morrison R. Waite, the Phœbe Griffin Noyes Library; turn to the left and cross the sapphire Lieutenant River (one of Lyme's five little rivers rippling deep or shallow as the tide flows and ebbs) and cross the low causeway dividing the lush meadow through which the stream plays hide-and-seek beneath the ripe smothering emerald grasses. Suddenly you come upon the broad Connecticut: north, bending lovingly close to the "Great River," are the homes and studios of Carleton Wiggins, Allen B. Talcott, and Clark G. Voorhees, within view of the pleasant white village of Essex on the opposite shore.

"Up river" is the wild, ancient tract of Tantummaheag bequeathed to Lieutenant Richard Lord, son of William Lord, "bounded west by the Cove, East by my brother Thomas Lord's land, South by Tantomehege brook." At the Neck the hay-fields are edged by rugged rocks, formerly the quarries of the Lords and of "John Coult,[1] Gentleman," who built homesteads hereabouts.

In the homestead of Lieutenant Richard Lord on the Neck was born the high-spirited and beautiful Ann Lord[2] who vowed to "jump out of the window" if not allowed

---

[1] Ancestor of the Colts of Hartford. Mrs. Samuel Colt the philanthropist, Mrs. Evelyn MacCurdy Salisbury of New Haven and Lyme, were among the founders of the Society of The Colonial Dames of Connecticut.

[2] Ann Lord's sister Elizabeth married Jared Eliot, Jr., son of the Rev. Jared Eliot of Killingworth, now Clinton, Conn., a great-grandson of the apostle Eliot.

to marry the man of her choice, the young Scotch-Irish ship merchant, John McCurdy. Her handsome "setting out" of mahogany and china remains in their homestead to this day. In recompense for stores lost in the burning of New London, John McCurdy—one of the governing committee in charge of the Revolutionary coastguard—received a grant in Ohio—Lyme of the Western Reserve.

> A daughter of John McCurdy married the Rev. Henry Channing of New London in whose family were spent the early days of William Ellery Channing; he probably often wandered over the picturesque rocks at the Neck, the home of her grandfather. Most appropriately the Channing Memorial Church was quarried out of these rocks of porphyritic granite, the gift of a nephew of Mrs. Channing, Judge Charles Johnson McCurdy, Chargé d'Affaires at Vienna, 1851–2.

It was midsummer, 1778; the American Revolution was almost at boiling point. Above stacked arms, under shadowy elms on the Green of Old Lyme, waved the white *fleur-de-lys*, and our shining yearling, the Stars and Stripes, first flung in united strength and beauty at Brandywine. Mingling with the rugged buff and blue were courtly and brilliant uniforms surmounted by the *tricorne*, the sword suspended by a knot of the blue ribbon of Saint Michel, and the Marquis de Lafayette in yellow satin waistcoat, the red and white trimmings of the blue coat fastened with gold buttons.

Major-General Lafayette had ordered a night's rest in Lyme for Varnum's and Glover's brigades on their quickstep to join the land forces of General Sullivan and Admiral D'Estaing's six frigates and twelve ships of the line in the recapture of the island of Rhode Island.

We have discovered no list of these French officers, yet doubtless De Gimat was there, the intimate friend and aid-de-camp of the Marquis, and chivalric Armand de la Rouerie, familiarly "Colonel Armand"; also De Pontgibaud, for he had succeeded in escaping from Château de Pierre-en-Cise, in order to fly to the United States, after having been deprived of his liberty like others of the young nobility by a *lettre-de-cachet*.

The McCurdy House, built about 1730, Property of Mrs. Evelyn McCurdy Salisbu
Here Washington was entertained April 9, 1776, and Lafayette, July 27, 1778.
The north chamber is preserved as of yore.

In the north chamber of yonder colonial house, Lafayette slept, accepting the hospitality of Lyme's Scotch-Irish patriot John McCurdy, he who had so vigorously circulated revolutionary broadsides written by Sons of Liberty, and moreover had dared to publish in the *Connecticut Gazette* the rebellious document against the Stamp Act written by Lyme's "incomparable Stephen Johnson," thus, as Mrs. Lamb says, "fanning the flame of Liberty with his broad purse."[1]

Lafayette much appreciated his reception in the country towns, and enthusiastically expressed his pleasure in the following letter to his valorous comrade of noble lineage, his beautiful young wife, the unselfish Adrienne de Noailles. She was first in applauding his course, his relatives being furious at his crossing the Atlantic to aid America. The devoted and anxious husband sent off this letter to Madame Lafayette in three parts, in three separate vessels, challenging every vicissitude—pirates, gales, English frigates:

"Everything is very like England excepting there is more simplicity here. . . . The American ladies are very pretty, very simple, and delightfully clean. Cleanliness prevails universally with the greatest fastidiousness, . . . The inns are very different from those in Europe; the innkeeper and his wife sit down at table with you, do all the honors of a good meal, and when you go you pay without any bargaining. If you don't want to go to an inn, you find country houses, where it is enough to be a good American to find a reception such as Europe only gives to a friend. . . . I hope that for my sake you will become a good American. It is a sentiment fit for noble hearts; for the happiness of America is linked to the happiness of mankind. . . . People must think I am very happy, but you are not here, dear heart." [2]

---

[1] Martha J. Lamb on the *Historic Home of Judge Charles Johnson McCurdy*, Magazine of American History, vol. 26.

[2] *Household of the Lafayettes*, by Edith Sichel: Archibald, Constable, & Co. and The MacMillan Company.

The ardent young Marquis, now making his first entrance into New England, was the cynosure of all eyes, just

*The First Congregational Church of Lyme, at the corner of The Street and Ferry
Lane. Erected, 1807. Organized, 1666. Burned, July 3, 1907.*

as on his second visit to Lyme after the vicissitudes of his
beloved France had pencilled lines in the face without
shrivelling the heart.

Enlisted as a volunteer at his own expense[1] and wounded

---

[1]After some years Washington encountered his opportunity to return

at Brandywine,[1] Washington and Lafayette had just
wintered together at Valley Forge, training uncouth volunteers and sympathizing with shoeless troops, and the man
of forty-five came to love as his own child this generous
boy so royally impulsive yet discreet. Rumors of the
romantic star that ruled his career, now luminous, preceded
him.

All in one moment Lafayette had decided to fly to aid
America. He first heard of the declaration of American
independence at a dinner given by his commander, the old
Marshal de Broglie. The guest of honor, the Duke of
Gloucester—then in disgrace with his brother, George III.,

---

in part our debt to Lafayette. On the tidings of his imprisonment at
Rochefort in 1792, Washington's first thought was the consolation of
the Marchioness and he wrote:

*"If I had words that could convey to you an adequate idea of my feelings
on the present situation of the Marquis Lafayette, this letter would appear
to you in a different garb. The sole object in writing to you now, is to inform
you that I have deposited in the hands of Mr. Nicholas Van Staphorst of
Amsterdam, two thousand three hundred and ten guilders . . . subject
to your orders.*

*". . . This sum is, I am certain, the least I am indebted for services
rendered me by the Marquis de Lafayette, of which I have never yet received
the account. I could add much, but it is best, perhaps, that I should say
little on this subject. Your goodness will supply my deficiency."*

[1]Fifty years later, when Mrs. Rives, wife of our minister to France, paid
a visit to Lafayette at Lagrange, she discovered that *the flag presented to
the General by the officers of the Brandywine, formed the tapestry of the principal salon, in an appropriate drapery of the picture of Washington.* Samuel
Topliff of Boston, in his pleasant and spicy travels was also impressed with
General Lafayette's interest in all things American. Every room in the
chateau "contained some memorial of America." On a fine green spot
was the beautiful race boat presented by the Whitehall boatmen of New
York. On displaying his farm, Lafayette related that an English nobleman had observed concerned a certain superior pig "that the General
could boast of having the finest one England could produce. 'Excuse
me,' said the General . . . . 'I must inform you it came from Baltimore.'"
Topliff's Travels. Edited by his granddaughter, Ethel Stanwood Bolton.
—The Boston Athenæum.

on account of his marriage,—regaled the party with the story of the Boston Tea Party and the denoument: Lafayette was afire for Freedom, and opposition from his king only incited him to ask aid from Franklin, who put him in the way of fitting out a ship; the Marquis escaped in the disguise of a postilion, and it is said he was recognized by the pretty maid of an inn, who nevertheless told the officers pursuing that Lafayette had gone by in a carriage.

Sailing from Bordeaux the youth landed at Charleston, S. C., where Von Hüger welcomed him. Lafayette's devoted comrades, the Comte de Ségur and Vicomte de Noailles, postponed accompanying him only because they had no money. It is said that Lafayette arrived one morning at seven while the Count was still in bed. "Wake up," he cried. "I am going to America to fight for Freedom. Nobody knows it as yet, but I love you too much not to tell you"; De Ségur lost not a minute in leaping out of bed and saying he would go too.[1]

Lafayette encountered reminders of the practical Franklin continually in New England; he had first seen the philosopher when page to the Queen at the scintillating French Court, where this youth stood a little aside and pondered, whilst his friends of Young Paris danced the minuet and picked up the coquettish fan. Marie Antoinette encouraged his originality. In the midst of the *Ancien Régime* enters the Envoy with black coat and unpowdered hair and the novel idea of freedom. The young Société d' Épée aux Bois, to the disgust of the old courtiers, embraced with fervor the plain manners of Benjamin Franklin in high marten cap, declaring they would discard toupées and adopt fustian. Every man of quality possessed a medallion of Franklin on a snuff-box or rapier.

---

[1] *The Household of the Lafayettes*, by Edith Sichel.

Rogers Lake, formerly Big Pond, Lyme

LANDMARKS: Rivers—Lieutenant, Duck, Black Hall, Mile Creek, Four Mile. Lyme once included Old Lyme, Lyme, East Lyme, part of Hadlyme. First settlers: Griswolds, Marvins, Elys, Lords, Lays, Noyes, Lees, De Wolfs, Champions, and others. *The Street*; 1 1-2 miles long, beginning at south end: Rev. Jonathan Parsons house and Parsons Tavern stood on site Charles Henry Ludington residence. First Congregational Church. McCurdy homestead, built not later than 1730. Purchased by John McCurdy, 1753. Black walnut trees planted before the Revolution. Mather homestead, (1790), now Parsonage of Congregational Church. The ancient and learned family to which Increase and Cotton Mather belonged. Boxwood School. Chief Justice Henry M. Waite house, residence Mrs. Joseph Perkins. The Noyes Library, on site of Noyes homestead, erected by Charles H. Ludington and Joseph Noyes Ludington in memory of Phœbe Griffin Noyes, the educator, daughter of Joseph Lord; address on Presentation Day made by Daniel Coit Gilman. Mrs. Noyes had one of the first art schools in the country. Gen. Sheldon-Joseph Lord house, Deming house (1729)—ancestors of the Demings and Champions of Connecticut. Reuben Champion built large vessels on the Connecticut. Judge Charles Johnson McCurdy house (1817). Noyes house (1790), summer residence of the Rev. Dr. William T. Sabine of New York. House of Judge Walter Chadwick Noyes (author on Trusts) on site Manse of Rev. Moses Noyes. On L'eutenant River, vessels built and West India trade carried on by

On Meeting-House Hill is one of the celebrated Franklin milestones[1] which in 1776 saw Washington pass into Lyme (where he spent the night of April 10th) on his way from Cambridge after the British had evacuated Boston; and also saw these French allies march on to Rhode Island. Perhaps General Lafayette saluted this little wayside post planted here by his philosopher friend, Franklin, when Postmaster-General of the Colonies; Franklin measured the miles by a machine of his own invention attached to his chaise, the ancestor of our cyclometer.

A story of Franklin when on one of his frequent journeys over the post-road from Philadelphia to Boston is told by Shepherd Tom Hazard. Arrived at an inn not far from Lyme one frosty night, Franklin found every inch of the blazing log pre-empted by village politicians swapping news, and thereupon ordered a peck

[1] On the old Bowery is a Franklin stone which reads, " 2½ miles to New York." It would seem when one reviews the mechanical and intellectual devices turning our wheels faster and faster that the earliest suggestions on all things which add to comfort were offered by Washington and Franklin. Franklin founded the first circulating library and the first fire insurance company in America.

John McCurdy and William Neilson of New York followed by Samuel and James Mather. " The Neck"; Lord house, summer residence of Robert C. Hall, Esq., of Pittsburg. Dr. William Lord house, property of James N. Brown, Esq., of Brooklyn. The Coult homesteads. Jumping Rocks, 80 ft. above valley. The " Stone house," chaotic mass of caverns, quarries of red porphyritic granite. McCurdy Avenue leads to Black Hall by way of Memorial Bridge across Black Hall River. Lay's Hill between Black Hall Creek and Duck Creek. Here John Lay and Isaac Waterhouse first settlers. Point beyond Black Hall owned by Prof. Daniel C. Eaton of N. H. Hamburg or "North Quarter" of Lyme: Home of Rev. Dr. E. F. Burr, author of "Ecce Cœlum." Here lived Dr. Samuel Mather, and Miss Caroline Ely founded a school. East Lyme: Widow Caulkins Inn. Lafayette dined here.

of oysters for his horse: the entire company followed the landlord to see the miracle. When mine host returned to say that the horse refused to feed on oysters, Franklin was discovered ensconced in the warmest corner, quite reconciled to a meal off the oysters himself.

The third house of worship on Meeting-House Hill came near destruction in 1780, because of woodpeckers boring holes in the roof; when the "watch" shot at them with his flint-lock musket the tow-wad set fire to the dry timbers. Tradition says that Hessians or light horsemen stationed in the town jumped on the roof like squirrels and saved the meeting-house, finally destroyed by lightning in 1815. In 1817 this church was succeeded by the present model of architectural beauty on the plain below. The painting of Old Lyme Church by Childe Hassam exhibited at the St. Louis Fair hangs in the Gallery of American Artists at Smith College.

NEW LONDON (PEQUOT), 1645

" New London, New London, New London, ahoy ! "   H. C. BUNNER.

LION GARDINER TO JOHN WINTHROP, JR., FROM THE ISLE OF
WIGHT

" Feb. 1652.

"Honored Sir:—

*" My love and service being remembered. are these
to thank you for the hay seeds you sent me, I sowed them and
sum came up. I have sent you a rarity of seeds which came,
from the Mohawks, which is a kinde of milions [melons,
probably the summer squash] but far excelleth all other. They
are as good as wheat for to thicken milk, and sweet as sugar,
and baked they are most excellent, having no shell. You may
keep them as long as anie pumpkins."*

Thus did the Lord of Gardiner's Isle exchange garden
civilities with the founder of New London and future
Governor of Connecticut, the Younger Winthrop, *preux
chevalier* and one of the great men of our Colonial age.
He had chosen for his grant—baronial in extent—Fisher's
Island and Pequot, rich in woodlands, a broad river, and
the finest harbor between New Amsterdam and Newport.
The worshipful John Pyncheon perceived the excellencies
of Pequot Harbor, and very early entered into correspondence with Winthrop, sending cattle in droves from Springfield "over the path to Pequot"[1] to be shipped.

Winthrop held exclusive privilege of grinding corn for

---

[1] On this wilderness path, which also branched to Wethersfield, stood
the Uncas fort, on the Rev. Gurdon Saltonstall grant of 1699. After the
Charter, was built the first English house on this Pequot path. Barber
says "the old well and crooked pear trees fix the site, and mány wonderful stories are related about what happened to this house in days
of old."

the Colony, and strange to say his mill is still in possession of the rock glen in the heart of New London, having survived the town's disasters from war and fire, the malice of Arnold, yellow fever and the decline of a fine West India trade.

The Salt Meadows.

To the Winthrop grant soon came from Gloucester on the Cape a "Welsh party" of Monmouthshire, led by the Rev. Mr. Blynman; these families, called to meeting by the beat of Peter Blatchford's drum from Cape Ann Lane, were Hugh Calkins, the Lesters, Allyns, Averys, and Coites,[1] who founded a shipbuilding industry, also the

[1]Joseph Coit, who became the first minister at Plainfield (the son of

5

Meades, Beebes, and Marshalls. Hugh Calkins's grant on
the bay adjoined Winthrop's Ferry Farm, which carried
the *Rope Ferry* privilege at Nahantick bar.

" Ye ferry over Great River," Groton ferry, " being a scow
with both sails and oars," was leased to Cary Latham,[1]
first at Groton Bank, and first to mow the meadows at
Fog-Plain. In 1705, the rents of the ferry were assigned
the grammar school, in part of the master's " yearly sallery.
provided nevertheless, that the inhabitants of the town
on Lords days, thanksgiving days, and days of humiliation,
shall be ferriage free."

The settlers like all staunch Puritans were severe on
themselves. Nathaniel Mather writes: " Of all the manifold
sins which then I was guilty of, none so sticks upon me as
that, being very young, I was whittling upon the Sabbath
Day." Many were summoned to court for offences almost
as trifling as whittling: " John Lewis and Sarah Chapman
for sitting together on the Lord's day, under an apple tree
in Goodman's orchard."

Hawthorne declared that any one of the black-browed
Puritans of the Hawthorne tree would have thought the
blossoming of an idler like himself sufficient retribution for his
sins. 'What is he?' murmured one gray shadow of my forefathers to the other. 'A writer of story books!' 'What kind
of a business in life, what manner of glorifying God, or being serviceable to mankind in his day

LANDMARKS: Court House (1784). Library (Richardson design); bas-relief of founder, H. P. Haven, by A. St. Gaudens. General Jedediah Huntington house; Collector of the Port and friend of Washington. His house fashioned after the style of Mount Vernon. " Ye Ancientist Burying Ground." Oldest stone to James Mudge 1652. Oldest inscribed tablet to Captain Richard Lord: " The Bright Starre of our Cavalirie." Memorials to Madame Elizabeth Winthrop, Rev. Simon

Joseph and Martha Coit), was the first native of New London to receive
a collegiate education, being a first graduate of the Collegiate School at
Saybrook, now Yale College.

[2] Captain William Latham commanded Fort Griswold in 1781 under
the district commander, Colonel William Ledyard.

Bradstreet, Deacon Clement Miner (1700), Deacon Joseph Coit. To founders Lester, Harris, Raymond, Comstock, Hough, Haynes, Chappell, Truman, Fosdick, Darrow, Dart, and others. St. James's Church, dedicated by Bishop Seabury, the first Bishop of Connecticut and Rhode Island. Mumford-Wolcott house (1792), the Parish House. Smith Memorial house (1799). The First Church of Christ. Distinguished ministers, Rev. Ephraim Woodbridge, Rev. Henry Channing, Rev. Abel McEwen. Huguenot house (1697). Soldiers and Sailors Monument, gift of a son of Joseph Lawrence. Major-General Burbeck house. Four Sister Elms (1812). Captain Guy Richards house (1739). The "Red Lion"; house spared in 1781 by p.eading of beautiful Molly Coit for her ·sick father. Latimer-Dr. Abel McEwen parsonage. Arnold-Marvin Wait house (1719). Birthplace of Hon. John T. Wait, on site of Gov. Saltonstall house. Captain Nathaniel Coit-Belden house. Denison-Chappell house (1785). Manwaring homestead stood on site of George Chappell's lot of 1650. Hallam house. Shaw's Neck between Bream and Close Coves, home-lots of Thomas Miner and William Morton. Foxon's hill, named for Foxon, deputy of Uncas at court, " the wisest Indian in the country." Nathan Hale Memorial School, Post Hill. Thames River bridge, widest drawbridge known. Tongue's Bank, Tongue's Cliffs. George Tongue was granted four poles of land before his house-lot on the bank." Collection of antiques at Groton, open to the public, by Anna Warner Bailey Chapter, D. A. R., of Groton and Stonington. Groton is the birthplace of Daboll's Almanac. Bill Memorial Library and Starr homestead. Early light-houses, New London district: West side harbor entrance Thames, built 1760. Lynde Point, west side Connecticut,

and generation may that be? Why, the degenerate fellow might as well have been a fiddler!' Such are the compliments bandied between my great-grandsires and myself across the gulf of time!"[1]

"Little Owl Meadow" was given to James Avery, who seems to have been the Miles Standish of New London. Together with John Morgan, Avery received bounties for wolves' heads. As Lieutenant he commanded the Pequot allies when Governor Josiah Winslow broke the power of the Narragansetts at their fort at South Kingston, R. I. Previously Lieutenant Avery with Mr. Brewster, Richard Haughton, and Samuel Lothrop had rescued Uncas when pursued by the Narragansetts to the head of Nehantic River. For £6, he purchased the first barn meeting-house (the men then sat on one side and the women on the other), become all too small for the settlers, who came from up the Mohegan or Pequot and across Great River (the Thames) "with flint-lock in one hand and the Bible in the other." Lieutenant Avery built at Poquonnock (South

---

[1] Introduction to *The Scarlet Letter*.

lighted 1803. Stonington Point, 1823. Morgan's Point near Mystic, 1831. Fisher's Island Hummock 1849. Floating Lights, Bartlett's Reef, 1835. Eel Grass Light on Fisher's Island Sound, total number of vessels passed in 1850, 17,697.

Groton) that quaint and famous farmhouse known as "The Hive of the Averys."[1] Eleven of the gallant Averys fell at Fort Griswold and are enrolled on the Groton monument.   Christopher Avery came with Governor Winthrop to Salem.   Groton was named for the home seat of Adam Winthrop, leader of the second Puritan emigration.

On September 6, 1781, sounded the boom of Fort Griswold's two regular guns of alarm and New London met her Waterloo.   The British were doubly exasperated by the capture in Long Island Sound of the rich merchant ship *Hannah;* Shaw's warehouse at New London was packed with her cargo, the most valuable brought in during the war, and other rich merchandise.   The scarlet coats, vowing vengeance, landed on both sides of the river, capturing Fort Trumbull, and spared but few houses.   In New London the very gutters ran rivers of fire, and Arnold, from " Ye Ancient Burying Ground," watched with bitter joy the destruction of the houses of "auld acquaintance" of his

---

[2] It is an interesting fact that kin of the New England Averys have established a homestead far south in Louisiana on one of the old Spanish grants, the island of Petit Anse ("Little Goose"), now Avery's Island, assigned originally to settlers from the Iberian peninsula (New Iberia is just north).   The island is famous for its salt mine, the peppery Tobasco sauce, and for its prehistoric relics and fossils imbedded between the overflows of salt.   Situated in the vicinity of that region pictured by Lafcadio Hearn in *Chita*, the island is of unusual charm, even in winter, rising above a wide sea of purple marshes, stretching to the Gulf and threaded by silver bayous; Acadian huts scattered here and there, in January, the green and the scarlet of the yupon berries in high contrast to the sere, flat rice-fields along the Têche.   The salt mine itself is a superb crystal cave, under artifical light flashing like diamonds.   General B. sent a brigade to destroy the mine; "we have razed the works, Sir, but we cannot blow up the earth," was the day's report.

boyhood and the attack of Fort Griswold on Groton Heights opposite: there

The summer home of Dr. Samuel R. Elliott, New London, built on the rock where the British landed. Dr. Elliott's home has long been a rendezvous for men of letters. Here (Miss) Edith M. Thomas spends her summers.

> *"Ledyard, the hero, held his men*
> *Up to their work with a grip of steel,*
>
> . . . .
>
> *Honor or life then honor first."*[1]

---

[1] Rose Terry Cooke.

A letter dated *"N. London, 7th Sep. 1781"* is eloquent:

Dr. Sr.

I have the Unhappiness to acquaint you, Genl. Arnold with about 1500 or 2000 Men Landed Here Yesterday Morning & have Burnt this Town from the Court House to Nathl. Shaw; House which was Sav'd & from Giles Mumfords House to Capt. Richards Store. . . . They Have Burnt your House & All Your Stores at Groton & Most of the Houses on the Bank. They Attack'd the fort at Groton with Great Spirit but were Repuls'd with Loss several times by Col. Ledyard who Commanded, who was Oblig'd to Surrender to Superior Force. after the Fort Had Surrendered they inhumanely Put him to Death as Also Capt. Peter Richards and a Number of Others. . . . The Enemy are Now Under Sail Going Away—Shou'd think it Best for you to Come Down—

I am With Great Affection Your friend

ZAB: ROGERS.

[Addressed:]

THOS. I. MUMFORD Esq.[1] Now at Hartford.

Arnold's birthplace being only fourteen miles distant, he had retained secret allies in the town, and gave orders that a certain house in Gingerbread Lane should be spared; it was accordingly chalked; the owner, like *Ali Baba and the Forty Thieves*, secretly chalked his neighbors' houses, and these all survived as "Widow's Row," in Gingerbread Lane. On the Parade all was destroyed.

By curious fortune the combustibles lighted by the British in the Manwaring house were extinguished with a barrel of soap, and at Shaw Manor by tapping a pipe of vinegar in the garret.

Nathaniel Shaw, Jr., the merchant prince of New London, acquired a fortune by shipping mules to the West Indies

---

[1] Thomas Mumford was one of eleven men of Connecticut who formed the project of taking Ticonderoga.

and importing molasses, brown sugar, and coffee.   In 1774
trade was ruined, for "mules would not sell for cash in the
West Indies or molasses in New England."

During the Revolution he advised in all naval affairs in
Connecticut, and forwarded opportune supplies of powder
to General Washington, who visited New London to counsel
with Admiral Hopkins, commander of the first naval expedition under authority of Congress.

The Hempstead Homestead built before 1678 by Robert or his son Joshua.
Residence of John L. Branch, Esq.

The mahogany four-poster in which Washington slept
is in the "White Room" of the Shaw mansion.   In the
stress of war-times, Mistress Lucretia Shaw filled her home
with cots for our soldiers.   In 1898, in the same hospitable
hall, a descendant, with the Lucretia Shaw Chapter, D. A. R.,
packed hampers for the war sufferers.

Nathan Hale "taught school" in New London and here enlisted under the inspiration of his renowned epigram. Other prominent patriots were Major-General Burbeck, later president of the Massachusetts Society of the Cincinnati, Richard Law, and Major William Hillhouse, members of the Governor's council, and Captain John Deshon (Deschamps).

The oldest house in New London is the Hempstead homestead,[1] in which was held the first assembly of the Society of Mayflower Descendants of Connecticut. In "The Antientist Book" of 1647 is written: "John Steubens and Robert Hempstead are chosen to view the fences for this year." Also Robert Hempstead mowed the meadows at Lower Mamacock.

Mrs. Branch has given us a series of pretty pictures in this quaint Hempstead home of eight generations, flanked by sweet-flag and violets, the "posy-beds" of great-aunt Patty, and the flowering quince hedge along The Lane, up which the ducks used to wander. In *The Manner of Life of Nancy Hempstead*, the inexperienced young wife of Joshua Hempstead appears disconsolate, not because her jelly "won't jell," but because in trying this first time to make bayberry tallow for candles, she skimmed the top off, and got nothing! Bayberry, unlike other fat settles to the bottom.

Aunt Patty Hempstead remembered the burning of New London, and how when they fled into the country, she led her little brother Joshua up the long hills of the Colchester Road, and lifted him to his feet when he stumbled; they slept that night in a barn on piles of sheep's fleeces. Great was the children's excitement when they returned, to find

---

[1] Names connected with this house are: Sheriff Hempstead and the Joshua who was a New England *Pepys;* also Mary Bolles Branch and Anna Hempstead Branch, to whom we are deeply indebted for certain delicate and sympathetic latter-day poems.

houses in ashes and their own home flooded with rum and molasses and strewn with broken cheeses.

After the war, prosperity sailed once again into New London in barrels of whale oil. There is still a flavor of whaling-days among the old "sea-dogs" who "call all

Ocean Beach, New London, Conn.
"Still shall a violet evening please the sea,
And a pale splendor satisfy the air."
—ANNA HEMPSTEAD BRANCH.

hands" to plum-duff at the Jib-Boom Club, and fall to reeling yarns as thrilling as at the Captains' Club of Nantucket. There is a fascination in sea-adventures after safe return, but imagine the horrors of fifty New London sail crushed between icebergs, or a crew cast on Desolation Island among sea-elephants.[1] When you see tide meeting

[1] A sketch of New London's whaling industry and the Captain is included in Charlotte Molineux Holloway's "The Old Whaling Port," *Connecticut Quarterly*, May, 1897.

tide under Race Rock Light, or view on the Shore Road the
wrecking-apparatus of "Captain Joe," the diver, big-hearted
and retiring, and hero of *Caleb West* (like Edmund Hosmer,
Emerson's philosopher-farmer, "the spicy farming sage" of
Concord, Captain Joe is of the finest "stock" the States
produce), you rest content to be a landlubber, and make the
most of summer by the sea, upon the sands of Ocean Beach
lazily watching the passing on the Sound, and, over the
Sound, summer reigns till gray November.

> " *So all day long the vine looks down,*
> *On the roofs of the quaint, old-fashioned town.*" [1]

Again, you stand on the ramparts of Fort Trumbull
looking up the Thames at sunset, a rosy haze melting into
violet, lights up the rich foliage, tints listless sails and Groton's emerald lawns sloping to the harbor's mouth.   In
the afterglow, Groton monument, the Fort Griswold embankment, and a gray schooner drifting riverward, are etched
darkly against the sky; the oars of a dory trail gold at every
stroke.   Dancing attendance on the evening star, light
after light flashes on the romantic horizon—"the street
lamps of the ocean."

From New London's wharves, there is a fine choice of
historic trips by water; you may steam to Greenport, or, if
it is not "skittish weather" outside, to Block Island.   Again
to Watch Hill, the fishing grounds of the tribe of Ninigret
who carried off the daughter of Wyandace of Long Island
during her wedding festivities.   The bride was rescued by
Lion Gardiner, sealing his life friendship with the Sachem.

Or visit ancient and aristocratic Stonington, touching
midway at the quaint hamlet of Noank framed in blue
water by Palmer's Cove and Mystic Harbor.   On a transparent day of Indian summer, it seems as if you might

---

[1] *The Song of the Van*, by Walter Learned, New London.

reach out and touch Fisher's Island and North Hill where the *Atlantic* went to pieces in '46; Mystic Island is close by and the Mason monument on Pequot Hill. You listen to the sound of hammers "*knocking away the shores and spurs*" of some noble ship, for on Mystic River is a large wooden ship-building plant. Gales Ferry, up river (every June the quarters of the Yale crew) is a lovely peninsula. By

The Town of Noank, with Palmer's Ship-yard, from Mason's Island

the mill-pond is the red, gambrel roof of the Richard homestead. Commodore Decatur was blockaded here with a prize ship. The British officers of The *Wasp* carried on many a flirtation in old Rodman Neil's kitchen, and at least one Gales Ferry lassie met her fate. A remarkable oak presides over the old farm of Adam Larrabee, often spoken of as "the friend of Lafayette."

On your trip up the Thames to the beautiful town of Norwich, "The Rose of Connecticut," you skirt the shore of Montville, the North Parish of New London, and will choose to return by the turnpike road or Mohegan trail, over which Miantonomoh fled before Uncas. Near the scene of the sachems' single combat, the tribe have lingered and it is but a few years since the last of the Mohegans departed to "the happy-hunting grounds." From these beetling cliffs, the warrior shaded his eyes to spy out the enemies of mighty Uncas, or to sight in shimmering Pequot harbor the white man's sails.

Behind the Indian church, not far from Chehegan boulder, spreads a magnificent view of the Thames Valley. The Uncas granite chair is near the River Fort and the favorite grounds of Uncas and his chiefs were the farms at Massapeag and Pamechaug, deeded in 1658 to Richard Houghton and James Rogers; one on Saw-Mill Brook was purchased by Samuel Rogers; these with Joshua Raymond were first settlers. Major Christopher Darrow, who distinguished himself in the French and Indian wars, belonged to the North Parish and Elder Zadoc Darrow to Waterford.

The Mohegans held seignorial rights of land and the Uncas heirs, in 1898, directed a suit against the town of Norwich, for encroachments upon their royal burying-ground and Yantic river-path. Sampson Occum, the Indian preacher, was renowned in England and Mohegans attended the Indian school at Lebanon, founded by Dr. Eleazer Wheelock, which finally merged through the generosity of Lord Dartmouth to the pagans into the Dartmouth College foundation.

The eight-mile walk from the pretty Chesterfield district to meeting in New London was said to be merely an agreeable recreation to the Latimers, "a tall and robust race," and one might agree with them, when the air is balmy with

clover and spiced with the sea. In North Parish (Montville) the *ride-and-tie* system prevailed: a farmer who took
his wife behind him on his good family horse and rode half-
way to the meeting-house, then dismounted and, fastening
his horse to a bar-post, travelled the last miles "on Shank's
mare," leaving his mount for the use of a neighbor and his
wife on the road behind.[1]

[1] *History of New London*, by Frances Manwaring Caulkins.   H. D.
Utley.

"The clover-blossoms kiss her feet
She is so sweet."
Song—OSCAR LAIGHTON.

NORWICH

In the long, long city of Norwich, you always meet the unexpected; the old town plot followed the windings of the romantic Yantic, the "noisy river" of rushing, falling water. Upstart hills and rocks, half-hidden in foliage,

Typical Road and Trout Brook in Vicinity of Norwich, Conn.
"Here is a bit for a painter, a lovely vista—the road dips into a little hollow, turns gently, and passes out of sight within the shadow of a wood."—BRADFORD TORREY

charm and bewilder the stranger. The first homes crept under them for shelter in picturesque abandon; the tiny meeting-house mounted guard on top of a cliff, and the bell hung from the crotch of a tree.

It would be impossible in less than two volumes to tell

the story of old Norwich. Her many, many colonial mansions are aristocratic from the door-knocker to keeping-room; behind the portals of "Long Society" are rich ancestral possessions—"as choice as hens' teeth" according to the old saying. If you would know Norwich "first families," open Miss Perkins's delightful story of the *Ancient Houses of Norwich*, rich in portraits, miniatures, and the original colored map of Norwich by Donald G. Mitchell, as it appeared to him in boyhood days.

LANDMARKS: Dr. Johnson-Lathrop house. Thomas Lathrop house. Coit homestead. Coit Elms, alluded to in "Autocrat of the Breakfast Table." Lydia H. Sigourney house. Home of Captain Joshua Huntington and Judge Andrew Huntington. White residence. General Jedediah and Ebenezer Huntington house. General Jabez and General Zachariah Huntington house. Farnsworth house, once residence of John Lothrop Motley. Slater house. Osgood residence. Amos Hubbard house. Sachem Park. Colonel Joshua Huntington house. Governor Samuel Huntington house. Old Burying-Ground. Brown Tavern, later Bela Peck house. Rock Nook Home, Gift of Moses Pierce, Monument to Major Mason. Old Witter Tavern—Hazard house, Bean Hill. Yantic Mills on site Backus Iron Forge. Winslow T. Williams house. Elijah Lathrop house. Vernett Lee house. Hon. David A. Wells house, N. Washington St. On East Main St., Home Gov. William A. Buckingham, now Club House of the Grand Army of the Republic. Old Hyde homestead, Navy Yard Lane. Old Burying-Ground. Cleveland house, former home of Grover Cleveland. Near Sachem Park is the Miantonomoh Stone on the Providence trail. The Crotch of the Rivers. The Hook of the Quinebaug. Scotch Cap Hill near where bounds meet of Norwich, Franklin, and Bozrah.

Four of the Presidents of the United States turn to Norwich as ancestral home. At Lebanon was the war office of Governor Jonathan Trumbull, of whom Washington would say when short of supplies: "We'll see what Brother Jonathan can do."

Who will not applaud the patriotism of Connecticut women, especially marked in Norwich! Was not Lydia Huntington even more beautiful in homespun, daintily embroidered by her own hand, than in foreign stuffs, scorned as bitterly as Revolutionary tea? The Norwich dames were famous for their exquisite paper work and shadow portraits, once so fashionable.

In this township the Indians had three rude forts: Fort Hill, the citadel of Waqueenaw, brother of Uncas; Little Fort Hill between Landing and Trading

Ising-Glass Rock. Wheel-Timber Hill. Butternut Brook. The Great Darke Swamp. Dragon's Hole at Kewontaquck.

coves belonged to Uncas, and a third stood at the junction of the Yantic and Hammer Brook. Cæsar Sachem was succeeded by Ben Uncas, "Major Ben," followed by Ben Uncas, 2d, who was brought up in the family of Captain John Mason, and the first to adopt our dress. To-day in that wild Mohegan country a city lies serene,

"*Guarded by circling streams and wooded mountains,*
Like sentinels round a queen." [1]

[1] Edmund Clarence Stedman.

WATCH HILL, R. I.
Here Burned Signal Fires.

THROUGH GARDINER'S BAY TO GREENPORT

"Launch thy bark, mariner!"

No short voyage along the New England coast is more historic than from New London to Shelter Island and Greenport, which seaport in Washington's day was on the shortest route from New York to Boston by way of Newport. It is particularly interesting on account of the new fortifications on Fisher's Island, Great Gull, Plum Island (the Isle of Patmos), and Montauk; these with Napatree Point completely shut out marauders from Long Island Sound. No forts command a more strategic position.

New London Light.
"A Street Lamp of the Ocean."

As the steamer leaves New London Light and Ocean Beach on her starboard bow and Watch Hill Light far to port, she comes abreast of Race Point, the dangerous long, low beach on Fisher's, and Race

81

Rock Light, the salvation of mariners, the masterpiece built
by F. Hopkinson Smith, transcending his other inspirations
even that of yesterday's brush, *The Glory of Venice.*

Fisher's Island was a Utopia when John Winthrop, Jr.,
wrote from thence to Lion Gardiner for advice about his
sick child; but the deer-stalked woodlands disappeared
under the great gale of 1815, which flung spray against
window panes eight miles inland. Deep under Fisher's
Island Sound, innumerable boulders are seen of the same
race as great Chehegan and others at Mohegan, which seem,
as it were, strewn by giants' play. Fisher's Island itself
is a mass of boulders covered by sand where the heavy ocean
surf arrested a glacier. It now is a part of Southold, Long
Island.

Great Gull and Little Gull are alight in the green water;
here the British fleet anchored in 1813 and blockaded the
port, after pursuing several American frigates into New
London harbor, that had come through the Sound, hoping
to slip out to sea by Montauk. No enemy could rendezvous
before the ten-inch disappearing guns on Plum Island.
Steer discreetly through Plum Gut, the narrow gateway
of Gardiner's Bay between Plum Island and Orient Point,
the southern prong of the fork of Long Island.

Tiny unexpected lakes glimmer about Montauk between
sandhills rolling like waves of the sea. An old squaw on being asked the road from Narragansett to Montauk, answered:
"Keep out of the woods and the water and you'll get to
Montauk." The last chief of the Montauks, despairing, is
said to have departed with three steps: to Shelter Island,
Orient Point, and to Montauk, throwing himself in the sea.

Orient Point was formerly Oyster Ponds and the scene
of Cooper's *Sea-Lions.* Cooper's hero was Roswell Gardiner,
and Lothrop says "one is tempted to call the first Lion
Gardiner a *sea*-Lion." He was a born leader of men without

" Like silent ghosts in misty shrouds
Stand out the white lighthouses high."
CELIA THAXTER.

Camp Wyckoff, 1898, 3d U. S. Cavalry.

Montauk Point Light,
Long Island.

83

boisterous ambition, a diplomat of the first water, with a quick decision and courage, the admiration of the savage. The Montauks remained always friendly to the whites, the tribe deferring utterly to Gardiner.[1] Wyandanch placed his son in his guardianship and left the territory of Smithtown to Gardiner, "the most honorable of the English nation here about us."[2] Gardiner was created by eminent domain Lord of the Isle of Wight by the Earl of Sterling, possessing a grant of all islands between the Hudson and Cape Cod; and Gardiner's Isle, 30,000 acres of concentrated romance, is possessed still by the Gardiners.

Gardiner's Bay was the prowling ground of Captain Kidd. When the Earl of Bellomont was Governor of New York (1699) he complained that Long Island was a "receptacle for pirates," and set a watch for Captain Kidd. But *his* was not the wickedest pirate bark that sailed high seas; he

---

[1] Gardiner's extraordinary insight into the leanings of the primitive American appears in his course with the harassing Pequot, the powerful Uncas, and his friendship with Wyandanch, "the wise talker."

Gardiner prevented the fiendish plot of the Narragansetts to unite the tribes and destroy the whites. The Narragansetts were shrewd in seeking help from the Long Island tribes, mighty in the financial world; the Five Nations came even from the Great Lakes to obtain coin in the "land of the periwinkle," the Montauks' bay-indented shores being long and rich in shells, and squaws many, to string the wampum.

Lion Gardiner, on going over one day to Long Island, by chance saw Miantonomoh and three of his great warriors talking secretly with the Montauk Sachem and his old counsellors. Wyandanch revealed to Gardiner that they urged him to give no more wampum to the English, and offered presents if he would join their schemes to become once again lords of the soil; otherwise, said the Narragansetts, " we shall be all gone shortly, for you know our fathers had plenty of deer and skins, our plains were full of deer, as also our woods, and of turkies. . . . But these English have gotten our land, they with scythes cut down the grass, and their hogs spoil our clam banks, and we shall be starved": Lion Gardiner said "you must not give wampum to Narragansett," and with Wyandanch's help circumvented their wiles.—Gardiner's *Pequot Warres.*

[2] Wyandanch continues in his will: "he apeared to us not only as a

gave Lady Gardiner Indian sweetmeats [1] for her children and cloth of gold—which she dared not refuse—in return for her good mutton. Kidd buried much booty (for which the unwise still go a-digging)—gold, silver, precious stones, silver candlesticks, gold bars and dust—and confided his secret to Lord John Gardiner (third proprietor), declaring that Gardiner was welcome to the treasure if he never returned, but if he ever called and found it missing, he would take his head or his son's.

The Earl of Bellomont sent an express to Lord Gardiner to deliver at Boston the treasure of "the sloop *Antonio*, Capt. Kidd, late commander, for the King's use." Gardiner delivered the treasure to appointed Boston dignitaries,— Samuel Sewall, Nathaniel Byfield, Jeremiah Dummer, and Andrew Belcher. This ended the Kidd episode, but less considerate pirates attacked Gardiner's Isle, slashing the proprietor's hands with sabres, and Lady (Allyn) Gardiner seized her silver tankard and fled to her maiden home in Hartford.

---

friend, but a father, in giveing us monie and goods, whereby we defended ourselves and ransomed my daughter and friends . . . we haveing nothing left that is worth his acceptance but a small tract of land which we desire him to accept of for himself, his heires—forever." Signed by Wyandanch, his mark,—an Indian shaking hands with a white man.

[1] The Kidd pitcher of Indian sweetmeats has descended through the Mumfords, Saltonstalls, Thatchers, Christophers to Mrs. H. Fairfield Osborn of New York from Lucretia Mumford Perry of New London, Conn.

EAST HAMPTON.

DURING the Revolution Gardiner's Bay, now a famous roadstead and favorite practice-ground for school-ships, was the pleasant retreat of a British fleet under Vice-Admiral Arbuthnot. They feasted on the rich preserves of Gardiner's Island, and the marks of dollars which they pitched for recreation are yet on the floors of the dining-room of the Manor.

Their depredations would have resulted far more seriously, had it not been for the tact of Parson Buell, father of the "Lady of the Manor," who invited the Britons to dine, went gunning with them, and accepted invitations on the flag-ship, the *Royal Oak*.[1] "Old Rebel," the young officers called him.

Sir William Erskine, who commanded the post, remarked one Saturday to Dr. Buell that he had ordered the men of the parish to appear on the morrow with their teams at Southampton. "Ah, yes, I am aware of it; but I am commander-in-chief on Sunday, and have annulled your orders." General Erskine graciously revoked the order. General Erskine said that, after the war, he should build a country-seat in "the garden spot of America"—in the rare old town of East Hampton.

"Down on the shore, the sunny shore!
Where the salt smell fills the land."

Among the officers billeted at Colonel Abram Gardiner's, East Hampton, were Lord Percy, Governor Tryon, Lord Cathcart, and Major André, who was much beloved, and the wine-glass exchanged by Major André with Colonel Gardiner is still treasured.

---

[1] Memorandum of Lion Gardiner.

A son of the house, Dr. Nathaniel Gardiner of the Continental Army, came home in disguise, on leave of absence. After "Dr. Nat" returned to his post André quietly remarked that he would have been pleased to have made that young man's acquaintance, but as a British officer, his duty would have compelled him to arrest him as a spy.[1]   It is said that Dr. Nathaniel Gardiner was ordered to attend Major André at Tappan the night before his execution.

Colonel Gardiner's grandson David was one of the President's party accidentally killed on the frigate *Princeton* in 1844.   His daughter married President Tyler.[2]   Their engagement had been a profound secret.   After the wedding breakfast, served at the Gardiner mansion in Lafayette Place, the bride and groom drove down Broadway behind four white horses and embarked on a ship of war.

Many besides Gen. Erskine have been infatuated with this "love of a place."   Pudding Hill is occupied by a beautiful summer home, and Thomas Moran set his studio among the honeysuckles; St. John Harper chose the Amagansett Road, the Albert Herters, the old Bridgehampton road, close to Georgica, a lake enchanting.

East Hampton's shining literary days began with Lyman Beecher, Cornelia Huntington, and General Jeremiah Miller.

It was an event in carpetless East Hampton when Mrs. Beecher covered the usual sanded floor with a carpet for which she spun the cotton and painted a border in oils with bunches of roses.   Old Deacon Tallmadge came to see

---

[1] "The Manor of Gardiner's Island," by Martha J. Lamb, *American Magazine of History.*

[2] The Gardiners have intermarried with Van Cortlands, Van Rensselaers, Livingstons, and Beekmans of New York, the Smiths of St. George's Manor, the Floyds, Thompsons, Sylvesters, Nicolls of Long Island, the Greenes of Boston, and the Conklings.   George Bancroft was a descendant and Gardiner Greene Hubbard, past president of the American Geographical Society.

Mr. Beecher and seemed afraid to come in. He stopped at the parlor door. " 'Walk in, Deacon, walk in."—'Why, I can't,' said he, ' 'thout steppin' on 't.' Then, after surveying it awhile in admiration, 'D'ye think ye can have all that, *and heaven too?*' "[1]

A sermon on *Duelling*, following the duel of Hamilton and Burr, made Lyman Beecher famous; he tried it first on his people at the hamlets of Amagansett and Montauk and finally sent it over to Gardiner's Island to be criticised by John Lyon Gardiner, his literary parishioner, before publication. On the return it was dropped into the water from the sailor's pea-jacket pocket and miraculously tossed up on shore above high-water mark and quite dry, being wound with yarn. The picturesque custom was to light a seaweed fire at Fire-Place, the point nearest Gardiner's Island, as a signal to the skiff of the Manor that visitors wished to wait on Lord Gardiner.

---

[1] *Autobiography of Lyman Beecher.*

OYSTERS SET ON SHELLS ON NATURAL BED.

SAG HARBOR.

THE first newspaper on Long Island was printed at Sag Harbor—*Frothingham's Long Island Herald,*—with the prelude:

> *"Eye Nature's walks, shoot folly as it flies,*
> *And catch the manner's living as they rise."*

Its columns are etchings of the times: "To be Sold. A valuable wench in her 19th year. She is very active and understands the whole business of a kitchen. Enquire of the Rev. Zachariah Greene of Southold" (1792). "Strayed, a lame geese, one wing cut. Benjamin Nicoll, Shelter Island."

A poor printer of Boston, David Frothingham, of the aristocratic family whose daughters were declared "the beauties of Charlestown," settled at Sag Harbor, after running away with Nancy Pell, a daughter of Pelham Manor ; he was finally lost at sea.

Lieutenant Daniel Fordham and nearly all the 2nd Regiment of the minute-men of 76, who fought in the battle of Long Island, were "raised in Sag Harbor." [1] The Fordham family purchased many acres of the Indians at Hempstead. Sloop *Polly*, Captain Nathan Fordham, plied between Sag Harbor and Albany. The valuable Indian implements picked up in the Hamptons by Mr. William Wallace Tooker the Indianologist [2] are the property of the Brooklyn Institute. He recently acquired at Barcelona

---

[1] *An Island Heroine: A Romance of Long Island,* by Mary Breck Sleight of Sag Harbor.

[2] Mr. Tooker's interesting "Aboriginal Terms for Long Island," "The country of the ear-shell," may be found in the *Brooklyn Eagle Almanac.*

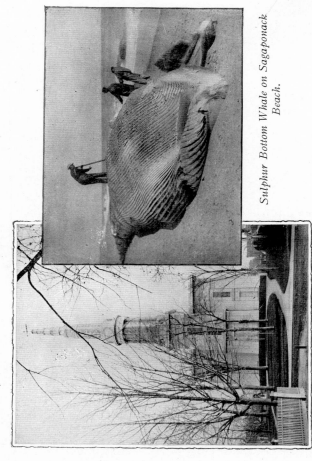

Sulphur Bottom Whale on Sagaponack Beach.

The Presbyterian Church, Sag Harbor.

90

Beach a peculiar semi-lunar Algonquin knife, called by the Esquimaux, Uloo.

Steaming slowly away from Sag Harbor in late afternoon, glancing backward across the pretty North Haven bridge, the Shinnecock Hills become violet as evening approaches. Sailing on through Shelter Island Sound over "the large inland sea, adorned with divers fair havens and bays and fit for all sorts of craft," as said Cornelius Van Tienhoven in 1650, a landing is made at Southold, and you catch an enticing glimpse of the village up Town Creek, one of the pretty inlets which attracted settlers when Southold became a part of the New Haven Colony.

On the final relinquishment of Long Island by the Dutch, there was a landing of ceremony at Southold. From across the Bay "where five hundred ships may safely ride abreast" approached the skiff with the "Keneticut" Commissioners, Ex-Governor Wyllys and Fitz John Winthrop, the English flag astern, followed by the Dutch in a barge manned by the colored servants from Sylvester Manor, both nations having been entertained over night on Shelter Island.

There are a few homesteads standing in Southold— Colonel John Young's of 1650, and those of the Benjamin L'Hommedieu and Boisseau families. The monument to the Founders stands on the site of the first meeting-house in the oldest burying-ground on Eastern Long Island. An interesting coincidence of the 250th anniversary celebration was the delivery of the oration by the Rev. Richard Salter Storrs, of Brooklyn, in honor of the town and church of his ancestor, the Rev. John Storrs.

In walking about the delightful little seaport of Green-port among the boat-builders, you question which is of the more intense blue, the sea or the sky. When Greenport was Sterling, Colonel George Washington stopped on his road to Newport, in 1757, at Lieutenant Booth's Inn standing

on Sterling Lane. His servant announced his boat, and
Washington, with much grace, took each lady by the hand,
saluted her with a kiss, gravely asked their prayers, and
bade them an affectionate adieu. This was related by
Miss Havens, one of the Greenport young ladies. Before
"Ye Clark House" hangs the original sign and quite after
the fashion of a quaint, delicious English country inn it is.
Greenport is as famous for its exportation of oysters to
Liverpool, as Orient for perfect potatoes.

TOWN CREEK, SOUTHOLD, L. I.

SOUTHAMPTON, 1640

THE pioneers who marched through Southampton forest, and stopped at the Old Town Pond, were from Massachusetts; and the Bay Colony became so infatuated with the soft climate (by virtue of which the inhabitants of Eastern Long Island attain fivescore years), that a vessel sailed regularly between Lynn and Conscience Point, Southampton. Governor Winthrop himself voyaged around Long Island in the *Blessing of the Bay*. If Southampton were beautiful then, it is surpassingly so now, for the fresh-water lake, Agawam, close to the roll of old ocean, is bordered by green lawns of tasteful homes; white skiffs skim the blue surface; a protecting sand-bar shines between the shore road and the salt surf; the lovely church, St. Andrew's by the Sea, is hard by; a life-saving station recalls wintry perils in contrast to the Meadow Club House, centre of serene summer pleasure. Along these superb Long Island beaches, some fifty years ago, were little whaling huts, and whale-boats on wagon wheels, ready to man at a moment's notice.

It would be impossible to mention the families of distinction from New York whose leisure days are spent by Southampton Beach, circling Agawam Lake, and about its sequestered Hampton Park, on the way to North Sea.

A few quaint roofs, the Presbyterian Church, built in 1707, and Wind Mill Lane show the antiquity of Southampton; the homesteads of the day of Rev. Abraham Pierson[1] and Rev. Robert Fordham, built facing the south, or the beach, have been turned to the main street, except the Job Sayre house, after whom Job's Lane was named.

The little village of Water Mill has its story and Canoe

---

[1] First minister of Southampton and first rector of Yale.

Still Life.
Westhampton, L. I.

Residence of Mrs. Wm. S. Hoyt, Shinnecock Hills.
The Oldest Wind-Mill of Wind-Mill Lane, Southampton.

Sayre Homestead, 1640.
Southampton.
Oldest Dwelling in New York
State.

Hercules Figurehead near Canoe
Place Inn (Erected 1730), Good
Ground, L. I.

94

Place, the narrowest path between Shinnecock and Peconic Bays, where the Indians carried their canoes across. In this region is a canal prehistoric to the white man, cut by Mongotucksee, great chief.

Unique among the airy Shinnecock Hills, an ideal art-village was originated by Mrs. Hoyt, somewhat after the French fashion, yet truly American, and with enthusiastic fervor the students paint moorlands, meadows, sand-dunes, woods, and tangled rushes of Long Island, boats stranded on sunset marshes and beached on its bays; also the gray huts and life of the Indian Reservation, for which Mr. William M. Chase, as instructor-in-chief, obtained the privilege.

The Manor of Shelter Island, New York.
The Horsford Summer Residence.

SHELTER ISLAND

THERE was a young poet of Orient who spoke of his native shore on one prong of Long Island as "enchanted ground," and truly on an enchanted sea floats the bewitching isle, *Manhansack Ahaquashuwamock*, being translated "the island sheltered by islands," hence Shelter Island; between Montauk and Oyster Ponds (Orient) it lies like a pearl clasped by its Long Island shell.

The founding of an historic house on Shelter Island by Nathaniel Sylvester came about during the trying Cromwell epoch when certain English estates were confiscated, and their owners, loyal to the King, took refuge in Holland and then purchased land in America.

Shelter Island was sold to the Sylvesters by Deputy-Governor Goodyear of the New Haven Colony for 1600 pounds of "good merchantable muscovada sugar." About this time Parliament issued a warrant for the arrest of Thomas Brinley, auditor of the king and much loved and trusted by the royal family; to his ancestral home in Staffordshire Charles II. had fled after his defeat and he was obliged to live in exile. His lovely daughter, Grissell, a girl of sixteen. was immediately claimed by her affianced one, Nathaniel Sylvester, and they took passage on the *Swallow* accompanied by Governor William Coddington and his bride, Anne Brinley, and Francis Brinley, her brother, founder of the Brinley family in America. In a terrible storm off Newport the vessel was wrecked and priceless heirlooms devoured by the greedy sea. The bridal pair escaped to live happily in their beautiful Manor adorned with scriptural Holland tiles and doors from Barbadoes, (the new home of a brother, Constant Sylvester) The scented "box" which they planted grew tall and precious as years rolled on and when the writer visited the garden a few years ago was still superb after two hundred and fifty years, probably the oldest box on the continent.[1]

Much friendly intercourse took place with their neighbors, the Winthrops on Fisher's Island, and a pathetic paragraph from Sylvester begs advice because the baby is sick and in danger of strangling, "and here we are quite out of ye way of help." Winthrop was presented with a hogshead of sugar by Constant Sylvester, the brother at Barbadoes. The sugar business was very lucrative and timber for hogsheads was furnished from Shelter Island.

Brinley Sylvester caused the present mansion-house with its avenue of cherry trees to be ornamented with elaborate carvings. On the death of his grandson, General Sylvester Dering, it was purchased by Ezra L'Hommedieu, and inherited by Professor Eben Norton Horsford of the L'Hommedieu line.

It appears that by chance an exiled Huguenot, Benjamin L'Hommedieu, settled at Southold, where the Sylvesters attended worship; one day he saw approaching two beautiful girls, Patience and Grissell Sylvester, in a canopied barge rowed by six colored servants. His heart was lost at first sight to Miss Patience, who became Mrs. L'Hommedieu. Quite as romantic was the sad parting at the old stone bridge of Grissell Sylvester with her fiancé, Latimer Sampson, proprietor of the estate known of late years as Lloyd's Neck. He went south to die, leaving his property to Grissell, who married James Lloyd[2] of Boston.

Nathaniel Sylvester bequeathed Sachem's Neck to a

---

[1] "The Manor of Shelter Island," by Martha J. Lamb, *Magazine of American History*, vol. xviii.

[2] Descendants are the Hillhouses and Woolseys of New Haven, Livingstons, Onderdoncks, and Brownes of New York.

friend, William Nicoll,[1] a patentee of Islip, who married a
Van Rensselaer.

The ancient landing-place of Sylvester Manor has borne
its part in the family history.   One may imagine the welcome of the Quaker exiles, George Fox and the persecuted
Southwicks, harbored and consoled by the Sylvesters.   At
these steps, worn by many feet, were received Governor
Dongan, also Sir Edmund Andros, and if you wish to know
how many meetings and partings of lovers they have seen
go and ask the babbling tide, the steps will never tell.   A
haunted mirror in the guest-chamber is said to reflect at
midnight some fair lady's image of " auld lang syne."

Other families of Shelter Island have been noted for
hospitality: the Nicolls, Derings, and Havens; but Shelter
Islanders loved not invaders.   When the pigs were about
ready to kill the British chose Shelter Island for a foraging
expedition.   The burning question was how could the pigs
be concealed, for pigs *will* squeal, and the ladies had before
seen pigs strung at the yard-arm.   A witty dame concocted
the brilliant idea of ripping up the feather beds and sewing
in the pigs, and these went comfortably to sleep while the
troops searched the house, thus preserving the winter's
bacon.

Veritably, Long Island is a long romance.   Its western
end shared closely in the social life of early New York.
There were the gay " bride-visitings" from one country house
to another,[2] and the most delightful balls and routs.   Washington himself regretted the snow-storm which prevented
a dance, because there were only two chariots in New York.
Picture the gallants in sheer ruffles and small-clothes aglint

---

[1] The   Nicoll   inheritance   is   the   W.   K.   Vanderbilt,   Jr.,   estate,   "Idle
Hour."

[2] *The Story of a New York House*, by H. C. Bunner, Charles Scribners"
Sons.

An October Day, Southampton Beach, Long Island.

"In glee the horses of the sea
Curved up in windy weather,

Shook their white manes at the window panes,
And then ran off together."   —LILLIPUT LEVEE.

with diamond buckles leading with formal grace through
the cotillion these statuesque dames, who wore their brocades
and filmy laces with the bearing of queens, not only because
of the aristocracy of culture, but on account of a judicious
application of the backboard in girlhood.

There was a pretty bride-*taking* from Long Island. It so
happened that Walter Franklin,[1] a man of fortune, was
riding in his chariot on an excursion through Long Island,
when he caught sight of a maid milking cows in a barn-yard.
He asked her who occupied the house. With great simplicity, she replied, "My father, Daniel Bowne; wilt thou
not alight and take tea with him?" The invitation was
accepted, and after three visits he asked her in marriage.
So the Quaker milkmaid rolled away to take possession of
the most elegant house in the city, on Cherry Street, near
Pearl. Her daughters swerved from Quakerism, and became
fashionable belles. One married De Witt Clinton.

---

[1] Uncle of Rear-Admiral S. R. Franklin and General Franklin. From
Memoirs of a Rear-Admiral. Copyright by Harper & Brothers.

GUILFORD, 1639

Omne tulit punctum qui miscuit utile dulci.
He makes a good breakfast who mixes pudding with molasses.

I sing the sweets I know, the charms I feel,
My morning incense, and my evening meal,
The sweets of Hasty-Pudding.
   .   .   .   .   .

Some talk of Hoe-cake, fair Virginia's pride,
Rich Johnny-cake, this mouth has often tri'd,
Both please me well, their virtue much the same,
Alike their fabric, as allied their fame,
Except in dear New England, where the last
Receives a dash of pumpkin . . .

But place them all before me smoaking hot,
The big round dumplin' rolling from the pot:
You tempt me not—my favorite greets my eyes,
To that loved bowl my spoon by instinct flies.

THE HASTY-PUDDING, by JOEL BARLOW, the "Hartford
Wit." Written at Savoy, 1793.

UILFORD is to-day your goal
out of New York. Along-
shore you have had fleeting
glimpses, ever since you sped
out of Stamford, of gambrel
roofs and lean-tos in Old
Fairfield and Stratford and
Milford ; yet, as the train
steams on east, leaving you
to saunter up Whitfield
Street into the heart of Guilford, you are surprised to be
apparently transplanted
backward into the seven-
teenth century; you instinct-

ively look around for some lady mounted on a pillion behind her squire to alight at the Old Stone House, assisted by an expectant cavalier in steeple-crown and rapier, or expect at least to meet in Petticoat Lane a yellow chaise. How oddly certain houses skew cornerwise to the street, each built by compass to face the east.   These old houses form

The Grace Starr House built in 1687 on Crooked Lane, otherwise State St., Guilford.

the meridian line or noon-mark "and every urchin on the lane can tell the dinner-hour by watching for the dead line which at twelve o'clock crosses the street like a scissors-blade."

There is a wedding to-day in the Stone House, the first in New Haven Colony; the teacher, young Master Higginson, is to wed Parson Whitfield's daughter Sally, and the merry board is set forth with rye bread, pork, and peas.

Sara Whitfield has a fair dowry and setting up, for Colonel Fenwick of Saybrook gave the lands of Hammonasset, which he bought of Uncas, to Guilford only on condition that his friend Mr. Whitfield should have a large slice. Lady Alice Fenwick also had presented Master Higginson, her fellow-passenger and sometime chaplain at Fort Saybrook,[1] with several valuable cows which she brought over from home.

Her passage was taken on a pilgrim ship of great importance to the Colony for the *St. John* of London, Captain Richard Russell, sailed direct to Quinipiac bringing Mr. Whitfield and many men of learning and means from Kent and Sussex, quite as disaffected with the government and Star Chamber as Davenport who writes to Lady Vere Sept. 28, 1639: "my deare child is safely arrived with sundry desirable friends—such as Mr. Fenwick and his lady, to our great comfort. Their provision at sea held good to the last—we sent a pinnis to pilot them to our harbor, for it was the first ship that ever cast anchor in this place. The sight of ye harbor did so please ye captain of the ship and all the Passengers that he called it Fayre Haven." It is said that these passengers, many of whom were younger sons, and became world-renowned, were put to great expense to procure a blacksmith for their new town, for "there was not a merchant or mechanic among them." They chose a place, Menunkatuck, about sixteen miles easterly from "Quilli-

---

[1] The Rev. John Higginson succeeded the Rev. Henry Whitfield in Guilford and then sailed for England, but was driven by adverse winds into Salem harbor, the chosen home of the famous pioneer, Francis Higginson—previously Vicar of Claybrook Church, Leicester,—where his father's people persuaded him to remain. He succeeded the Rev. Hugh Peters, who had returned to England only to be tried at the "Old Bailey," and sentenced "to be hung, drawn, and quartered for treason."

piack" (New Haven), lying between Ruttawoo (East River) and Agicomick (Stony Creek), "and there set down." The long-since-departed early companions of Whitfield's house were the homes of Governor Leete, William Chittenden by West River, Robert Kitchel on the corner of Petticoat Lane, and that of the Chief Magistrate, Desborough,[1] afterwards Keeper of the Great Seal of Scotland under the Lord Protector. John Hoadley, one of the "seven pillars"

The Samuel Hubbard House (1717) on the home-lot of Jacob Sheaffe, Broad St., residence of John B. Hubbard, Esq.

of Guilford, became chaplain of Cromwell's garrison in Edinburgh castle; Guilford appears more nearly linked to events under which the Protectorate evolved itself, than any town of the new colonies. Henry Whitfield himself, one of the most eloquent clergymen that came to Connecticut, driven by the bitter persecution of Archbishop Laud, relinquished a rich living at Ockley in Surrey where his

---

[1] The other "deed signers" were John Bishop and John Caffinge. The Kitchels founded Newark, N. J., with Abraham Pierson and his Branford

The Stone homestead (*residence of Miss Anna M. Stone*) *built in 1740 on the site of Governor Leete's house; in his barn, tradition says, the Regicides or "Judges" lay concealed. Opposite is the Simeon Chittenden homestead, "Cranbrook," on the home-lot of William Chittenden, a founder of Guilford and native of Cranbrook in Kent; the estate is the summer home of Simeon Baldwin Chittenden, Esq.*

Sea-Holly or Marshmallow on the banks of West River.

house concealed such persecuted men as Cotton, Hooker, Nye, and Davenport; the climax arrived when Whitfield refused to read from the Book of Sports. The exodus of non-conformists would have come about seven years earlier had not Laud's predecessor as Archbishop of Canterbury, George Abbot, exercised sympathetic leniency to the clergy of Puritan leanings.

Mr. Henry Robinson says that "Guilford was born with a book in her hand,"[1] the founder Whitfield having published a second edition of a "little bundle of sermonettes dedicated to Lord Brooke, full of quaint conceits or poesies." And this was in the day of Shakespeare, Milton, and rare Ben Jonson. When Whitfield returned from New England he wrote his plea to Parliament for Indians, "for the good of the souls of the poor wild creatures . . . going up and downe with the chains of darknesse at their heels."

Benjamin Franklin purchased fifty copies of the first essay of the Rev. Jared Eliot of Guilford and Killingworth [present Clin-

LANDMARKS: The First Church (1830); first building erected 1643, first tower clock in America, 1726. (Historical sermon by Rev. F. E. Snow on "The Old Meeting-Houses of First Church," "Religious Herald," Jan. 26, 1899.) The Old Stone House built by the Rev. Henry Whitfield, 1639, property of the State of Connecticut. Contains museum of antiquities. On the land apportioned to the Rev. John Higginson stood the homestead of the son of the apostle Eliot, Rev. Joseph Elliott, who married a daughter of Governor Brenton, and, 2d, Mary, daughter of Governor Wyllys (1664) at Elliot Corner; property of Edward Eliot. The present house was built (1726) for Abiel Eliot who married Mary Leete, great-granddaughter of Gov. Leete. Their granddaughter was the mother of Fitz-Greene Halleck. In this house is an Eliot "Court-cupboard" rare. The Green-Charles Fowler house (1735). Major

followers. William Chittenden was known as Lieutenant, fought in the Netherlands, and was an ancestor of Governor Thomas Chittenden of Vermont and the Hon. Simeon Baldwin Chittenden, representative to Congress. Jacob Sheaffe, a grandson of the Canon of Windsor, William Wilson, and one of the "seven pillars" of Guilford Church, sold his rights and established a notable homestead in Boston. Jacob Sheaffe of Boston purchased the old Wentworth Mansion at Portsmouth, N. H., for his daughter Nancy, the wife of Charles Cushing.

[1] *Guilford and Madison in Literature*, by Henry P. Robinson of Guilford, a descendant of Thomas Robinson, 1666, and the Rev. Henry Whitfield.

Lathrop-Ralph D. Smyth house on house-lot of Thomas Jones, pioneer. Christ Church was organized at the William Ward house, near present residence of Miss Annette Fowler facing the Green; Broad Street: Timothy Stone house (1740). Daniel Hubbard house(1717); residence of John B. Hubbard. Tuttle house (1781), property of Miss Clara I. Sage. Chittenden homestead. Samuel Desborough's home-lot on "Mr. Desbrough's Lane" (Water St.), purchased by Dr. Bryan Rossiter, 1651; William Dudley residence. Fair Street: Russell-Frisbie house, residence of Benjamin C. West. Davis house (1759). Griffing house, residence Henry Eliot, and Mrs. Sarah Fowler. Birthplace of Frederick A. Griffing, a leading founder of the New Haven & New London Railroad; its first President and associated for many years with John I. Blair of New Jersey in the building of western railroads; the largest business man Guilford has produced. Johnson house (1746). Birthplace Samuel Johnson, Jr. Stewart Frisbee house, residence Edward M. Leete. Guilford Institute and High School. Gift of Mrs. Nathaniel Griffing. York Street: Samuel Robinson homestead (1752). Shelley-W. N. Norton house (1775). West Side: Dr. Sproat-Spencer house (1700), famous button-ball trees. State Street: On Henry Doude home-lot, Anne Kimberly-Benton house (1740). Titus Hall homestead (1696). Comfort Starr homestead (1764); home of the Seven Starrs, Seven Sisters. Philo Bishop house (1671). Union Street: Kimberly homestead (1732). Collins-Cook house (1700). Boston Street: Loyzelle-Burgis-Morse house. Caldwell-Lathrop house (1760), whence descended a branch of the L'Hommedieus of Norwich and Lathrops of New York and New Rochelle. Fiske-Wildman homestead. Clapboard Hill or "Dudley Heights." Justin Dudley house. Alderbrook

ton, founded by Edward Griswold, who came from Kenilworth, England]. Of Guilford's shaking meadows Eliot writes: " I began last Fall (1747) to drain another meadow of forty acres up in Guilford woods. This was a shaking meadow; a man standing upon it might shake the ground several rods around him. It seemed to be only a strong sward of grass laid over a soft mud of the consistence of pan-cake batter. There is reason to believe that the shaking meadows have been formerly beaver ponds . . . I was pitied as being about to waste a great deal of money . . . I ditched it, the ditch serving as a fence, and then sowed red clover, foul meadow grass, English spear and herd grass. If life and health be continued, I design to try liquorice roots, barley, Cape Breton wheat, cotton, indigo seed and wood for dyeing; as, also watermelon seed, which was originally from Arch-Angel, in Russia." His "darling subject" was the planting of mulberry trees for silk culture in Guilford, of which we are reminded in "Mulberry Farm," long the home of Eliots and Footes.

Cemetery; Fitz-Greene Halleck's grave. Moose Hill: General Eli Fowler-Kelsey house (1760). Fowler homestead (1765); birthplace of Sophia Fowler, a deaf-mute, the wife of Rev. Thomas Hopkins Gallaudet; her sons were Rev. Dr. Thomas H. Gallaudet, pioneer in the instruction of deaf-mutes, and P. W. Gallaudet of New York City and Dr. Edward M. Gallaudet. Nutplains: John Miles-Hall house (1745), residence of Dr. N. Gregory Hall. Davis homestead (1646). Parmelee house (1750). Evarts house (1756). Phelps house (1748). Sachem's Head: "Shaumpisheu Farm," Guildford, property of Mrs. Thomas H. Landon, for several years summer home of Bisho) Woodcock of Kentucky. Egleston and Crampton houses on Long Hill Road to North Guilford. Whealen house, old road to North Branford. Hungry Hill, Bluff's Head. Note: It is impossible to mention all Guilford's houses. There are at least 84 Pre-Revolutionary houses in Guilford and 46 in East Guilford (present Madison) and 13 in North Madison. Bassett homestead of six generations (1680).

MADISON: The five most ancient houses standing in the pleasant town of Madison are the James Meigs-Bishop house (1690), Boston Street, North Bradley homestead, Hammonasset (1680), Deacon John Grave house (1680), residence of Miss Mary E. Redfield, Captain Griffin-Scranton house (1759), and the Deacon John French-Captain Meigs house (1675). The Wilcox and Watrous houses of 1770 and the Hand homestead (1764). First meeting-house erected 1705, "between John Grave's house and Jonathan Hoit's." John Grave was chosen to beat the drum, "for twenty shiling a year."

The most distinguished pupil of Jared Eliot was Guilford's "studie-man," the Rev. Samuel Johnson, first president of King's (later Columbia) College. Bishop Berkeley said that he was "one of the finest wits in America."[1] "Through him," says Dr. Andrews, in his *History of Christ Church, Guilford,* "came about the extended use of the service of the Church of England in Connecticut, Samuel Smithson, of Mulberry Point, having loaned Dr. Johnson a Prayer Book, one of the 16 volumes comprising his library. Johnson was called by President Dwight the "father of Episco pacy" in Connecticut.

Teaching was hereditary in the Johnson family, but this was a farming community, and the farmers who kept sheep sent wool to the Johnson mill to be fulled, colored blue with indigo and black with logwood; a blue homespun coat with brass buttons was the pride of every old gentleman.

Master Samuel Johnson, of a later generation, was a fierce

[1] Other early writers in Guilford were the Rev. John Cotton, son of the famous John Cotton who "prayed in Indian," like Roger Williams, and also Samuel Hoadley: educated at Edinburgh and father of the Arch-

Samuel Robinson homestead of 1752, on site of the home-lot of 1664 of Thomas Robinson; residence of Henry Pynchon Robinson, Esq., York St.

CLINTON: Jared Eliot homestead. Redfield-Stevens house. Hill-Stevens homestead, Prospect Hill. Stanton house, John Stanton Collection of Connecticut antiques; on this site were held sessions of future Yale University by the Rev. Abram Pierson, first rector, when the foundation was in Saybrook.

Federalist and believing the country to be "going over to Infidelity and Revolution," he set the urchins this copy; "Demons, Demagogues, Democrats, and Devils." His favorite pupil was Fitz-Greene

bishop John and the Bishop Benjamin Hoadley; Rev. Thomas Ruggles, who left a manuscript history of Guilford. The Hon. R. D. Smyth wrote the *History of Guilford*, 1877. A later history is by his grandson, Bernard C. Steiner, now head of the Enoch Pratt Library, Baltimore. Other writers—Charles Wyllys Elliott, Rev. Abraham Chittenden Baldwin, and the poet, George Hill.

Halleck,[1] to whom he presented Campbell's *Pleasures of
Hope*. Johnson was unusually thin: and being much
bothered by a persistent tin pedlar to buy finally said;
"Have you a pair of tin boots?" "Yes, just to fit you,"
and brought out a pair of tin candle-moulds.[2]

Many are the tales of the country store. One day came

*Ruttanoo brook or East River Nutplains. Close to the bridge, the little boat
was always found waiting by the children of the Ward, Beecher, and
Foote families. Across the bridge on the pasture slope is the family
burying ground.*

[1] Whittier wrote lines to *Fitz-Greene Halleck* "at the unveiling of his
statue," ending:

> "But let no moss of years o'ercreep
> The lines of Halleck's name."

[2] Samuel Johnson (great-nephew of Dr. Johnson) wrote the first school
dictionary, 1798. One copy remains in the British Museum, one at
Yale University, and one in the Hartford Athenæum. His grandfather
Nathaniel (1744) was warden of Christ Church.—Samuel Johnson, Jr.,
and his Dictionaries, by Henry Pynchon Robinson, *Connecticut Magazine*, 1899.

a little boy with three eggs to barter: "Please, Sir, a penny's worth o' rum, a penny's worth o' gum, and the rest in sal-soda."

The village much admired Miss Catherine E. Beecher, and even to-day they talk of her driving down to the Green

The hospitable side-porch of the Foote homestead. Built by George Augustus Foote. He afterward removed to Mulberry Farm giving the Nut-plains farm to his sons. "Farming is the only business a man ought to follow," said he.

from Nutplains to buy a spool of thread of Miss A. lest some one else should buy it of a man, when a woman was in business.

A lady summoned a jack-of-all-trades to repair her fence. After contemplation he enquired, "Well, marm, will you hev it hen-tight or cow-tight?" "As we have n't any hens, I think cow-tight will do."

After the railroad was built, a Guilford worthy scorned the train, for, said he, "My white Dolly is safer when she stumbles, than the rail cars when they go down an embankment."

NUTPLAINS

A serene and lovely hamlet in Guilford is at Nutplains, where hickory and walnut trees unite with ancient elms to guard the spacious street. The eldest elm is one hundred and sixty-two years, and that noble one standing before the Meigs farm was planted by the grandfather of Fitz-Greene Halleck. The Indians used to fish all up and down both sides East River, and you could not walk across the lot without picking up an arrow-head. On the hither side of the "Iron Stream" rises "Fence Rock," so steep that the cattle cannot get up it on account of the ledges; volcanic action is evident in the valley.

Long ago, two homesteads stood in Guilford, one at Nutplains on the banks of Ruttawoo Creek, and the other on the north corner of Guilford Green, being closely related to each other, and to our literary annals. On the Green was the home of Eli Foote, whose wife was Roxana, the daughter of General Andrew Ward.

It was General Ward's regiment that remained at Trenton to deceive the enemy by keeping up the camp-fires, while Washington withdrew the army. It is related of Colonel Andrew Ward, who served in the Old French War, that he took his grog rations in silver and brought home six table-spoons engraved Louisbourg.

When Eli Foote died, General Ward took his ten grand-children home to Nutplains, one of whom, Roxana, became Mrs. Lyman Beecher. General Ward used to laughingly say of his three eldest granddaughters, that when the girls first came down in the morning, Harriet's voice would be heard—"Here! take the broom: sweep up: make a fire: make haste!"

Betsy Chittenden would say: "I wonder what ribbon it's best to wear at a party?" But Roxana (who became the mother of Harriet Beecher Stowe and Henry Ward Beecher) would say: "Which do you think was the greater general,

Hannibal or Alexander?" This incident is related in the *Autobiography of Lyman Beecher*,[1] perhaps the best picture of early days in Connecticut bequeathed to us. The quaint fascinating wood-cuts of the various homes at New Haven, Nutplains, East Hampton, Litchfield, and Andover make it all very real. Miss Catherine Beecher drew from memory the Ward homestead—"Castle Ward" the children playfully called it.

Roxana Foote (Beecher) the mother of Mrs. Stowe, spinning flax and conning French verbs, at "Castle Ward," Nutplains.

General Ward brought up his grandchildren on the most meaty and inspiring of intellectual pabulum, for he had the delightful custom of reading aloud with remarks and discussion. He read the whole public library through, but was of rather careless habits in household matters. He came home from the Legislature "with his saddle-bags loaded with books on one side and nails on the other. So, when

---

[1] *Autobiography, Correspondence, etc., of Lyman Beecher, D.D.* Edited by Charles Beecher. Copyright by Harper & Brothers.

8

he had taken his hammer and gone all over the place mending and patching, he would come in and read all the books." It was said of Eli Foote also: "Give him a book and he is as happy as if he owned Kensington Palace." So that his children's children had by rights a "born faculty" for pen and pulpit.

The girls' favorite sport was the spinning-mill built by General Ward in a ravine on a little brook with machinery for turning three or four spinning-wheels by water-power.

Roxana learned to speak French fluently from a refugee from San Domingo who settled in Guilford, and she studied as she spun flax, tying her book to her distaff.

The Ward house of delightful memories has disappeared but the tiny river flows on. You may cross the bridge, close to which the little boat was always found waiting by the children of the Ward, Beecher, and Foote families for four generations.

Lyman Beecher and Roxana Foote were married at Nutplains by Parson Bray. "Nobody ever married more heart and hand than we," said Lyman Beecher. He had met Roxana when staying with his uncle Lot Benton at North Guilford, where Lyman's passion for fishing developed, and grew rampantly; even after he became famous he would occasionally come in to the weekly lecture at Litchfield fishpole in hand and rest it against the pulpit. Mr. Beecher says:

"The first time I went fishing, Uncle Benton took me down to Beaver Head, tied a brown thread on a stick, put a crooked pin in it and worms, and said 'There, Lyman, throw it in.' I threw it in and out came a shiner. . . . I always liked 'training day' because I could go fishing. Fished all day till dark, and felt sorry when night came."

The Indians lingered long in Guilford after Whitfield's

The front entrance of the Foote homestead, Nutplains, residence of Mrs. Andrew Ward Foote. Here Harriet Beecher (Stowe) and all the children used to visit "Grandma Foote". Here she heard first the ballads of Sir Walter Scott.

"The lovely little white farm-house under the hill was such a Paradise to us, every juniper bush, every wild sweetbrier, every barren sandy hillside every stony pasture spoke of bright hours."—H. B. S.

band came, for they loved the creeks, their canoe-paths. The Totokets crept down over the trail—the shortest road to the beach—from their picturesque village "to pick clams and oysters" on the shore, stopping often at the pure and delicious spring on the Murray farm.

According to the legend of the farm the master of the old Jonathan Murray house once fell ill, and was cured by a passing Indian witch-doctor. On leaving she thrust her staff of buttonwood into the ground, vowing that "as long as this branch shall flourish so long shall the land go to the blood,

but a curse shall fall on him who cuts it down." This buttonwood tree yet gives grateful shade to the wayfarer. This was
the home of Mr. W. H. H. Murray, long known as "Adiron-
dack Murray," the first to reveal the charms of the Adiron-
dacks. Neck River runs at the foot of the farm, on which
the first millwright built.

The story of Sachem's Head is of the days of Uncas who

The little District School with wood-house,
North Guilford.

clung to his rights in the Hammonasset lands "to hunt,
fish, use trees for canoes, rushes for flags" in the deed of
sale to Colonel Fenwick. Uncas was leading Captain
Stoughton's troops on their chase of the Pequots when he
discovered that the wicked old Mononotto (who had disputed with him over the territory of New London) was in

hiding with his warriors on the (Guilford) shore towards Stony Creek. Uncas waylaid them as they attempted to escape by swimming across Bloody Cove, shot the chief, and placed his head in the crotch of a tree.

From Sachem's Head in 1777, Colonel Return Jonathan Meigs (of a Guilford family) led an expedition against Sag Harbor in sloops and whale-boats; they succeeded in burning all British vessels in the harbor, stripped a foraging party of De Lancey's Brigade, and captured the hospital on Brick Hill.

A month later three ships of the enemy landed at Sachem's Head and burnt Solomon Leete's house. In 1781 the British landed at Leete's Island, burning the house of Mr. Daniel Leete; they advanced toward Guilford and were repulsed by Captain Peter Vail and Lieutenant Timothy Field.[1]

Agnes Lee, the wife of Captain Samuel Lee of the Harbor Guard, was a noted foe to Tories. Powder was stored in the attic: one dark night a Tory knocked at her door, when Captain Lee was on duty; "Who's there?"—"A friend."— "No, a friend would tell his name," answered Mrs. Lee, and fired. An hour later, an old doctor of North Guilford was summoned to attend a mysterious gun-shot wound. When the British landed at Leete's Island, Captain Lee fired the agreed signal; "Grandma Lee responded by blazing away on the cannon set at the head of Crooked Lane, for she had not a son, and Uncle Levi was a cripple."

During the War of 1812 the story goes that as George Griswold was hoeing corn on his farm at East Creek, the church bell rang violently and the flag was raised on Clapboard Hill; snatching his sword Griswold mounted his black horse, gathered the militia company, a score of men with

---

[1] In 1688, the tyrannical days of Andros, commissioners were sent from Hartford to obtain the charter concealed at Andrew Leete's but Captain William Seward marshalled his company, and with drawn sword escorted them out of town.

rusty muskets. On reaching Leete's Island, they saw a
vessel manning her boats to make a landing. Realizing
that they would be no match for the invaders, they manœu-
vred by marching down through a hollow, then up in sight,
then down and around again until the enemy became impressed that the Guilford forces numbered nigh on a thousand men. At the same time the one "nine-pounder" at

*The birthplace of David Dudley Field, D.D., "The Woods" district, East
Guilford, present Madison, Conn., built by his grandfather, David
Field, in 1725.*

the Green fired shot after shot, and the British changed
their tactics and spread sail and away. Lieutenant Griswold's sword still hangs in his homestead.

Several Deerfield colonists sought a haven on the Sound,
where there was little danger of awakening to find a toma-

hawk flourished over one's head.   No family suffered more
than the Fields, many of whom were carried to Canada.
Ebenezer Field came to East Guilford and married Mary
Dudley, a descendant of two Governors of New Haven
Colony; David Dudley Field was born in "The Woods"
district, was graduated at Yale, then became pastor at
Haddam.   Captain Timothy Field, his father, served under
Washington, and either abroad or on the farm appeared in
"cocked hat," short breeches, long stockings, and bright
silver shoe-buckles.   He was Sergeant-major of the Sev-
enth Regiment of Connecticut, and after the defeat on Long
Island, was stationed between Fort Washington and East
River to watch the British troops which held the city of
New York, and took part at White Plains.

Many interesting and historical homesteads stand in
Madison and North Madison.   The beautiful green town
street is adorned by the Memorial Library to Erastus
Scranton.   John Scranton came with Mr. Whitfield in
1639.   It is said that six brothers settled here "within speaking distance."   The first minister, the Rev. John Hart, was
the sole member of the senior class of Yale in 1702, and the
first regular graduate.   When the Rev. Jonathan Todd
"was upon trial, in order to setel," Capt. Janna Meigs
(otherwise "ye Worshipfull Janna Meigs"), Deacon John
French, and Left. Thomas Crutenden were chosen to treat
with Mr. Todd upon his "principels."

NORTH GUILFORD

"Still sits the school-house by the road.

Within the master's desk is seen,
Deep scarred by raps official;
The warping floor, the battered seats,
The jack-knife's carved initial."

WHITTIER, *In School-Days.*

At the summit of Long Hill road lies a quaint and pretty

village, North Guilford with its district school. Here all
the world seems fashioned for Whittier's barefoot boy; his
is the feast of freshest berries and hickory nuts, wild-
flowers, scarlet strawberries and golden pippins, woodchucks
and shiners. It was in Quinebaug Outlet that Lyman
Beecher caught his first perch, and one may imagine the
jolly spelling-school and frolics at huskings—no law was
ever kept so well as that of the red ear, while the dry husks
rustled and sweet-cider went round. What heroes from
this woodland sprung! Many a boy became eminent who
learned the Rule of Three in "the great barn of a school in
North Guilford," though "nobody ever explained anything,
we only did sums," says Lyman Beecher; all the sons of
the village blacksmith Michael Baldwin became prominent.
Abraham Baldwin aided Milledge to found Georgia University, and his pet sister Ruth, with whom we are best
acquainted through the songs, madrigals, and letters of Joel
Barlow, poet and philosopher, was of a great piquancy,
amiability, and beauty, making her an object of admiration
in the polite circles of Europe. She ensnared the heart of
the poet when he was at Yale College in the remarkable class
of 1778,[1] inspiring a remarkable passion, which survived an
adventurous career, during which he negotiated the treaty
with Algiers and became minister to France, when Napoleon
was France. He writes to his love ever with merry badinage,
philosophy, and tenderness. An early letter, when she is
on a visit to North Guilford, affects jealousy. (The Bald-
wins were then living in New Haven.) "Do, Ruthy, tell

---

[1] Barlow excelled in mental rivalry even such men as Oliver Wolcott
(Governor Oliver Wolcott, one of the signers of the Declaration of Independence, married Lorraine, daughter of General Augustus Collins of
North Guilford) Noah Webster, Zephaniah Swift, Uriah Tracy, and Josiah
Meigs. His favorite tutor was Joseph Buckminister, who took charge
of the class when sent to Glastonbury during the Revolutionary disturbances.

me sincerely," he urged, "don't some of these mountain swains invite you to ramble in their green retreats, entertain you with fine stories about Arcadian nymphs and rural innocence? . . . But you must remember, *ma amie*, that your old friend Apollo was a poet as well as a shepherd and in winter time the most likely place to find him will be

The Birthplace of Gilbert Munger, Opening Hill, North Madison, Conn.
A painting of Niagara Falls ordered by the Prussian Government first made him world-famous. Munger's paintings of Venice were exhibited in London on the entreaty of Ruskin. The reigning Duke of Saxe-Coburg-Gotha conferred on him Knighthood with the title of Baron.

at college, so I advise you to return to New Haven as soon as you receive this letter. . . .[1]"

Ruth's father objected to her "rhyming lover," in spite of his position as chaplain in Poor's Brigade, but Barlow returned to New Haven when the army was in winter

[1] *Life and Letters of Joel Barlow, LL.D.*, by Charles Burr Todd, G. P. Putnam's Sons.

quarters and they were secretly married and—forgiven.

On Joel Barlow's first visit to Paris, he writes that he was "accompanied by Master George Washington Greene, twelve years old, who goes to Paris for his education, being addressed to the Marquis de Lafayette." General Greene's youngest son, and the son born to Lafayette during the Revolution, were both named George Washington. "This fact abided with Lafayette, and after General Greene died, he applied to Mrs. Greene to allow him to take her son George to France, where he might be educated with *his* George, so as to perpetuate the love which had illustrated the lives of their fathers." This came about as they wished, but unfortunately a few weeks after young Greene's return home, when on a pleasure party, the yacht capsized and all perished.

Mrs. Barlow was in the first weeks not enamored of Paris; she writes to Mrs. Dr. Dwight at Greenfield Hill: "O, it is altogether disagreeable to me. It is only existing. I have not an hour to call my own except when I sleep. Must be at all times dressed and see company. . . . We are pent up in a narrow, dirty street surrounded with high brick walls. . . . O, how ardently do I wish to return to America." Paris being unsafe in 1791, they removed to London, where they were frequent guests of Copley in Hanover Square, and saw much of Trumbull and Benjamin West.

In later years when Mrs. Barlow lived on their beautiful estate Kalorama—where Jefferson and Madison had often consulted with the statesman, Joel Barlow,—her thoughts turned backward to girlhood days in Connecticut. She saw the village smithy, the school-children watching the flaming forge and the wonderful yellow sparks struck from her father's anvil; the drives to the shore, the gathering of driftwood on the sand-beach, the steaming clam-chowder, each child so hungry that his spoon of clam-shell seemed silver-lined. In winter, light snowflakes falling, merry sleigh-rides, the horn sounding and bells tinkling, on frosty nights, ending in a frolic with blind-man's-buff, twirling the plate, and forfeits; and once more an eager hunt for snowdrops and pussy-willows coaxed out by that shy coquette, the bewildering New England Spring.

> "*Hark, 't is the bluebird's venturous strain,*
> *High on the old fringed elm at the gate—*
>   .   .   .   .
> *Dodging the fitful spits of snow,*
> *New England's poet-laureate!*"
>
> ALDRICH.

Late in the year of our Lord 1773, an unknown horseman, half-frozen, stopped to bait his horse in Guilford. It was the first patriotic ride of Paul Revere. He brought the audacious news to Connecticut that King George's tax-laden tea had just been salted down in Boston harbor by unknown Mohawk champions of Liberty, and it would seem as if Paul Revere's own war-paint as patriotic promoter of the affair was of so deep a dye that it could never be scrubbed off. Dr. Holmes says

> "*The waters of the rebel bay*
> *Have kept their tea-leaf savor.*
> *Our old North-Enders in their spray*
> *Still taste a Hyson flavor.*"

Revere was quickly off over the turnpike to Philadelphia, bearing secret dispatches to men who were soon to set the country seething by speeches, in that first Continental Congress.

This assembly met at the suggestion of the "father of all the Yankees," as Carlyle called Benjamin Franklin, who had written from London to the Massachusetts Assembly

The Lot Benton house at the sluice at the foot of Harbor St.; removed from the north end of Guilford Green by a yoke of 35 oxen ; residence of Captain Jeremiah Rackett.

that it was full time to meet and act. Virginia was the first in sending forth trumpet summons.

What next! Ebenezer Hurd, the fortnightly post-rider out of Saybrook, had ridden forty-six years through New Haven to New York and back, and never "heerd tell sech doin's." Every good man along the Sound rose daily expectant and took down his rusty flint-lock and the boys' guns from their hooks on the summer-beam to set them "hendy"; mother surreptitiously rubbed them up a bit with tears in her eyes.

It was before daybreak on Friday, April 21, 1775, that Lieutenant Israel Putnam's cry "to arms" echoed in Middlesex County, Connecticut; just as the cry of Paul Revere on his midnight gallop had roused Middlesex County in Massachusetts. Lieutenant Putnam received at the plough his message from Israel Bissell (who had ridden so hard from Watertown to Worcester that his horse fell in his tracks) and handed it over to the regular New York post-rider; people hastened from distant farms into Guilford,

Branford, and New Haven to hear the news of the Lexington fight and Minute-men began to strap on haversacks for the long march to Boston, while the post sped on covered with mud and foam through Milford, and Stratford; Sunday at noon the Lexington message was countersigned at Fairfield by Jonathan Sturges. On and on the war messenger

The Worthington Bartholomew house 1774, on the Boston–New York turnpike; residence of Rev. Dr. George C. Griswold. A remarkable "apple-tree elm."

rode through Norwalk, Stamford, Westchester—down Bowery Lane, past Governor Stuyvesant's pear orchard, the Tea-Water Spring,[1] and over the Kissing Bridge,[2] shouting his news regardless of Tory scowls, clattering down Broadway to Bowling Green.[3]

[1] Water drawn from this pump was said "to make better tea" than from any well in New York.

[2] Toll: "Salute your partner."

[3] The historic Green of the Burgomaster, centre of Nieuw Amsterdam, the heart of old New York.

What an excitement in the market-place ("T'Marck felt")![1] The Whigs repeated it in the very ears of His Majesty George III., who might well have risen in his leader stirrups with haughty amazement at the audacity of his Colonial subjects. The New York loyalists disdained to countenance the facts and waited for confirmation. Meanwhile Isaac Low signed the message. On Tuesday at two of the clock arrived a second war dispatch, indisputably endorsed by Pierrepont Edwards at New Haven on Monday at nine and one half o'clock. The Long Island ferry awaited impatiently the news packet near Fly (Fulton) market. From end to end of Long Island stirring scenes ensued— from Brooklyn Heights to Easthampton and among the retainers of the Lord of Gardiner's Isle. Town meetings from Faneuil Hall far South rang with "Liberty!" Troops assembled and Washington was summoned to command.

[1] Site of the present New York Produce Exchange.

The door-knocker of " Mulberry Farm," the Jared Eliot–Foote house. This knocker was removed from an older house on Guilford Green.

NEW HAVEN (QUINNIPIAC), 1637

" There was a wood, in which now the little ones gather in spring, and in autumn, heaping baskets of nuts. There was a strip of sea in sight, on which I can trace the white sails as they come and go without leaving my library chair ; and each night I see the flame of a lighthouse kindled. "

IK MARVEL at Edgewood, New Haven.

A GREAT charm of the City of Elms is the reach of blue sea—"Adrian's Sea," a poetical and appropriate pseudonym for Long Island Sound. The sea gives a final touch of kingly grace to the old New Haven Colony, and to her towns entangled 'mid lofty rocks, wooded hills, and tidal rivers.

The stranger within New Haven's gates is immediately impressed by the vista across the broad and beautiful Green, flanked by row upon row of superb elms planted largely by the people under the leadership of James Hllhouse.[1]

Three churches of varying creed now stand upon the aforetime Puritan market-place, where the austere stocks and whipping-post once nodded to the Town Pump and aided the one meeting-house—surmounted by its Indian Watch Tower—in discipline of Church and State. Unlike Boston Common, the New Haven Green was designed, says the Rev. Dr. Bacon, not as a park, but for buyers and sellers, for such public uses as were

Library Tower, at Yale. Ivy grown from the grave of Sir Walter Scott.

[1] Many of the elms planted between 1787 and 1796 came from the Hillhouse farm in Meriden. The Rev. James Austin planted inner rows on the Green. Among those who as boys participated were Judge Henry

reserved to the Roman Forum and the Agora at Athens. Nevertheless, being convenient, as on Boston Common, cows were pastured on the Upper Green, and a student

United Church on the New Haven Green, erected 1815. The Law School of Yale University on Elm Street.

transported one to the belfry of the Old Chapel, at which the unhappy cow protested as loudly as *The Pope's Mule* of Avignon.

Pressing close upon the colonists' Green are classic, ivy-

Baldwin, Ogden Edwards, and President Day. The first meeting-house stood where the flag-pole is, and Ezekiel Cheever's school-house hard by.

gowned halls, half concealed by the elms of the long Temple
Arch, and in the quadrangle hidden by these younger halls
of Yale University are the plain bricks of beloved South
Middle (Connecticut Hall), the sole survivor of "old Brick
Row." Facing the Green on the north is the Pierpont
house and other of the older homesteads of the city.

Contemplating the present community of tolerance one
may scarcely countenance the fact, as written in the Town
Records, that in the rigid years when this veritable Green
was subject to Blue Laws, Elder Malbon caused his daughter
Martha to be brought before three magistrates and sentenced to be publicly whipped,[1] because with her cousin
she attended a forbidden house-warming escorted by a
young man! Another delinquent was whipped for the
diabolical outrage of lighting his pipe on the public street
from a pan of live coals. Others were branded on the
forehead for theft. It was many years before the punish-
ments of the old country were discarded. The closing
scenes of Decker's *Old Fortunatus* [2] the villain in the stocks,
is akin to actual dramas of Colonial days in America, the
gate to which has been thrown open to us with Hawthorne's
key.

It has been a strange procession of years, this passing
from under a royal sceptre to the government by the people;
from Puritan edicts to our fraternal age, in which fellows
of all climes and creeds are "well met" on Yale's campus
It is the prettiest climb imaginable by woodland ways
to the summit of East Rock, for which the poet Hillhouse [3]

[1] Recorded by the Town Clerk and included in Mr. Cogswell's interesting
historical novel, *The Regicides*.

[2] *Old Fortunatus* was marvellously well presented in the rich garb of the
day on the grounds of Tufts College, by the undergraduates, in June,
1906.

[3] James A. Hillhouse, the son of James Hillhouse to whom New Haven
is so much indebted, was the author of *Percy's Masque* and other dramas.

of Sachem's Wood, suggested the name of "Sassacus" and for its twin, the West Rock, "Regicide." At your feet, submerged under countless elms lies a bustling city, its core the old "Nine Squares," stockaded and with guardhouses. You may draw imaginary lines around the Green and the other "quarters": Yorkshire quarter, Herefordshire quarter, and Mr. Gregson's and Mr. Lamberton's quarter, and the Governor's quarter which held Theophilus Eaton's mansion of nineteen fireplaces. Eli Whitney built his

The Soldiers' Monument on East Rock.

house in a portion of the Governor's quarter. President Stiles remembered the thirteen fireplaces in Mr. Davenport's house, for these built large houses to correspond with their accustomed style in London. Governor Eaton like Governor Edward Winslow of Plymouth played the part of diplomat and explorer for the new Colony.

At one corner of the Green, close to the inlet where the company landed, once stood a mighty oak on "Widow

Hannah Beecher's lot,"[1] at the present corner of Chapel
and George streets; here the planters assembled on the first
Lord's day to listen to the celebrated London preacher, the
Rev. John Davenport. The stump of this great oak severed
by time from its canopy of leaves, held the anvil of Nathaniel
Beecher. His grandson David used the same anvil placed
on the same oak stump.

> He lived well according to the times and laid up four
> or five thousand dollars. In those days, six mahogany
> chairs in a shut-up parlor were considered magnificent:
> he never got beyond cherry. He was one of the best read
> men in New England. . . . Squire Roger Sherman
> used to say that he always " calculated to see Mr. Beecher,
> as soon as he got home from Congress, to talk over particu-
> lars." He kept up with his student-boarders in their studies,
> and was very absent-minded: coming in from the barn he
> would sit down on a coat-pocket full of eggs, jump up, and
> say, "Oh wife!" "Why, my dear," she would reply, " I
> do wonder you can put eggs in your pocket." [2]

The bricks stamped *London* discovered in razing the
Atwater homestead recall the ballasting of the good ship
Hector and her consort with building bricks, for John Daven-
port and his opulent company. On the shipping lists the
names of men of note appeared in disguise, for the ship was
liable to be searched by order of the Lords of the Privy
Council for non-conformists obnoxious to the Government.[3]
It was with a sigh of relief that the port was cleared with

---

[1] In seating the meeting-house in 1646 the first seat was assigned to
Old Mrs. Eaton, and Widow Beecher was on the list of those "permitted
to sit in the alley (upon their desire) for convenience of hearing."

[2] *The Autobiography of Lyman Beecher.*

[3] Doubtless the names of Davenport and Eaton were not on the lists.
These had long been concerned with colonial projects, holding an interest
in Winthrop's *Arbella*, which led the fleet of 1630 to Salem.

all sail set and the ship's bow pointed toward Governor Winthrop's town, ere King James, alarmed at losing from his kingdom so many subjects rich in brains and property, published a decree forbidding men of their value to pass to plantations in his new Colonies without a license.

The good people of Boston besought the influential company of the "famous Mr. Davenport" to abide in

The old home of Roger Sherman, "The Signer" and the first Mayor of New Haven. The house was built by him in 1789 and stands on Chapel Street, near High, remodelled into stores.

Massachusetts. Newbury even agreed to give up the town. But the Bay was in a hubbub on account of the controversy precipitated by Mistress Anne Hutchinson[1] and at that moment Captain Stoughton returned from the campaign against the Pequots with the same glowing accounts as Captain Underhill, who wrote that "Queenapiok hath a fair river, fit for harboring of ships," etc., and his

---

[1] Mistress Hutchinson was banished and the master of the *Dove*, Captain Richard Lord, was fined for bringing over "the troublesome Anne Hutchinson."

The Pierpont House erected 1764-7, Elm Street.

This house was pilluged and used as a British hospital, July 5, 1779. Now the home of the Rev. Anson Phelps Stokes. On its walls hang rare prints and other Yale memorabilia. East is the Jarvis house of 1767. West stood the house of the Rev. James Pierpont, a founder of Yale.

interested audience, the London company, finally decided
to purchase lands beyond Saybrook. The first winter in
New Haven messages to their friends in Boston were probably carried by Indian runners, whom Roger Williams had
known to run eighty miles or more on a summer's day.

Strange adventures were those of the Regicides Major-
Generals Whalley and Goffe. Royal commissioners pursued them from Boston to New Haven and three times
orders for their arrest arrived. Twice concealed at West
Rock, on the boulders of Judges' Cave they carved the
days of the calendar. Feigning to go to Manhattan, they
returned to the house of the Rev. John Davenport. In
another refuge at Hatchet Harbor in the Woodbridge Hills,
provisions were conveyed to them by Richard Sperry; they
took the Indian trail over which Thomas Tibbals had led
the colonists to Wepowagee (Milford). Here they remained
two years (Judge Treat was in the secret), concealed in the
Tomkins house, never venturing out even in the orchard.
This game of hide-and-seek must have been an uneasy and
chilling period of existence; finally they fled to Hadley,
where the Rev. John Russell protected them for the rest of
their lives. The third Regicide, Colonel John Dixwell,
never dared reveal his identity in New Haven; although
he lived here from 1673 to 1689. The stone above his grave
behind Centre Church on the Green [1] is marked simply,
J. D., Esq. Mrs. James Pierpont used to wonder what her
good husband found to talk about at such length—across
the fence—with the mysterious "James Davids."

On the Lexington alarm the Governor's Guard of New
Haven and a company of volunteers, Benedict Arnold as
Captain, hastened to Cambridge. Nathan Beers, Jr., was
with them and was afterwards one of the guards of Major

---

[1] *Chronicle of New Haven Green,* by Henry T. Blake.

André. The original pen-and-ink sketch of Major André drawn by himself with the aid of a mirror and given by him to Jabez Tomlinson of Stratford, officer of the guard at Tappan, was passed to Nathan Beers of New Haven, and is in the Yale Library. The Beers elm on Hillhouse Avenue is

Collins Homestead, 1694,
West Haven.

Savin Rock, Long Island Sound.
Where the British Landed. West Haven.

the loftiest of its kind. The Jocelyn[1] portrait of Nathan Beers descended to his grandson Dr. Robert Ives.[2]

Extracts from the *Connecticut Gazette* in war-times:

July 5, 1775. His Excellency, Gen. Washington, Major-Gen. Lee, Major Thomas Mifflin, on their way to the Provincial camp near Boston, "were escorted out of New Haven by

---

[1] Nathaniel Jocelyn the portrait painter, was born in New Haven in 1796. His miniature was painted by G. Munger in 1817. "A Patriarch of American Portrait Painters," by Ellen Strong Bartlett, *The Connecticut Magazine.*

[2] William Ives came over in the *Truelove* to Boston in 1635, and joined the New Haven company. His son Joseph Ives married Mary Yale.

a great number of inhabitants, two companies dressed in their uniforms, and a company of young gentlemen belonging to the Seminary . . . whose expertness in military exercises gained them the approbation of the Generals."

June 28, 1780. " Yesterday passed through this town on their way to join the American army, the Duke Laezon (Lauzun) with his Legion, consisting of about 600. The strictest order and discipline was observed among them."

Nov. 29, 1781. Notice of meeting of the Commissioners concerning the confiscation of the estate of Benedict Arnold, " late of New Haven now joined with the enemies of the United States of America," at the dwelling house of Pierpont Edwards, Esq.

The invasion of New Haven was accomplished by Generals Garth and Tryon; when the fleet appeared off Savin Rock on July 4, 1779, one signal of alarm was the lantern hung in the old Woodbridge oak. Tryon landed at Lighthouse Point and Garth marched his forces across West Haven Green; the families in the first houses they entered were compelled to prepare them a good dinner; in the old Kimberly house[1] bullets mark their passage. Parson Williston, made prisoner, was released by gallant Adjutant Campbell's order.

Great was the excitement in New Haven. Colonel Sabin called on the militia, and Captain Phineas Bradley fortified West Bridge. Ex-President Daggett of Yale[2] peppered away solus at the British near Milford Hill: an English officer, surprised at the curious independence of the old gentleman, cried out. "What are you doing, you old fool,

---

[1] A quaint portrait hangs in West Haven of Mary Kimberly Reynolds, gowned in satin-petticoat, lace sleeves and cap, a peculiar ring on her forefinger with Masonic devices. The ring, lost in a cornfield, was recovered twenty years later.

[2] President Dwight wrote a famous national song of 10,000 lines during the Revolution.

An Old-fashioned Garden, Milford, Conn.
"Grandmother's gathering boneset to-day;
In the garrett she'll dry and hang it away,
Next winter I'll 'need' some boneset tea—
I wish she would n't always think of me!"
                                    EDITH M. THOMAS.

firing on his Majesty's troops?"   "Exercising the rights
of war," said President Daggett.   "If I let you go, you
old rascal, will you ever do it again?"   "Nothing more

likely," said the professor.   He was dragged out from his cover and injured fatally.

The Blue Meeting-House parsonage was ransacked. Many houses were pillaged and Madame Wooster,[1] wife of General David Wooster, first Major-General of the Connecticut troops, who fell at Ridgefield, was roughly treated; she sent her niece on horseback to Farmington with an escort, and stood by the guns with Prissy, who would not desert her mistress.

Mrs. Seeley of New Haven was a great Tory.   She walked out of church when a thanksgiving was offered after Bunker Hill.   "I came here to learn the way to heaven, not to Bunker Hill," said she.

General Garth departed by New Haven's celebrated Long Wharf, considered one of the great enterprises of that age.   It is made up of the parts of the Island of Malta, the Rock of Gibraltar, ballast from Sicily, gravel from Dublin, and rocks from St. Domingo and other islands of the West Indies.   Commodore Hull ran a West Indiaman from this port, prior to his command of "Old Ironsides."   On Long Wharf the "Merchant Princes"[2] congregated on business; and on rainy days, called "rat days" from the immense number driven out of their holes by the high tides, the merchants discussed trade at the Tavern, and pledged the success of the army.

---

[1] Mrs. Wooster was a daughter of President Clap of Yale, lineal descendant of John Howland and Mary Whiting of the Governor Bradford line.   The Mary Clap Wooster Chapter, D. A. R., is named for her; a sketch of Mrs. Wooster is in the volume *Patron Saints of Connecticut Chapters, D. A. R.*

[2] "Long Wharf has produced such men as Elias Shipman, Henry Daggett, Ward Atwater, Thomas Ward, Solomon Collis, Benjamin Prescott, Lockwood De Forest, Russell Hotchkiss, Timothy Bishop."   Thomas Rutherford Trowbridge, a Secretary and President of the New Haven Colony Historical Society, wrote with authority on the *Ancient Maritime*

Professor Ezra Stiles wrote in his *Every-day Diary* in 1777 concerning his election to the Presidency of Yale College: "An hundred and fifty or an hundred and eighty

The William Walter Phelps Gateway at Yale.

Young Gentlemen students is a bundle of Wild Fire not easily controlled or governed, and at best the Diadem of a

Interests of New Haven, his family being long connected with shipping interests.

President is a Crown of Thorns." President Stiles liked the intensely aristocratic laws of English Universities, and frowned down the Freshmen when they complained of the fags put upon them. When he was inaugurated, the procession returned to the Chapel in the following order:

The four classes of Undergraduates consisting of 116 students present; Bachelors of Arts: the Beadle and the Butler carrying the College Charter, Records, Key, and Seal: the Senior presiding Fellow; one of the Honorable Council and the President Elect; the Reverend Corporation; the Professors of Divinity and Natural Philosophy; the Tutors; the Reverend Ministers; Masters of Arts; Respectable Gentlemen.

Many interesting customs are continued at Yale. The ivy-covered buildings of the Skull and Bones, Scroll and Key, and Wolf's Head reveal no secrets, but on Tap Day in May the undergraduates assemble at the Senior Fence on the thrilling occasion of passing down the honors of the Senior Society by "tapping" on the campus, and a severe "go to your room" from the Senior to the lucky Junior, chosen for dignity of character, by tradition's decree. Exclusive rights of fence have increased as the fence diminished. President Timothy Dwight abolished the mediæval system of "fagging" for the freshmen and the "Bully" is no longer elected to rule in disputes between "town and gown."

Steeple crown hats are seen no longer in Chapel at 5 A.M., but the unique and dignified custom of "bowing to the President" takes place at the close of morning prayers. The President descends, and proceeds up the Senior aisle, the Seniors bowing from the waist to the floor as he passes. In early days the students were fined for any misdemeanor. One of the early penalties was a fine of one penny "for tardiness in coming to prayers." "Scholars when in their

chambers shall talk Latin."
" Every undergraduate shall be
called by his Sir-name unless
he be the son of a noble man
or Knight's eldest son."[1] In
1742 it was ordered that the
steward shall provide the commons for the scholars—"for
supper 2 quarts milk and one
loaf of bread for four. When
milk cannot be had then apple
pie wh. shall be made of $1\frac{3}{4}$
pounds of dough, $\frac{1}{4}$ pound hog's
fat, 2 ounces sugar and half a
peck of apples." After all is
said, those who live in Kipling's
" pie belt" assert that nothing
can surpass in flavor a *good*
apple pie. A farmer was over-
heard to say on sending a wagon
load of melons to the metropo-
lis, " Would you believe it, them
dudes in the city ruther'd hev
melons than pie for breakfast!"

When Jonathan Edwards was
a student at Yale, he wrote to
his father at East Windsor for
a pair of dividers, also a book
on the Art of Thinking. " P. S.
What we give a week for board,
is £0. 5s. 0d."

In contrast to the present

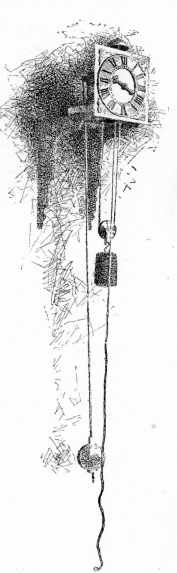

Wag at the Wa'.

---

[1] " Orders and appointments to be
observed in ye Collegiate School in

*A Sheffield Tea-Service Used in the old Maltby Mansion,
Fairhaven, Conn.*

splendid buildings and scientific equipments at Yale University, Lyman Beecher's account is interesting. "Yale College then [1793] was very different from what it is now. The main building then was Connecticut Hall, three stories high, now South Middle College. . . . As to apparatus . . . there was a four-foot telescope, all rusty: nobody ever looked through it, and if they did, not to edification. There was an air pump, so out of order that a mouse under the receiver would live as long as Methuselah."

At the base of East Rock in a romantic vale, Lake Whitney and Mill River trail like a serpentine ribbon. At the head of tide-water stand the picturesque mills of Eli Whitney, where he retrieved his fortunes by the manufacture of firearms, because his early and mightiest invention brought him nothing but vexation of soul. The writer saw the crude hut on the banks of a pleasant brook in Augusta, Georgia, in which Mr. Whitney first experimented with his cotton-gin. The story is told by a granddaughter of Gen-

Connecticut." From the Field Papers in possession of the Connecticut Historical Society. Also Professor Dexter's *Yale Biographies and Annals.*

West Rock, New Haven.

"My Farm at Edgewood."

The Home of Donald G. Mitchell—"Ik Marvel."

eral Nathanael Greene of the consummation of Whitney's experiment at the beautiful and hospitable *Dungeness* on Cumberland Island, over-canopied with live-oaks and olive-trees. Mrs. Greene had become interested in Mr. Whitney's enterprise and invited him to spend the winter at *Dungeness,* "where an abundance of cotton and quiet were assured." One morning he descended headlong into the drawing-room from his workshop in the fifth story and excitedly exclaimed, "The victory is mine." In deep sympathy, guests and hostess went with him to see the model in motion, by which Whitney was to change the industrial history of the world. For a few moments the miniature saws revolved without hindrance, and the separation of the seed from the cotton wool was successfully accomplished; but after a little the saws clogged with lint—the wheel stopped and poor Whitney was in despair. "Here 's what you need," exclaimed Mrs. Greene, and instantly seized a clothes-brush, and held it firmly to the teeth of the saws. "Madam," said Whitney, overcome with emotion and speaking with the exaggeration of gratitude, "you have perfected my invention!"

On a secluded and sweet upland at the edge of a hillside wood lives the dear companion of all youth, and good Americans in particular—Ik Marvel. His "farm at Edge-wood" faces what appears to be a thick wood pierced by belfries, spires, and towers in high relief against purple hills; the picture's frame is composed of Mr. Mitchell's own beautiful shrubs and trees.

Passing through the Dutch door into an hospitable hall, a familiar portrait of our host in his youth reflects the eternal charm of the pensive humor of the *Reveries*. To a querying

---

[1] "Recollections of Washington and His Friends," as preserved in the family of General Nathanael Greene, by Martha Littlefield Phillips, *Century Magazine*, January, 1898.

world, the *Bachelor* answers: "I should think there was as much truth in them as in most Reveries." One can but look at his library with emotion, and the room of ancestral portraits. From its window is a view of the Woodbridge hills, commemorating a family name, and who but a man with such a Scotch grandfather as Donald Grant could have spiced with a piquant savor that comparatively prosaic period of American Letters,—from the *Mayflower* to Rip Van Winkle,—"when the need to do things . . . seemed so much larger than the need to write about them"!

New Haven holds possessions unique in America: The Center Church on the Green, modelled after St. Martin's in-the-Fields with the Crypt; the Jarves and Trumbull Galleries of Yale, and Hillhouse Avenue. Sachem's Wood,[1] high among the oaks, the stately home of the author of *Percy's Masque*, faces the avenue at one end, and the handsome building of the New Haven Colony Historical Society[2] the other. Hillhouse Avenue was private property until 1862, and annually on some October night Mr. William Hillhouse and Mayor Skinner used to stretch the chain across the entrance.

The silvery bell of Battell Chapel calls the study hours as you walk by the Sheffield Scientific School, past the Avenue's historic houses, to obtain a view from Sachem's Ridge and the Winchester Observatory. Conspicuous is the beautiful

---

[1] Senator James Hillhouse (father of the poet James A. Hillhouse), who planted these elms in 1792, was often called the "Sachem" because of his Indian complexion, and a joke of his Congressional confrères related to a hatchet he kept in his desk. His favorite toast was "Let us bury the hatchet." The Hillhouse estate has recently become the property of Yale University, and a part of it will be devoted to the Yale Forestry School. *Hillhouse Avenue, formerly Temple Avenue, from 1809–1900*, by Henrietta Silliman Dana, is an interesting sketch of its homesteads.

[2] The Historical Society building is a memorial gift of Henry F. English. Open to the public from 9 to 5.

tower of Christ Church,[1] a rare example of fourteenth-century Gothic, and soon will rise the new Library building of Yale.

> Most notable in the Yale Library is the Salisbury Collection of Oriental Languages and Literature. Professor Lanman alludes to Edward Elbridge Salisbury as the "life and soul" of the Oriental Society. He was the founder of the Oriental chair at Yale long filled by the eminent William Dwight Whitney.
>
> Men of Yale distinguished in letters and science are legion; Andrew White in his *Autobiography* says: "Yale had writers, strong, vigorous, and acute; of such were Woolsey, Porter, Bacon and Bushnell, some of whom, . . . had they devoted themselves to pure literature would have gained lasting fame."
>
> Of the collections in the Peabody Museum,[2] Huxley says that Professor Marsh's Extinct Mammals of North America are surpassed by no other collection in the world. Woolsey Hall contains the Steinert Collection of Musical Instruments.

In the Yale Art School Building (the gift of Augustus Street), is the finest Gallery of early Italian Masters in the country. James Jackson Jarves was inspired in his selection of rare works adorning the Chapels of the Old World. It would be out of the question to gather together anything

---

[1] The architect of Christ Church was Henry Vaughn. The beautiful chancel window was designed by C. E. Kempe.

[2] Indispensable to the traveller is the *Guide to New Haven and Yale University*, with maps, and including the old houses. As supplementary reading carry also the *Historical Sketches of New Haven*, by Ellen Strong Bartlett. Miss Bartlett's illustrations of the Trumbull Gallery and the Center Church are comprehensive, including even the Tablets to the Pastors, which are of unusual historic interest; to Nicholas Street, a graduate of Oxford University; to Chauncey Whittlesey, member of the Colonial Assembly, to James Dana and the rest.

A *Manual of the Geology of Connecticut* with map has been compiled by William N. Rice, Ph. D., L.L.D. and Herbert E. Gregory, Ph. D.

PATRIÆ PATER

Washington.

From a photograph by William Radford of an Engraving by Rembrandt Peale after his own Portrait of Washington. The artist made the Engraving, and then apparently added the leaves around it. The painting hangs in the National Capitol.

approaching it now, beginning, as it does, with the first known Italian painter Giunta of Pisa, down through Veronese, Taddeo Gaddi and Spinello. The frames alone are a rich study. One spans ages of thought in stepping from the Jarves Gallery into the Trumbull Gallery, in which we meet face to face the men of Washington's day (Colonel Trumbull was very exact in his likenesses). One is an eye-witness of the events of the Revolution dramatically presented by the Aid-de-camp of General Washington; among patriots and heroes are Laurens, Knox, Rochambeau, Schuyler, Mifflin, Colonel Wadsworth and Governor Jonathan Trumbull, Jr., whose daughter Harriett married the celebrated Professor Silliman the elder; and surprisingly beautiful miniatures of charming women, belles of that day—the graceful Eleanor Custis, piquant Peggy Chew, and the Hartford beauty, Mary Seymour Chevenard.

Trumbull's full-length portrait of Washington represents the Chief at the moment when resolved to retreat into the country from the banks of the frozen Delaware. (This portrait, originally painted for the city of Charleston in 1792, was presented to Yale by Governor Trumbull, General Jedediah Huntington, the Honorables John Davenport, Benjamin Talmadge and Jeremiah Wadsworth.) Washington writing to Francis Hopkinson on the subject of his sittings for an earlier portrait says: "It is a proof, among many others, of what habit and custom can effect. At first I was impatient at the request and as restive under the operation as a colt is of the saddle. The next time I submitted very reluctantly, but with less flouncing. Now no dray moves more readily to the thill, than I to the painter's chair." *Lossing*.

Washington visited New Haven in 1789, on his tour through New England.

The city offered all hospitality and honor to the great

Washington, recently inaugurated as head of the new republic. In scanning the pages of Washington's own account of his tour, one notes illustrious Connecticut names. It is a striking fact that at New Haven, the three chief magistrates who received President Washington were all Signers of the Declaration of Independence—Governor Samuel Huntington, Lieutenant-Governor Wolcott and the Mayor, Roger Sherman.

Powder-horn decorated with a drawing of New Haven Green and a troop of horse, and inscribed, "Moldrum. In the 42d Royal Highland Regiment, His Powder Horn made at Crown Point, November 17, 1759. In the Anson Phelps Stokes Collection of antiquities of New Haven.

THE TOUR OF GENERAL WASHINGTON IN 1789[1]

[In part; from New York to Springfield]

" [New York] *Thursday, October 15th, 1789.*

" Commenced my Journey about 9 o'clock for Boston and a tour through the Eastern States.

" The Chief Justice, Mr. Jay—and the Secretaries of the Treasury and War Departments accompanied me some distance out of the city. About 10 o'clock it began to Rain, and continued to do so till 11, when we arrived at the house of one Hoyatt, who keeps a Tavern at Kingsbridge, where we, that is, Major Jackson, Mr. Lear and myself, with six servants, which composed my Retinue, dined. After dinner, through frequent light showers we proceeded to the Tavern of a Mrs. Haviland at Rye; who keeps a very neat and decent Inn.

" The Road for the greater part, indeed the whole way, was very rough and stoney, but the Land strong, well covered with grass and luxuriant crop of Indian Corn intermixed with Pompions (which were yet ungathered) in the fields. We met four droves of Beef Cattle for the New York Market, (about 30 in a drove) some of which were very fine—also a flock of Sheep for the same place. We scarcely passed a farm house that did not abd. in Geese. . . .

" Their Cattle seemed to be of good quality, and their hogs large but rather long legged. . . .

" Friday 16th.

. . . we breakfasted at Stamford, which is six miles further (at one Webb's). . . . At Norwalk, which is

---

[1] Extracts from the *Diary of Washington:* From the first day of October, 1789, to the tenth day of March, 1790. From the *Original Manuscript* now first printed. New York, 1858. By permission of Estate of James F. Joy.

Benson's Tavern, Fairfield, Conn.
From "An Old New England
Town."

Copyright by M. O. Wright
The Village Elms.

The Oldest Inhabitant.

"The bird notes invite you to come and live in the garden of nature."
"An oriole queries 'Will you? will you, truly?'
The meadow lark answers 'Spring o' the year, Spring o' the year.'"
MABEL OSGOOD WRIGHT.

ten miles further we made a halt to feed our horses. To
the lower end of this town Sea Vessels come. . . .

"From hence to Fairfield where we dined and lodged
. . . we found all the Farmers busily employed in
gathering, grinding and expressing the Juice of their apples;
. . . The Destructive evidences of British cruelty are
yet visible both in Norwalk and Fairfield; as there are the
chimneys of many burnt houses standing in them yet.
The principal export . . . is Horses and Cattle—
salted Beef and Pork—Lumber and Indian Corn to the
West Indies."

"*Saturday 17.*

"A little after sunrise we left Fairfield, and passing through
Et. Fairfield breakfasted at Stratford, . . . a pretty
village over near Stratford River. . . . At this place
I was received with an effort at Military Parade; and
was attended to the Ferry . . . by several Gentlemen
on horseback. Doctor Johnson of the Senate, visited me
here, being with Mrs. Johnson in this town (where he formerly resided). The [Housatonic] Ferry is near half a mile;
and sometimes incommoded by winds and cross tides.
The navigation of vessels for about 75 tons extends up to
Danby."

"From the Ferry it is about 3 miles to Milford, . . .
In this place there is but one Church, or in other words, but
one steeple—but there are Grist and Saw mills, and a
handsome Cascade over the Tumbling dam. . . . From
Milford we took the lower road through West Haven, . . .
and arrived at New Haven before two o'clock. . . .
By taking the lower Road we missed a Committee of the
Assembly, who had been appointed to wait upon and escort
me into town—to prepare an address—and to conduct me
when I should leave the City as far as they should judge
proper. The address was presented at 7 o'clock—and at
nine I received another address from the Congregational
Clergy of the place. . . . I received the Compliment
of a visit from Governor Mr. Huntington—The Lieutenant

Governor Mr. Wolcott and the Mayor, Mr. Roger Sherman."
"The City of New Haven occupies a good deal of ground,
but is thinly, though regularly laid out and built. The
number of Souls in it are said to be about 4000. There
is an Episcopal Church 3 Congregational Meeting Houses
and a College, in which are at this time about 120 Students
under Auspices of Doctor Styles [Ezra Stiles].   .   .   .

*he first House built outside the Palisades, Milford, Conn.   Residence
of Mrs. Nathan G. Pond.   Property of Charles W. Beardsley.*

The Exports from this City are much the same as from
Fairfield &c., and flax seed, (chiefly to New York)."

"Sunday, 18th.
"Went in the forenoon to the Episcopal Church, and in the
afternoon to one of the Congregational Meeting-Houses.
Attended to the first by the Speaker of the Assembly, Mr.
Edwards, and a Mr. Ingersoll, and to the latter by the

Governor, the Lieutenant Governor, The Mayor and Speaker."

" These Gentlemen all dined with me (by invitation), as did Genl. Huntington, at the house of Mr. Brown, where I lodged, and who keeps a good Tavern. Drank Tea at

From the Connecticut River Wethersfield is a view of delight ; her Christopher Wren spire nestles among the trees, and white stones of the old burying ground, like a flock of sheep on the hillside, appear quite English and pastoral.

the Mayor's (Mr. Sherman.) Upon further inquiry I find that there has been about . . . yards of coarse Linen manufactured at this place since it was established—and that a Glass work is on foot here for the manufacture of Bottles. At 7 o'clock in the evening many Officers of this

State, belonging to the late Continental army, called to pay
their respects to me. By some of them it was said that the
people of this State could, with more ease pay an additional
100,000£ tax this year than what was laid last year."

"*Monday 19th.*
"Left New Haven at 6 o'clock and arrived at Wallingford
(13 miles) by half after eight o'clock, when we breakfasted,
and took a walk through the town. . . . At this place
(Wallingford) we see the white Mulberry growing, raised

*The old Home of the Hon. John Webster, Fifth Governor of Connecticut,
Hartford.*

from the seed, to feed the Silkworm. We also saw samples
of lustring (exceeding good) which had been manufactured
from the Cocoon raised in this Town, and silk thread very
fine. This except the weaving, is the work of private
families, . . . and is likely to turn out a beneficial
amusement. . . . We arrived at Middletown, on Connecticut River, being met two or three miles from it by the
respectable Citizens. . . . I took a walk round the

Chief-Justice Ellsworth Mansion, Windsor, Connecticut.
Life-size Portrait of Chief-Justice Ellsworth and Abigail Wolcott Ellsworth.

Town, from the heights of which the prospect is beautiful. Belonging to this place, I was informed (by a Genl. Sage) that there were about 20 sea vessels. . . .

"Having dined, . . . passing through a Parish of Middletown and Weathersfield, we arrived at Hartford about sundown. At Weathersfield we were met by a party of the Hartford light horse, and a number of Gentlemen from the same place with Colonel Wadsworth, at their head, and escorted to Bub's Tavern, where we lodged."

" *Tuesday 20th.*

"After breakfast, accompanied by Colonel Wadsworth, Mr. Ellsworth and Colonel Jesse Root, I viewed the woollen Manufactory at this place, which seems to be going on with spirit. Their Broadcloths are not of the first quality, as yet, but they are good; as are their Coatings, Cassimeres, Serges and Everlastings; of the first, that is, broad-cloth, I ordered a suit to be sent to me at New York—and of the latter a whole piece, to make breeches for my servants. . . .

"Dined and drank tea at Colonel Wadsworth's and about 7 o'clock received from, and answered an Address of, the Town of Hartford."

"Wednesday, 21st.

"By promise I was to have Breakfasted at Mr. Ellsworth's at Windsor, on my way to Springfield, but the morning proving very wet, and the rain not ceasing till past 10 o'clock, I did not set out till half after that hour; I called, however, on Mr. Ellsworth and stayed there near an hour— reaching Springfield by 4 o'clock, . . . examined the Continental Stores at this place, which I found in very good order. . . . A Col. Worthington, Col. Williams, Adjutant General of the State of Massachusetts, Gen. Shepherd, Mr. Lyman, and many other Gentlemen sat an hour or two with me at Parson's Tavern . . . which is a good house."

Charter Oak Chair.
Senate Chamber, Hartford.

DEERFIELD (POCUMTUCK), 1670

" . . . in the broad interval
Through which at will our Indian rivulet
Winds mindful still of sannup and of squaw,
Whose pipe and arrow oft the plough unburies,
Here in pine houses, built of new-fallen trees,
Supplanters of the tribe the farmers dwell. "

EMERSON.

"It is agreed that an Artiste be procured upon as moderate terms as
may be that may lay out the Lotts at Pawcomptuck to each proprietor
according to their Lawefull interest. "—*Resolved at Dedham Town Meeting.*

ON a terraced plateau of a valley within a valley were
builded the homes of Deerfield. The Pocumtuck tribe
once swarmed this vale, council seat of the Connecticut
River Confederacy: these with their allies defied Uncas
and the Mohegans in the Thames Valley: but the power
of the belligerent Pocumtucks was finally broken by their
recent comrades in arms, the fiery Mohawks, whose wigwams
lay distant two suns beyond Hoosac on the hither side of
Beverwyck (Albany).[1]

If you will but climb to the north of Fort Pocumptuck—
from which the tribe was dislodged and annihilated in
North Meadows by the Mohawks in revenge for the murder
of their ambassador, Prince Saheda,—past Sachem's Head
and Bear's Den to the Poet's Seat, you find yourself high
above the gorge where Pocumtuck stream—our Deerfield
River—turns abruptly and enters the Connecticut, by
piercing Pemawachuatuck, the *Twisted Mountain:* it severs
the Great Beaver's tail, driving royally through a craggy

---

[1] The first large Dutch settlement on the site of Albany, rich in beaver
was named after Beaverwyk or Beaverville of the Fatherland. The
beaver no longer build dams in Holland.

ate feathered by mountain pine. Here you may feast
n the mellow landscape of both lesser and greater valleys.

FROM THE POET'S SEAT

See, below the historic Albany ford, how—between
elds of tasselled corn—the slender Deerfield bends en-
reatingly toward the rugged and sometime menacing
oot-hills of Hoosac, where is the boiling spring, its well-
ead; while the superb Quonetacut (home of the Sococquis,
s Count Frontenac called the river Indians) runs smiling
ne entire length of old Deerfield township,[1] some twenty-
ve miles, and on and on, broadening as it runs between
ne blooming tobacco fields toward the cherished patent of
ords Say and Sele and Brooke, at last to lose itself in
drian Block's "Great Bay."

Look over the blue hills and far away to the north: the
eigneurs' territory of New France is intrenched behind a
undred leagues of waving tree-tops almost unbroken except
y Le Merde Iroquois (Lake Champlain) with its ominous
oint à la Chevelure or Scalp Rock (Crown Point). For a
entury, savage war-parties glided out of the glorious St.
awrence down the Sorel or Richelieu River, across Lake
hamplain, over the Winooski, and into the Connecticut
o attack the Massachusetts Reach.

Again from your Poet's eyrie you can discern but one
hite man's road, through which aid might come to the
order during King Philip's War, that is, the *Old Bay Path*,
rodden out by Thomas Hooker and by Pynchon on his
ay to the Boston Council from Springfield, and later by
roops from the Bay who marched double-quick to the
escue of Quaboag, Aggawam, Nonotuck, Squakeag, and
orwothuck. The word frontier is a cynonym for *peril*,
hich in our Colonies appeared as a living Red Peril.

---

[1] Brookfield, Springfield, Northampton, Northfield, and Hadley.

How daring a deed to set one's hearthstone [1] on the North
west frontier at the extreme outpost of Deerfield! [2] It wa
to fly English colors in a hollow square composed of wil

The Samson Frary house on home-lot of 1698, residence of Miss C. Ali
Baker. Section added in 1748 for Town Hall with high carved cornice
The kitchen has a huge summer-beam. Key-stone of fire-place arch is
double-sized brick. Benedict Arnold stopped here, when a tavern, to pro
cure beef for his troops. Oldest house in Connecticut valley.

---

[1] Deerfield's hearthstones nearly all came from "Hearthstone brook.
not far from Cheapside bridge.

[2] Early Deerfield included Greenfield, Gill, Conway, and Shelburn
averaging 9 miles in width below the great bend at Peskeompskut (Tu
ner's Falls); it was bounded by present Northfield, Bernardston, Leyde
and Colrain on the north; by Montague, Whateley, and Williamsbur
south; Connecticut River separated it from Sunderland, Montague, Ewin
and Northfield; west are Claremont, Buckland, Goshen, and Ashfiel
where George William Curtis and Charles Eliot Norton held feasts

forests and savages. Yet, Pocumtuck's stream overflowing Deerfield's verdant plain, sheltered by the Great Beaver, was to the Colonist as another Jordan in a new Land of Promise.

At least so thought Deerfield's pioneer, Samuel Hinsdell of Hadley, whose rude plough—impatient—disturbed the placid green level of a breadth and beauty truly remarkable. Hinsdell had "made Emproument" of several acres, before Lieutenant Joshua Fisher and Timothy Dwight arrived to gauge the famous "8000 acre grant" of western land with which the Colonial Council had reimbursed Dedham; a generous slice, for leading men grumbled audibly at yielding up their superior Naticke meadows to Eliot's Praying Indians.

Lieutenant Fisher had passed by the "Chestnut country" (now the beautiful town of Lancaster) because too many farms had been pre-empted; riding on over the Bay Path, the ambassadors had mounted the Connecticut ten miles above Hadley to these rich Pocumtuck meadows celebrated throughout the Province, because Major John Mason,[1] by purchasing the corn-crop of 1638, and persuading the Pocumtucks to paddle forty canoe-loads to Hartford, saved Connecticut from starvation.

The Dedham men reported few Indians and fair grazing on the hillsides "Easterlie and Westerlie"; also that the

---

eason. At Leyden Hills, Henry Kirke Browne the sculptor was born, also in the vicinity, Chester Harding, William M. Hunt, and Larkin G. Mead.

[1] This was a unique affair altogether, for never before in the history of conquest did a victorious General beg food from the brothers of the vanquished; and these, Major Mason, Mr. William Wadsworth, and Deacon Stebbins, who ascended Connecticut Valley one hundred miles to buy corn, were the first Europeans to enter Deerfield Valley.

LANDMARKS: Arms Corner house-lot (1698), south end of Deerfield Street. Tablet. West Lots. Christopher Stebbins house (1712), home and studio of Augustus Vincent Tack. Col. John Hawks-Hoyt house (1810). Barnard house, residence Henry Childs. Childs-Russell Williams house, residence Mrs. Elizabeth Williams Champney, studio of the late J. Wells Champney. Squire John Williams house. Birthplace of Bishop Williams. Mehuman Hinsdale house (1760), residence of the Misses Whiting. Ephraim Williams house, residence of William Williams. The Old Albany Road. Dickinson Academy. Benoni Stebbins lot. Site of Old Indian House or Hoyt Tavern. Tablet. Now home of Mrs. L. B. Wells. The First Church (1824), fifth building on site. Joseph Stebbins house (1768), Captain of Company in 7th Regiment under Colonel Brewer, fought at Bunker Hill. Commission signed by John Hancock. Residence Hon. George Sheldon. Williams house (1750), remodelled, residence Miss Louise Billings. Jones homestead (1750). John Sheldon homestead (1708). Broughton lot ran west to Broughton's Pond; Broughton family massacred, 1693. East Lots, North End. Stebbins homestead. Ebenezer Hinsdale house (old house in 1750). residence Mrs. E. C. Cowles. Allen house. Site Colonel David Field house and store (1754-85), engaged in fur trade with the Mohawks, and was Chairman of Committee of Correspondence and Safety, Delegate to Constitutional

meadow land of Pocumtuck hath a flavor akin to our beloved home-lots circled by the alluvial Charles, despite one striking difference, Pocumtuck is close-hipped by a curling, zigzag ridge. That east ridge of danger to old-timers! Why was the settler blind! Could he not see how these very hills of enchantment were eyries for the savage and his hill-locked home an easy prey? Of what use his turreted green-log fort and twenty leafy look-outs above? In open season, from the budding of the creeping azalea to the fall of the mahogany shield of the oak, some pair of tree-hidden eyes—never wearying—watched the farmer's goings and comings with plough, sickle, or to mill[1]; not even a chicken strayed outside the stockade unmarked by an arrow.

Nevertheless, each proprietor only saw in anticipation his luxurious crops bending under the

[1] One brilliant summer day, 1695, a party of villagers rode to mill through South Meadows with bags of grain thrown across their horses. (Joseph Barnard, first town clerk, Godfrey Nims, first constable escaped from the famous "Falls Fight," Henry White and Philip Mattoon). Deep in town affairs, unnoticed was the whirr of the meadow lark, the scarlet wing of the blackbird, or the song-sparrow, "All is vanity—vanity—vanity." Suddenly from an alder ambush sprang Indians and Barnard was fatally wounded at "Indian Bridge." Tablet.

Convention. David Sheldon house, residence Mrs. Samuel Childs. The Manse or Willard house. Orthodox Parsonage on site of Deacon Thomas French house (1703); previously lot of Quentin Stockwell (1673) where Mr. Mather, the first minister, boarded. Samson Frary house on home lot of 1698, residence of Miss C. Alice Baker. The Godfrey Nims lot, Home of the Deerfield Society, residence of the Misses Miller. Lane to Memorial Hall (1799) containing Museum. Orlando Ware house. Site Catlin homestead, 1778–1874. The Catlins established a rope-walk and made pewter buttons. Barnard House. Arms Corner. Stillwater Gorge. In 1746, after surrender of Fort Massachusetts to Gov. Vaudreuil, Indians crossed Hoosac Mountain by the Indian path and waited in hiding behind some haystacks in Stebbins Meadow near the beautiful Stillwater Gorge.

References: Sheldon's "Deerfield." "True Stories of New England Captives," by C. Alice Baker. Sketch of George Fuller in "Six Portraits" by Mrs. Schuyler Van Rensselaer. "George Fuller, His Life and Works." Sketches by W. D. Howells and others.

Events in Deerfield, according to early history: First grant, 1669; began to settle at Pocumtuck, 1671; Captain Lothrop's defeat, 1675; began to re-settle, driven off, 1677; commenced settling second time, 1682; settled a minister (Mr. Williams), 1686; town destroyed second time, 1704; number of inhabitants, 280; killed at the sack, 47; taken prisoners, 122; slain on the way to Canada, 19; never returned, 28; redeemed from the enemy, 62.

western breeze from the Sunsick Hills, little dreaming that Deerfield's rich harvest of five years hence was inadvertently to become a primal cause in precipitating the blackest day New England had as yet seen—that September tragedy when Muddy Brook changed its color and name. It is Bloody Brook to this day.

The Indian title was purchased of the Sachem Chaud[1] through the good offices of the great man of the Middle Connecticut Valley —Worshipful John Pynchon of Springfield — soldier, diplomat, and fur-trader.

The old squaw Mashilisk, mother of Wattewwaluncksin, marked Deerfield's south bound "To ye Lower Point of ye hill called Wequamps and by ye English Sugar loafe Hill"; Mashilisk's Wequamps (the picturesque southern knob of Pocumtucke Range, an especial glory of Hatfield towering sheer above pretty Sunderland Ferry) is of high prehistoric dignity; Agassiz says that the Connecticut River once occupied

---

[1]Chaud reserved "Liberty of fishing for ye Indians in ye Rivers or waters and free Liberty to hunt Deere or other Wild creatures and to gather Walnuts, Chestnuts and other nuts things etc. on ye commons."

Deerfield Plain and swept forcefully around Sugar Loaf, evidence of its seething tracks being a huge "pot-hole" on the craggy slope.   The valley legend of the Great Beaver (East Mountain) as related by a Pocumtuck Indian tallies with the conclusion of Agassiz.   This fragment has come down to us:

> "Many, many suns in the past, ere the wigwams of our tribe stood here, a great lake rippled wide and long across the land.   In its waters a giant beaver sported, and ravaged all the countryside.   Mighty Hobomok, wroth, vowed that the wicked one should die.   With an oak cudgel he struck across the beaver's neck—just there, O Netop [pale face], in the hollow between head and shoulders.   The fearful creature sank gasping to the bed of the lake and his carcass turned to stone."

The back of the petrified beaver [1] rises to a dizzy shelf, Pocumtuck Rock—"the East Eye"; another vigilant sentinel watching over Old Street is Arthur's Seat, "the West Eye," 1000 feet above tidewater, near Shelburne line in the Sunsick Hills.

The traveller of steady head will delight to stand on Pocumtuck Rock sheer above Eagle Brook Plain, Wisdom and the Old World and the Mill, and sweep his field-glasses up Old Street and North Meadows of pathetic history toward Cheapside, Country Farms, and hidden Greenfield, besides Turnip Yard at the final slope of Great Beaver's back; south, below Wapping or Plumbtree Playne (whence the captive Hursts were carried to Sault au Recollet), far

---

[1] The geology of this region is interesting.   A rare collection of the curious blue "claystones" found largely on the *left* bank of the Connecticut at low water has been made by the scientist, Mrs. Jennie Arms Sheldon and illustrated in her volume, *Concretions from the Champlain Clays of the Connecticut Valley.*   The flora hereabouts is included in *Wild Flowers of the Northeastern States* by Ellen Miller and Margaret C. Whiting of Deerfield.

The Fall in Deerfield Old Street.

That there shall be a highway for the common street laid out six rod in breadth . . . beginning on that side toward Eagle Brook and so on to run Northerlie . . . one teare of lot fronting on the said common Street Easterlie and another teare of Lotts fronting on the said Street Westeslie. . . . The Dedham Committee on laying out the Town Plott, 1671.

out beyond the Bars, Indian Hole, Squaw Hole, Bars Long Hill, the Grindstone, and Sugar Loaf, spread out in Nonotuck Valley the meadows of Old Hatfield and older Hadley; finally the brother peaks Mount Tom and Mount Holyoke stop the way, picturesque guardians of "Long tidal River," Quinetahacut.

DEERFIELD TOWN PLOTT

The Artiste divided Deerfield Town Plott into long, narrow strips, the southerly end of it being "att a little brook called Eagle Brook," extending to the falling ridge of land at Samson Frary's cellar on the north; each planter was obliged to set a stake "with the two first letters of his name, fairly written"; if found wanting, he was fined 12d. The Worshipful John Pynchon bought out the Rev. John Allyn of Dedham, thus owning the largest strip—54 cow commons and 4 sheep commons (5 sheep or goat commons being equal to 1 cow common).[1]

Four years passed of peaceful tilling and gathering of harvests, then a runner left direful news at farmhouse doors —that King Philip had at last yielded permission to his young braves to begin depredations in the village of Swanzey while the householders were sitting under the famous Welsh preacher, Pastor Myles, in ye little Baptist Church at New Meadow Neck. Worse yet, Nipmucks—after having ambushed in a narrow defile the peace ambassador sent by the Colonial Council, Captain Edward Hutchinson—had attacked Quabaug (Brookfield) with fire-arrows; the "treacherous heathen"—as Captain Thomas Wheeler calls the Nipmucks in his extraordinary *True Narrative*—"bound their

---

[1] The Dedham men largely sold their rights; Serg Fuller owned 20 cow commons; Isaac Bullard 11; Rob't Ware and Nathaniel Fisher 15; Joh Bacon 7; Jnh. ffarington 18 and 2 sheep commons, etc. Governor Leverett sold his for £6 current money and several barrels of tar.

arrows with cotton rags and brimstone, lighted them and shot at our roof"; then, "those cruel, blood-thirsty heathen" rammed against the house a fire-wagon, devised by a pair of cart-wheels piled high with flax, hay, and candle-wood. The besieged—some twenty men, fifty women and children—raised a few logs for a rampart and were holding feather beds against the windows; a holocaust was imminent when Major Willard's company appeared.

The Indian fighter, Captain Mason, Captain Richard Beers, and Lieutenant Thomas Cooper with dragoons and Indian allies arrived to aid terrorized Middle Connecticut Valley.

A critical moment! Should Mohawks choose to unite with the eastern tribes all those villages lying between the trading-post Warranock or Westfield (the jealous rival of Springfield in fur barter) and feeble Squakheag or Northfield, a veritable hot-bed of Indians, repeatedly deserted and repeatedly garrisoned—in 1688 by Sergt. Bigelow and Capt. Jonathan Bull of Hartford, sent by Gov. Andros,—would without doubt be caught in the vortex of massacre; especially Deerfield, so daringly planted on the canoe path of the Long River. No "darsnt's" appear in *their* vocabulary.

Moreover Red-skin allies were oft-times like snakes in the grass. Attawamhood declared that the Indians made "fools of the English," signalling their approach to the enemy by bird calls. Game was plenty hereabouts in season, but it was often starvation on long scouts to our regulars trained to a full knapsack; they were not able like the Kentucky Rangers or *coureur de bois*, to march on a handful of parched corn, or like Indians to enjoy ground nuts and boiled moccasin. An English commander, in the Old French War, on a far western trail beyond Albany, in lieu of starvation accepted Indians' pot-luck and was horrified to see a human hand ladled out—"his hosts were breakfasting on a dead Frenchman."

French battalions were often in trouble because they scorned to lay aside in the wilderness the rich foppery and courtly magnificence of the Old Régime. Yet the French were apt in cementing friendship with the savage. Even the splendid Count Frontenac, who commanded his army from a litter in old age, stooped to gambol in their wild dances to show his good fellowship.

> "*Crowned Quebec on her Citadel*
> *Fierce wild tales of her youth can tell.*
>
> .   .   .   .   .
>
> *The young sweet land of La Nouvelle France*
> *Has its share of Old World romance:*
> *But sobered by time are sword and gown.*"
>   *The Old Régime,* "SERANUS."

THE FLOWER OF ESSEX

> "*The fields shall grow yellow with ripened ears, and the red grape shall hang upon wild brambles.*"—VIRGIL. *Ecl., iv.*

The larder at the seat of war stands empty. Commander-in-chief Pynchon answers the starvation question by orders that his wheat at Deerfield be threshed—upwards of three thousand bushels,—and detached Captain Lothrop of the Bay to convey the provender to Hadley; "seventeen of ye principal inhabitants of Deerfield" volunteered as teamsters. Escorted by the very flower of Essex, the wheat wagons rumbled out of the village over the old Hadley road across South Meadows and Bars Long Hill. A crisp September air dispersed all megrims of lurking danger and the merry little procession crossed Eagle Brook—yonder stream of golden shallows and playful cascades, child of Pemmawachuatuck's cooling height—and let down the

The Allen Homestead, Deerfield Old Street, residence of the Misses Mary and Frances Allen.
Here, outside the stockade stood the Dame School; in King William's War, Dame Hannah
Beaman and her little pupils fled to the fort under a rain of arrows and bullets from Indian
allies of Baron de Saint-Castin ot Pentegoet (Castine, Maine). The enemy was repulsed by
Captain Wells.

169

Bars.[1]   (Now the Bars district is written down as of a bitter
and sweet history, first as a field for scalping-parties, and of
late the scene of Genius's peaceful victories in color—the
almost unrivalled color and American charm of George
Fuller.)   Another half-hour and the road led the commissary
relief-party through a bog, fringed with wild grape tangles
and scarlet dogwood—just such grape vines as delighted
the Norsemen.   Guns were carelessly left on the grain-bags
whilst heedless yeomen jumped down to supplement the
hasty sunrise breakfast with at least one luscious cluster—
"which proved dear and dead grapes to them," says Cotton
Mather.   In a twinkling out of the innocent marsh rose a
shower of poisoned arrows and the harsh, distracting war-
whoop, close-pressed by tomahawks and scalping-knife
of eagle-plumed warriors, whose tawny backs had been
indistinguishable from the mire.   Captain Mosely rushed
in too late.   Of the valiant husbandmen only John Stebbins[2] escaped, and all New England mourned with Deer-

---

[1] The Bars Gate was closed each day in the fall to fence the cattle so
they might feed in the valley until snow-time, after coming down from
the summer hill pastures, where the stock was allowed to run at large.

At all roads, gates had been set up except that leading from Hatfield
into South Meadows, where there were a set of bars; this Deerfield district
was the scene of the Bars Fight.

Here Edward Allen and his wife were killed by Indians;   Samuel Allen
also on the meadows north of the Burk homestead, "while valiantly
defending his children."   Eunice was tomahawked but recovered; the
boy Samuel was taken but rescued because of the gratitude of a squaw.
These were oral historians of fearful events.   The Allen homestead became
the studio of George Fuller, who was born in the Locke house opposite,
now the home of George Spencer Fuller, Esq.   Enneking says: "Many
Americans beside Whistler rank high as simon-pure impressionists; among
them George Fuller takes the highest rank."

First gate-keepers: Eleazer Hawks had charge of the Bars, John
Broughton of the north gate, Samuel Northam the middle gate, Jonathan
Wells at Eagle Brook, Ephraim Beers at Wapping.

[2] John Stebbins, the only man known to come out whole from the
massacre, was grandson of Rowland Stebbins, the family's founder in

Photograph by Frances and Mary Allen.

The Old South Door

Of ye Nims homestead, through which Revolutionary volunteers went out to war. De Rouville's Indian allies tragically burned the first house on this lot, that of Godfrey Nims, cordwainer, and "captivated" Mistress Mehitable Nims and little Abigail; now the home of the "Blue and White" Society, residence of the Misses Miller.

field, for were not "six and twenty children made orphans all in one little Plantation?"—moreover, brave Captain Lothrop and his "choice company of young men none of whom were ashamed to speak to the enemy within the gate" lay slain.

The Bloody Brook still ripples by the black mountainside." [1]

(From Sugar Loaf's rock chair above, tradition says that King Philip watched the fray, as he actually did watch the burning of Seekonk seated in a great arm-chair.[2])   To Moseley's aid came Major Treat, being out on a north scout; the Indians retreated, crossing the river at the glorious gorge of Stillwater shouting: "Come, Moseley! Come! you seek Indians, you want Indians, here's Indians enough for you!"

They stopped only to wave the garments of the English before the families of their victims in Deerfield fort: Captain Appleton sounded the trumpet, and the miscreants disappeared up the trail through Wisdom and Greenfield at the right of the present Eunice Williams monument.

DEERFIELD OLD STREET

Sauntering along witching Deerfield Old Street and up the slight rise of Meeting-House Hill, you read beneath each gable and lean-to, and carved door flecked with elm

---

America.   Lothrop lost men from Lynn, Romney, Cambridge, "Ould Newbury"; John Parke of Watertown received a pension, £2. 10s., for a wound in the elbow.

[1] The ballad of *Bloody Brook* was read by the author, Edward Everett Hale, at the anniversary of 1888.   Previously Edward Everett, "our first citizen" as Dr. Holmes called him, delivered one of his incomparable orations at Bloody Brook, and is by interesting coincidence descended from a settler of Dedham—Richard Everard.

[2] King Philip's arm-chair is preserved by the Antiquarian Society of Rehoboth.   See *Old Paths and Legends of New England*, Vol. I., chapter on Rehoboth; also *Swansea*, for the opening of King Philip's War, and *Dedham*.

shadows, tales of strange captures and stranger escapes by the old men, sturdy youths, and winsome maids of border days; for eighty-nine years of long winter evenings house-mothers shuddered at the shrieking blast lest it smother a war-whoop, and called to "father" to draw the shutter bars. Yet, when one family was devoured by Indians, another, by sheer pluck, built a house on the ashes of the first.

Two child neighbors were carried into captivity, to meet later as strangers, fall in love, and marry at Sault au Recollet fort; one little Abigail, daughter of Godfrey Nims, baptized into the Catholic faith and called *To-wat-a-go-nach* by the squaw *Ganastarsi* with whom she lived; the other, her sweetheart, Josiah Rising, was carried from the house of Mehuman Hinsdell, "twice captured by Indian Salvages," known to-day as "The Harrow" of the *Blue and White* group, standing south of Dickinson Academy; the latter is built on the site of Parson Williams's parsonage, burned at "The Sack," which stood hard by ye Old Indian house, whose ponderous, battered oak door with tomahawked hole —through which Mistress Ensign Sheldon was shot in her chamber—is conspicuous in the Deerfield collection at Memorial Hall (having been saved by Dr. Slade[1] of Chestnut Hill).

Pathetic there is the worn, wee shoe of the little captive, Sally Coleman, four years old, one of the spoils of Ashpelon's raid, and in the first party led to Canada. Sally dropped its mate in a brook during the long journey. By unresting demands, Benjamin Waite and Stephen Jennings had

---

[1] Visitors and historians are immeasurably indebted to the zeal of the Honorable George Sheldon in making accessible here at *Memorial Hall* a remarkable objective history of Deerfield and Pocumtuck Valley. Mr. Sheldon's History is a monument to Colonial heroes, many of whom would otherwise have been lost in obscurity. Mr. Sheldon has also published *The Journal of Captain Nathaniel Dwight; The Little Brown House on the Albany Road; The Flintlock Used in King Philip's War* and other monographs of Deerfield.

ransomed their families and the little girl travelled home to
Hatfield by Lake Champlain, Lake Saint Sacrement (Lake
George), and the Albany Road, but not before seeing Sergeant Jonathan Plympton, who had fought stoutly with
Moseley's troop, led unmoved to the stake by his friend
Obadiah Dickinson. This tiny, battered shoe is expressive
of unwritten pioneer martyrdoms, and is as precious to pa-
riots, as was to pilgrim of scrip and staff, the finger encased
in silver of the greatest of the seven thousand virgins in
the beautiful Church of St. Ursula.

Quentin Stockwell says in his dramatic relation that it
was through Chief Ashpelon's intervention that all were
not tortured or burned.

"We were like to starve. All the Indians went a Hunting
but could get nothing: Powwow'd and got nothing, then
they desired to see what the Englishman's God could do.
I prayed, so did Sergeant Plympton. . . . The Indians
reverently attended Morning and Night: next day they
got Bears." One bear's foot served five captives for twenty-
four hours.

Count Frontenac benevolently sent four Gentlemen of
his Household and a guard to escort the captives across the
border. Benj. Waite writes from Albany to Hatfield to
hasten aid: "*Stay not for the Sabbath, nor for the shoeing
of horses. We shall endeavor to meet you at Canterhook
[Kinderhook], it may be at Housatonuck [Great Barrington].
We must come very softly because of our wives and children.*"

That was a triumphant and pathetic procession welcomed
in broad Hatfield Street led by the rescuers carrying each a
babe, born in bondage—Captivity Jennings and Canada
Waite. Some were much altered by hardships; one mother
did not recognize her own boy, so she sang the child's favorite hymn, and he ran into her arms.

Old Street's mellow serenity this leafy month is intensi-
fied by contrast to "Injun days." On both sides of the

road, hiding among huge elm roots which break the sod, the dandelion doubles its yellow crest and long-stemmed purple violets open wide eyes at a stranger's intrusion thus early in summer. A whiff of rich fragrance from the haughty Persian lilac in a front door-yard brings back February days in tropical New Orleans where you discern an unaccountable delicate odor, long ere you arrive at the source of the sweetness—the rose-trimmed arch gate or the sweet-scented olive tree a block away. There at your left, on the old Sheldon place, half-way between the church and North Meadows, is an apple-tree bank. The pink and white blossoms have but recently fallen on the tribe's sepulchre here overlooking the river. How marked is the savage understanding of the beautiful! That which Thoreau says of Old Bedford of Middlesex, is true of this Deerfield bluff: "*The land still bears the scar here, and time is slowly crumbling the bones of a race. Yet without fail every spring since they first fished and hunted here, the brown thrasher has heralded the morning from a birch or alder spray, and the undying race of reed-birds still rustle through the withering grass. But these bones rustle not.*"

You delight in the springy earth path running straight to its close in a triple row of maples on the North Terrace and seat yourself under a leafy green umbrella facing the Leyden Hills, North Meadows in the interval between.

The country path compels reverie, just as gray asphalt and red brick incite that peculiar exhilaration of great human marts where mind flashes electric and creative under counter-currents; but once irresistible Spring enters the City she turns hurrying feet toward the calm hills against the blue.

The hush of the mowing-land is broken by an ox-cart's creaking as it trundles along against the dark low back-

Looking across North Meadows from Old Street, toward Pine Hill, whence Indians Approached Deerfield Village.
A Rift in the Clouds above Cheapside.

175

ground of Pine Hill. The farm-boys cool off under the nooning oak, "the Dinner Tree," so-called by Deerfield school-children as far back as Revolutionary Days. A bird of velvety coal-black wings and white breast sets his tall reed swinging next a burdock by the brook and whistles softly in free, careless joy, for are we not both guests of Lowell's "frank-hearted hostess"—*June*, "whose roof is every spreading tree"!

> "*A week ago the sparrow was divine;*
> *The bluebird, shifting his light load of song*
> *From post to post along the cheerless fence,*
> *Was as a rhymer ere the poet come;*
> *But now, oh rapture! sunshine winged and voiced*
> .   .   .   .   .   .
> *Gladness of woods, skies, waters, all in one*
> *The bobolink has come.   .   .   ."* [1]

Tragedy holds you on the green bank all the long afternoon; you count certain treacherous footsteps creeping with cruel intent toward village stockade; again, footsteps retreating, as one train after another of lagging captives cross Deerfield North Meadows, at this moment surpassingly beautiful in two-mile reach flecked with flowers. No fence of the owners interrupts the shaded sea of color, only Plain Swamp Brook sweeping toward Cheapside, the pretty hillside village, formerly Green River and an important post at the head of Connecticut River navigation, now possessed of seven bridges across her three rivers.

Looking backward many suns into a half-legendary mirror, the beat of tom-toms mingles with cries of aboriginal battle, as Mohawk drives Pocumtuck out of his Fort Hill stronghold and slaughters him in his corn-field. Pine Hill's skirts were again and again smirched with red during

---

[1] *Under the Willows*, James Russell Lowell.

Anglo-Saxon possession, yet she lifts her rounded green head serenely oblivious to world tumult. Under King Philip's sceptre Pine Hill saw the spoilers of Bloody Brook fly past under swamp and sugar maple of flaming red and gold, and at the opening of Queen Anne's War witnessed the approach of Sieur Hertel de Rouville and his four handsome brothers with a band of Caughnawagas and Abenakis.

The exceeding great ambition of his Majesty Louis XIV., punished in the War of the Spanish Succession, was the indirect cause of the flood which overwhelmed a few inoffen_sive villagers in the Massachusetts Province of Queen Anne, Deerfield's disaster being but the tail-end of a tidal wave of European discord. The policy of "Good Queen Anne" lay less in war than in distributing her famous "Bounty," of which our colonial churches possess tokens, and in stimulating Pope, Swift, and other wits of the Augustan age, who assembled at Wills' Coffee-house in Covent-Garden; yet through her romantic fondness for a lady of her bedchamber —the strong-minded Sarah, Duchess of Marlborough— Anne, last of the Stuart dynasty, was persuaded to declare war against France.

Responsively, in New France Governor Vaudreuil began depredations at "Guerrefille," glad of any excuse to bind as allies the vacillating and wolfish Abenakis, panting for more plunder and victims; this tribe might so easily go over to the English, their villages on the Saco and Kennebec being dangerously nigh Governor Dudley's Boston. Moreover, the French dared not rouse the Iroquois, so the Governor sent a war-party three thousand miles from Royal Mount to bag a handful of New England farmers instead of bigger game at Albany.

It happened that in 1704, "the old-fashioned frump, a ery hard winter had laid in great stores of snow with great ving winds." A February thaw had crusted the snow

12

in one boundless ice-sheet, circling the forty-one houses of our Puritan outpost, and, as the blacksmith said, "it was cold as the north side of a Jenooery gravestone by starlight." Sieur de Rouville left the Pickomegan (Green River) and advanced along the Deerfield, halting to reconnoitre under the west pines; the *trappeur* drew his pointed toque and gray cloak more closely under the bitter chill preceding dawn; discarding snowshoes, the half-starved band again advanced, carrying plentiful cords to bind the fluttering English birds whom they should snare, and now and again stopping, that the crunching under so large a body might appear but the rising and falling of the wind. Up they crawled on the natural ladder of a huge drift meeting the top of the palisade. A dreamless sleep enwrapt the innocent village, likewise the sentinel lulled by a mother's song to a teething babe; this one night, alack the day, Colonel Peter Schuyler's warning [1] was forgot and Parson Williams unheeded, having cried wolf too often. Raging with desire for food and plunder, the "red varmints" dropped within.

The blockhouse of Sergeant Benoni Stebbins [2]—bullet-proof by virtue of bricks between sheathings—was aroused by the awful war-whoops and death-cries of its neighbors.

---

[1] The vigilant commander of the northern militia, Colonel Peter Schuyler, Mayor of Albany, had forewarned Deerfield of the designs of French and Indians, says Chancellor Kent. Colonel Schuyler understood and had more influence with the Confederacy of the Five Nations than any other man. He chastised the Canadian French for destruction of frontier settlements. (New York Historical Society Collections.) Colonel Schuyler also (in 1710) presented through the Duke of Shrewsbury to Queen Anne the "four Indian Kings," who created a great sensation in London.

[2] The Stebbins garrison sheltered several families: Deacon David Hoyt (later captured and starved to death at Coos Meadows, now Newbury Vt.), Joseph Catlin, and Benjamin Church were there: the women melted all the silver and pewter, and the enemy was kept at bay three hours until aid arrived under Captain Jonathan Wells, who drove the invaders to Pine Hill.

*Ell of the John Sheldon Homestead, Deerfield, Mass.,
Home of Five Generations, and Handed down to the
Hon. George Sheldon.*

ilence Hoit "peeped cautiously out of a little dormer-
indow. Deerfield village was roaring with flames, the
ky and snow were red, and leaping through the glare came
he painted savage, a savage white face and the waving sword
f a French officer in their midst."[1]

---

[1] *Silence, and Other Stories*, by Mary E. Wilkins Freeman. Copyright,
98, by Harper & Brothers.
The vivid drama of *Silence* is akin to experiences of many a maid in the
ench and Indian wars, and Miss Wilkins has by her art made fiction
pear more true than reality itself.

Hatfield, Hadley, and Northampton interpreted the glare
in the heavens as Indians and flew to the rescue, meeting
distracted John Sheldon, half-frozen, bringing news of the
Sack.   At Chicopee the friends of Sheldon's sweet young
wife, Hannah Chapin, nodded to each other, saying, "Now
truly, she hath sad need of that pelisse," for they, in jest, had
quilted the future bride's wedding cloak of double thickness
three months before, laughingly saying: "in case the
Indians should carry thee off to Canada."   Hannah Chapin
proved herself a heroine, for the leap out of the window of
Ensign Sheldon's house (always, after that night, the Old
Indian house) sprained her ankle, which destined her to
captivity, yet she tore a blanket in strips to protect John
Sheldon's feet and urged him to leave her and alarm Hatfield.   The pioneers drove out the enemy, and the remnant
of the town took refuge at Captain Wells's without the
stockade, he having a palisade all his own.

Footsteps on the creaking snow of Deerfield Street and a
light swish of petticoats, it is *Silence* looking over the
meadow to the north.   "David!   David!   David!" she
calls, her fair wits slipping away with each step of her lover
toward Canada.   Widow Bishop, hastening after, harshly
admonishes her to go to spinning: "There is scarce a yard
of linen left in Deerfield."   Seven months later, according
to Goody Crane's prophecy, the moon an hour high, *Silence*
at last recognizes David returning across the meadow with
a white sheep's fleece over his shoulders.

> *Go, gentle gales, and bear my sighs along*
> *The birds shall cease to tune their evening song,*
> *The woods to breathe, the waving woods to move,*
> *And streams to murmur, ere I cease to love,*[1]

---

[1] Pope wrote his *Autumn Pastoral* that same remarkable year of 170
when the genius of Prince Eugene and the Duke of Marlborough won
Blenheim, and the renown of British arms was rising to an unsurpassed

CARRIED CAPTIVE TO CANADA

Watch our forlorn captives fording Green River's icy current, running at too swift a pace to freeze, yet in midsummer, how deliciously cool and transparent. John Williams walks erect and austere among the French, who exult not in their victory, being sobered by the repulsiveness of Indian warfare, and the savages' broken promise to De Rouville to fight like civilized Frenchmen. Little Eunice is carried carefully by Whistling Serpent[1] and her youngest brother Samuel dragged on one of the sledges (recovered at Brattleboro) over frosted lake and river, for children are valuable assets as future converts[2] to the governing faith of the *seigneurs:* likewise the boy can hunt and fish for his indolent owner. The mother Eunice, drenched and fainting, is put to death by her Indian master. Blind with grief, Parson Williams stumbles on, laden with smoked moose and suffering painful cramps of *mal à la raquette*, yet cheering his fellows by reciting from the Good Book. The savages threaten them with burning alive, should one escape. What an extraordinary experience for the followers of John Cotton and Increase Mather! At evening the bivouac in the forest: the snow swept aside in a circle, around a fire crouch hardy Canadians hooded like Capuchin monks, and savages fantastic in war-paint, remnants of their last dance

---

itch of glory.   Neither General nor Poet probably cast half-a-thought on contemporary wars or loves across the Atlantic.   Yet, a few years later, England talked of nought else than the presentation at Court of the American Kings, and the *Spectator's* sparkling satires on the Mohawk petitioners.

[1] "Whistling Serpent" is the name given to Eunice's Mohawk master by Mrs. Champney, who has written Eunice's strange adventures for children—*Great Grandmother's Girls in New France*.   Mrs. Champney talked with descendants of the Caughnawagas and searched Jesuit Relations."

[2] Jesuit zeal possessed converts among Iroquois of the Saut and Mountain, Abenakis of the Chaudière, Hurons of Lorette, Algonquins of Three Rivers.

*The Stoop of Parson Williams Homestead on road to
Albany, built in 1707 by the town for their "Redeemed Captive," to replace his parsonage burned
in the Sack. The salary of the Rev. John Williams, a Harvard graduate was payable in pork,
wheat, and Indian corn.*

in the Mission Square of Sault St. Louis (Caughnawaga).

Hither to Kanâwaké — "By the rapid" — they carrie
Eunice, child of Puritans, and the Jesuit taught her to forge
her catechism, to the grief of her father.   Like the little cap

---

[1] Kanawâké, or Caughnawaga, is situated at the head of Sault St. Lou
Rapid opposite Lachine, about twelve miles from Montreal.

tive Mary Field,[1] daughter of the courageous Field pioneers who braved several Deerfield massacres, Eunice espoused an Indian,[2] taking also to her heart the wilderness customs and dress. Perchance she sang also the songs of *ancienne mère-patrie* which floated from the passing raft, or that plaintive Caughnawaga song—"Rinonwes rinonwes, Ra-keni" (translated by a son of a Six-nation-chief, John Waniente Jocks, in *Songs of the Great Dominion*):

MAIDEN:
"Well, father, what is thy word?
My spirit is now to marry."

FATHER:
"Ashamed be thou, my child—
Thou whom I hold my little one,—
Thou art yet too young;
Thou canst not get thee thy food."

MAIDEN (in the words of the chorus):
"I love him, I love him, father,—
That young man."

---

[1] The father of Mary Field (a son of the Deerfield pioneer Zecheriah) fought the enemy in the North Meadows, hoping to rescue his family, all captured or killed in 1704. He then pulled up stakes and travelled down river to East Guilford (Madison) on Long Island Sound, following his brother Ebenezer, the ancestor of David Dudley Field. A cousin, John Field, married Sally Coleman, the little captive of the shoe. The Memorial Hall tablet to the Field pioneers was placed by Marshall Field of Chicago.

[2] No entreaties could coax Eunice Williams or Mary Field to dwell again among their kin. Eunice tarried several times at Longmeadow, Mass., with her brother, the Rev. Stephen Williams, as he records in his Diary: "Uncle and Aunt Edwards [the parents of Jonathan Edwards, from Windsor] and so many friends came to visit us, and our neighbors sent in so plentifully that we had even a Feast. . . . At evening our young people sang melodiously that was very Gratefull to my Sister and company and I hope we are something endeared to her." In 1761, Eunice brought to Longmeadow her daughter Catharine (Flying Leg) and husband Grand Chief Onasategen (François Xavier).

From under the cross-crowned parish steeple at Caughnawaga, the girl Eunice looked out upon the romance of French
colonization and Indian legend.

Above the twisting waters of Lachine, Eunice saw on the
opposite bank across the broad heart of the Lake of St.
Louis bounded by the dim forests of Chateaugay and
Beauharnois, a crumbling trading-post, built by the chiv-
alrous Samuel de Champlain, later the residence of La Salle
on his Seigniory, awarded by the Sulpitians[1] to him whom
Louis XIV addressed as "*Our dear and well-beloved Robert
Cavalier Sieur de la Salle.*"

They named the settlement La Chine to celebrate the
Seignior's South Sea dream, to be the first traveller westward, ho! by this road to China.   Instead, La Salle, ever
a wall of adamant under jealous persecution, threw open
a Great West and a Great South, guiding America into her
richest possessions.   Then came the struggle for a Continent, and

"*The lilies withered where the Lion trod.*"

The golden girdle is severed with which the practical
La Salle, neither martyr nor dreamer, bound the north
dominion of New France to a superb new south territory
—Louisiana,—and both to Versailles; yet our fresh-water
seas and the Mississippi are one eternal link, the other, the
sentiment of La Belle France which clings alike to both
the frost-land and the land of palms and roses.   The
stranger who has passed Carnival days in Canada or Louisiana perceives a distinct flavor of the Old Régime: whether
at the buoyant storming of Montreal's Ice Palace with
showers of light, and the festival of furs and color on skates,
or in that gay atmosphere of delicious mystery in which

---

[1] "La Salle and his successors became feudal proprietors of La Chine,
on the sole condition of delivering to the Seminary, on every change of
ownership, a medal of fine silver, weighing one mark."—*La Salle and the
Discovery of the Great West*, Parkman.

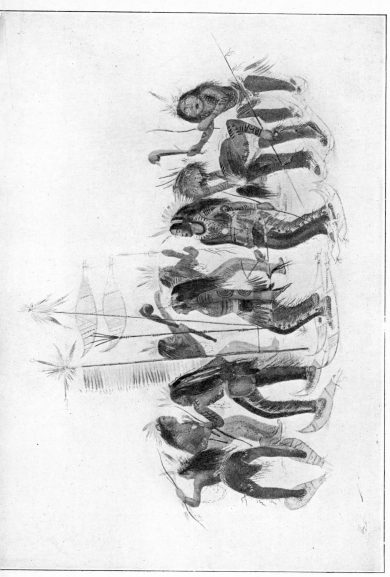

The Snow Shoe Dance (From Life by G. Catlin).

At the first appearance of snow the Indians celebrate the joyous event by a dance, with a song of thanks to the Great Spirit—around an ornamented pair of snow-shoes, elevated with the appropriate flags and spears of the band.

185

move the significant pageants of *Comus* and *King Rex* at
New Orleans. Where else on this continent is such an
exuberance of gayety possible, as in these cities possessing
so large an heritage of Latin blood!

Not far from Caughnawaga, Chambly, and Sorel, on the
Island of Montreal, was Sault au Recollet Mission, the
"Oso" (au Sault) Fort of hated memory to Deerfield[1] men

> "*Faintly as tolls the evening chime*
> *Our voices keep tune and our oars keep time.*
>
> *We'll sing at St. Ann's our parting hymn*
> *Row, brothers row, the stream runs fast,*[2]
> *The Rapids are near* . . . . . ."

who made entrance here only by running the Mohawk
gauntlet, as Mehuman Hensdell and John Arms (once
offered in exchange for Sieur de Verchères) knew to their
cost. Other captives were at the Iroquois fort at Oka on
the Ottawa, not far distant from Lachine and St. Anne Bout
de L'Isle. At the Rapid of St. Anne we still hear the echo
of Tom Moore's "Canadian Boat Song" set to the rhythm of
his boatmen as they sang and rowed the poet through the
magnificent scenery of the St. Lawrence.

---

[1] Many New England maidens founded Canadian families. A daughter
of Deerfield's blacksmith and town-clerk, Deacon Thomas French; became
the ancestor of the first Archbishop of Quebec, her daughter having
married a Plessis of Metz in Lorraine, founders of "The Tanneries of
Belair," outside the gates of Montreal.

Miss Baker's Deerfield ancestor, Abigail Stebbins, was led captive to
the house of her husband, Jacques Desnoyon, a bushranger of Boucher-
ville, her godfather being "the High and Mighty Seigneur Phillipe de
Rigaud, Marquis de Vaudreuil, Chevalier de L'Ordre Militaire de St.
Louis." Miss Baker succeeded in tracing eighteen captives in spite of
their names being altered to a defiant degree on records; those at Caughnawaga in Indian were translated for her by the Curate, Mr. Forbes.—
True Stories of New England Captives, by C. Alice Baker.

[2] To this shrine of the "Saint of the green isle," voyageurs never omit
their offering.

At Oka on "Utawas tide," in the Church of Notre Dame de Lorette, were wedded [1] the Deerfield playmates, now converts, Josiah Riseing (baptized Ignace Raizenne) and Abigail Nims. A domain was granted them on account of the example of their piety, and a few miles' drive over sand dunes and the road cut by the New Englander Riseing through his primeval forest will bring you to their old home under the espionage of the Two Mountains on beautiful Lac de Deux Montagnes.

Fortunate were Quentin Stockwell and Parson Williams to be carried first to Chambly, the Seigniory of François Hertel, "The Hero," father of Hertel de Rouville. The Hertels showered kindnesses on the prisoners, and attempted to buy Stephen Williams of his Indian master. Here Thankful Stebbins at sweet sixteen married a soldier of the camp—"La Vallee," and nobles of the Old Régime stood sponsors for her children. With other New England girls and boys, Thérese Steben had been graciously granted citizenship by Le Grande Monarche. Their petition to His Majesty was latterly discovered by Miss Baker behind a little tailor's shop in Quebec.

Parson Williams was sent far from Eunice down the river.

In a poem to Lady Charlotte Rawdon, Moore has also woven bits of legend of the Canadian tribes, and the poetical belief of the Hurons that the spirit departed to the Country of Souls is changed into a dove. Parkman relates a legend attached to a floating island in Lake Superior (Lac Frontenac); here no Indians dare land, for when their forefathers picked up the wonderful, round stones (copper) to heat their food, some Great Manito, or God of the Waters, thundered: "Who are these that steal the toys of my children!"

[1] The Riseing marriage in 1715 is recorded by Father Quère, with this addition: "who wish to remain with the Christian Indians not only renouncing their nation, but even wishing to live *en sauvages*." (On the other hand several French captives collected by Colonel Partridge at Deerfield for exchange doggedly refused to return to Canada.) The most distinguished child of Abigail Nims Riseing—Marie Raizenne—became Lady of the Community of the Congregation.

After being threatened with torture by an Indian convert at the Abenaki fort, St. Francis, because he would not kiss the crucifix, he was purchased by Governor Vaudreuil and courteously lodged at his Montreal house: then paddled down to Quebec, picturesque with the frowning bastions of Fort Frontenac, transformed from wood to stone by La Salle when autocrat here, by favor of Count Frontenac and his followers, the best canoe men in America.   After two years of adventure Mr. Williams was exchanged for the pirate, so-called, Captain Baptiste, and sailed for Boston.[1]   Eleazer Williams, then a Freshman at Harvard, with his chum, Thomas Prince, walked seven miles by way of the Neck to hear his father preach at Thursday lecture.

Deerfield's Old Manse stands a bit aloof in its dress of deep yellow and green doors, as the keeper of a thousand secrets. There is scarcely a crack in cornice or window-seat or yellow pine floor seasoned for thirteen years.   Its Northeast Wing's dormer window saw the six children of Samuel Carter "captivated" in 1704, and the birth of Joseph Allen, father of the famous Captain of Green Mountain Boys. Then the Allen house became "the wing" of Lawyer Sam Barnard's great house (entailed) and saw the sisters Nabby and Rachel and Sally weaving and sewing long seams for their wedding-day: arrayed in sky-blue silk they stood up together in the parlor one Sunday of 1792, with three bridegrooms from Greenfield in sheer ruffles and knee-buckles.

You don't think of them there in the Manse at high noon
As you pass : go again by the light of the moon,

---

[1] At Boston, Aug. 16, 1706, Samuel Sewall writes: "Spake that a suit of Cloaths might be made here for Mr. Williams. . . . Talk'd thoroughly with Cotton Mather about selling Henchman's House: . . . tells me Mr. Williams to preach the Lecture. . . . I invited the Gov. to dine at Holms's."   To this dinner Mr. Williams and Ensign Sheldon were invited.

The Old Manse, Deerfield.

"Built on honor" for Joseph Barnard in 1768, and home of the Parsons Willard. Residence of Mrs. Madeleine Yale Wynne and Miss Annie C. Putnam. The hip-roof Wing was the Samuel Carter House of 1694, sacked, 1704, and the lot was previously owned by Joseph Gillet, killed at Bloody Brook. Miss Wilkins wrote "Giles Corey" here. The Manse suggested the mysterious "Little Room" of Mrs. Wynne.

> *And you will say they are yet in town :—*
> *And in their old home with the moon shining down,*
> *As it did long ago.*[1]

Dr. Willard's chaise stopped at his parsonage opposite the Hoyt Tavern (Old Indian House) one eventful day of

---

[1] *Nabby and Rachel and Sally*, by Isabel H. Williams, included in the Story of the Old House by Catharine B. Yale. Mrs. Yale's pretty picture of the Manse is written *con amore* and illustrated with drawings of its quaint interior, the English piano, "the only one in town," and the silver tankard made to order by Paul Revere for Joseph Barnard, now among the church silver. A silver spoon of one of the brides in blue is treasured at the Manse.

1807 and the lilies of the valley opened wider their fairy bells as he lifted out his bride, "the lovely Susan Barker" after a four days' journey from old Hingham. One may imagine her on the first Sunday, the observed of the village, dressed in fawn-colored spencer and white skirt, wearing a Leghorn hat trimmed with white. She was "of a lovely graceful figure, and charming innocence of face and expression." Susan Barker[1] was one of that original family who remained loyal to the King fifty years after the Revolution, friends of Mrs. Judge Lyman of Northampton. The latch of the great gate of the Manse fell more often to Judge Lyman and his loaded carriage and pair than any other of the expected and unexpected guests. Emerson, Sumner, Dr. Henry Ware, Sr., Parkman, and the Rev. John Pierpont were visitors. Mrs. Willard's table overflowed, for any respectable traveller felt at liberty to stop at the minister's for dinner, just as at the hospitable Dominie's on the Hudson.

Miss Willard tells us that her father eked out his salary "by tutoring youths of the best Boston families—the Jacksons, Codmans, and Thorndikes": often Harvard delinquents were rusticated into the good man's care. The story goes that "one of the Lowell tribe," a cousin of the poet, Edward Jackson Lowell, being called before the Harvard Committee, said, "Gentlemen, please be as quick as you can, as I have my horse out here and he is very uneasy." This was deemed most impertinent, and they immediately took action and rusticated him to Parson Willard's.[2]

---

[1] See chapters "Hingham" and "Milton" in *Old Paths and Legends of New England*, Vol. I.

[2] The Rev. Samuel Willard lived in the Manse nigh on fifty years except a few years at Hingham, when occupied by Rev. Adolphus Dickinson, and Colonel Wilson and his four romantic daughters who pored over Scott, Byron, and Miss Austen in the old garret.

Many interesting names appear among Mr. Willard's contemporaries appointed to councils on his ordination: Rev. Dr. Abiel Holms (father

Miss Wilkins picked her first four-leafed clover at the Manse, near the old walk of diamond, colored stones selected by the blind parson, and Deerfield is the scene of her *Old Lady Pingree*. To an enthralled "Ghost Club," at The Manse, Mrs. Wynne first told the story of the mysterious *Little Room*,[1] this witching tale was passed on and on, until on its début in print, many readers exclaimed, "Why, where have I heard of that Little Room! Can it be plagiarized?"

THE OLD ALBANY ROAD

Take good heed of the weather-worn sign *To Albany* and follow Deerfield's sunset path down Hitchcock or Middle Lane to the old Albany ford, and to Broughton's Pond crested with lily-pads. A century and a half ago this was not a grass-grown lane but the King's highway to the Hudson and the Great Lakes, and you might have saluted Captain Nathaniel Dwight as he left his quarters in the Williams house to lead Hampshire County troops against Canada.

Mark on the left the stoop smothered in lilacs dedicated to flirtations ever since Aunt Spiddy Hoyt built it with eggs she sold, and not with her good man's profits on "wigges and foretops." The neighbors thought "Aunt Spiddy's Contrivance" "a great extravagance." Her son, Gen. Epaphras Hoyt, as high sheriff, wore a blue brass-buttoned coat, cockade, and crimson sash—he wrote here his *Indian*

---

of Dr. O. W. Holmes), the Rev. David Osgood of Medford, Rev. Daniel Chaplin of Groton, Rev. John Barnard of Salem, Rev. Jesse Appleton, N. H., Rev. Abiel Abbott of Beverly, also Rev. Roger Newton of Greenfield, and Rev. Theophilus Packard, Scribe.

Richard Hildreth was born at the Manse; Hawthorne says on his first visit to the "noble hall" of the *Boston Athenæum* that "The most remarkable sight, however, was Mr. Hildreth, writing his history of the United States   .   .   .   as quiet and absorbed as he would be in the loneliest study;   .   .   .   It is very curious thus to have a glimpse of a book in process of creation under one's eye."—*American Note-Books*.

[1] *The Little Room and Other Stories*, by Madeleine Yale Wynne.

Wars.   Deacon Hitchcock's boy Edward (afterward President of Amherst) and "Uncle Eph" used to fly from Aunt Spiddy's broom on cleaning and baking days to their study in the big elm.   Many a gander-party foregathered before

the blaze o' winter nights swapping war stories: Sergeant John Hawks, the hero of Fort Massachusetts, gran'ther Hoyt,[1] and Deacon Nims; moreover Deacon Justin Hitchcock, the next-door neighbor, the fifer who marched with Captain Locke's minute-men would tell how Captain Stebbins captured the baggage train of General Burgoyne and how he had compelled many a Tory to sign good resolutions.

Sign of the Burk Tavern, Bernardston, one of the garrison houses of the cordon of forts commanded by Colonel Ephraim Williams.   In Memorial Hall, Deerfield.

Deerfield's Tory minister, Mr. Ashley, had spoken of the doom of those Americans fallen at Lexington, as being fearful in the next world. A week later he found his pulpit door spiked up. Turning to Deacon A., a blacksmith, he requested him to undo the fastening, who, with a very proper gravity, replied that he did not

[1] Jonathan Hoyt was bought for twenty dollars from his Indian master on the streets of Quebec by the son of Governor Dudley.   The Indian came later to visit his boy, to whom he was devoted.

use his hammer on the Sabbath. Finally an axe was procured.

Another day an incensed patriot neighbor jostled him. Mr. Ashley queried why this rude treatment, saying, "You should not rebuke an Elder," etc. He replied: "An elder, an elder!—if you had not said you was an elder, I should have thought you was a poison sumach."

A dweller on Old Street many years before his death had a copper coffin built for himself, declaring emphatically, "I'll be d—d if I go snappin' raound hell in a hemlock coffin."

At Shelburne Falls—formerly Deerfield Northwest—some one remarked that the water in the river was very low. "Yaas," drawled a bystander, "it lacks a quart of being any water in it."

This "Little Brown House on the Albany Road" is one of Deerfield's studios, the village being absorbed in Art with Crafts. You may hear the clack of looms and the file at the smithy, the plane of the cabinet-maker, the rustle of the basket-weavers' reeds and willows. Marvellous early patterns come to the "Blue and White" fraternity from the tide-water families of "Virginny," and the New England West, to live again in delicate hand-made dyes and tufted coverlets.

There are interesting painted walls in Deerfield and Bernardston. In *Old-Time Wall-Papers*, by Kate Sanborn, is a capital reproduction of the scenic wall-paper in the parlor of the Ebenezer Hinsdale house on Old Street.

An heirloom.

NORTHAMPTON (NONOTUCK) 1654

" Enterprise, traffic, factory wheels, steam whistles, busy industries, en-riching and enlivening the people, have not spoilt the landscape, or robbed the recesses, roads, foot-paths, and bridle-paths of their romance, their love-liness, their legends, their traditions or their poetry."—The Connecticut River Valley, by the Rt. Rev. FREDERIC DAN HUNTINGTON.

BELOW Deerfield, the broad, fair Connecticut glides out between Mts. Toby and Sugar-Loaf at sweet Sunderland —village of the plain—and sweeps in magnificent curves through Nonotuck Valley toward Mt. Tom and the Great Falls at South Hadley.

It would seem as if the river endeavored to display its silvery beauty to greatest advantage while within range of the kingly mountains, Holyoke and Tom, and to double the area of unrivalled meadows for the pioneer. In this valley of Nonotuck, or *Midst of the River*, lie the towns of Old Northampton, Hadley, and Hatfield. On the 1831 map of Nonotuck (drawn before the river left its "Old Bed" at Northampton) the Connecticut loops in a splendid double ox-bow; the north six-mile loop is the Hadley "Honey-pot," the south bow incloses the Hockanum meadows at the foot of Nonotuck, the north spur of Mt. Tom, named by President Hitchcock of Amherst, "the Mountain of the Blest."

Stedman's tribute to Northampton, written from "High Ridge," Williamsburg, contains these lines:

> "There still the giant warders stand,
>   And watch the currents downward flow,
> And westward still with steady hand
>   The river bends her silver bow."

If you would wish to see this caressing play of mountain

At Hockanum under the Shadow of Mount Holyoke.

An Interval on the east side of Connecticut River.

"The plough with wreaths was crowned."

and river, follow the meadow road from Northampton to
Hockanum Ferry and summon the weather-beaten flatboat
from the opposite shore by horn—old style—(Ill-betide
the would-be passenger who is unable to blow a horn, he
must wait for the next comer.)

> As you ride to the ferry cross meadow, on your left
> the earliest divisions of the coveted alluvial meadows are
> Venturer's Field, which extended from Walnut Trees to
> Pomeroy Terrace, King's Hollow, Webb's Hollow, Bark
> Wigwam near Shepherd's Island, once a part of the Shep-
> herd farm of 300 acres, and Old Rainbow where you might
> once have seen reaping hooks in use. In Northampton
> it was a common saying, that one's social position was
> assured if he owned meadow land and was a member of the
> "Old Church" of Mather, Stoddard, and Edwards.
>
> Those who journeyed in Indian days were challenged
> at the gate of the Northampton palisades; [1] these being
> under repair in 1680, the town ordered that married persons
> should build 3 rods of palisades each, and single persons
> 2 rods.

The hamlet of Hockanum, established on a very narrow
shelf between Mount Holyoke and the river, is very lovely;
verdant farms and orchards decorate the gentle upward
slope to the forest wood-lots on the mountain range.   In
this region Cooper placed the scene of *The Wept of Wish-
ton-Wish;* Ruth Heathcote, or Narra-mattah, is the captive
heroine who, according to the tale, weds the Chief Canonchet
of the Narragansetts.

If you choose to follow the level road north 'long river

---

[1] The western line of fortification extended from the rear of the main
building of Smith College and President Seelye's house to Miss Tucker's
(formerly Rev. Gordon Hall's, owned in 1780 by Gen. William Lyman,
a member of Congress), thence to Henshaw Avenue; thence to west of
the house of Henry R. Hinckley on Prospect St., built in part by the
Rev. Solomon Stoddard in 1684, and by his son, Col. John Stoddard.

through Hockanum,[1] you will turn with the great bend into historic Hadley's Elm Street near Goodman's Ferry. (This ferry was the old stage-route, the way by which Springfield traffic coming up the east side entered Northampton.) Just one wine-glass elm picked from West Street's four royal rows, unmatched on the continent, would be the vanity of any city.

Who would not wish to have witnessed that most imposing of all musters in Hadley's mile-long street, when the entire militia of Western Massachusetts was ordered out by General Ebenezer Mattoon, an officer at the battle of Saratoga! Or the marching into Hadley in 1895 of the Third Corps and the old soldiers from the regiments of Major-General Hooker, to honor "Fighting Joe's" birthplace; its gray gambrel has lately been burned; the Academy here, where General Hooker was educated, was founded by Governor Hopkins.

Mere striplings were these elms when daring Parson Russell harbored the Regicides Goffe and Whalley. Continental troops were stationed within the eight-foot stockade to repulse Indians jealous for their maize fields. The legend of the "Angel of Hadley" is connected with General Goffe, who, according to tradition, mysteriously appeared sword in hand in the midst of an Indian attack of 1675, and led the people to safety.[2]

The Indian fort southeast of the town, where Fort River flows into the Connecticut from Amherst and "Indian Hill" opposite, are supposed to be aboriginal battle-grounds.

---

[1] North from Hockanum Ferry is the home of Clifton Johnson, the sympathetic illustrator of life in old New England.

[2] Elbridge Kingsley's picture representing the "Angel of the Lord" at Hadley meeting-house is reproduced (with other of his remarkable engravings of Hadley West Street, on which he lives) in the *Souvenir* book published on the meeting of the Third Corps Union. Included also is, *How Fighting Joe Hooker took Lookout Mountain*, by Clarence Hawkes, the blind poet of Hadley.

Whately Glen.

From a wood-cut by Elbridge Kingsley.

197

because the Connecticut year after year uncovers curious Indian weapons.

In North Hadley, *Under a Colonial Roof-Tree*, Frederick Dan Huntington, the beloved Bishop, was born. His daughter, Miss Arriah Huntington, lives at the old place, and has given us a vivid picture of this finest type of a Valley homestead,[1] built by Captain Moses Porter in 1752. An unusual feature is the generous "stoop" extending the whole western length of the house; the table is set there for the reapers, the churning and other work carried on there in summer time; at nightfall it becomes a grateful retreat after the day's labor. "Through the stillness we may hear the tread of horses' hoofs crossing the bridge by the mill a mile away."

Hadley toward the east, or Hadley Third Precinct, is the beautiful town of Amherst.[2] Rev. David Parsons was the first minister and among the first settlers were the families of Cowles, Dickinson, Hawley, Ingram, Chauncey, Nash, Scoville, and Wells.

THE SOUTH ROAD TO MOUNT TOM

To-day, you choose the south road from Hockanum Ferry, and discover that most charming of pine-crowned cliffs—Titan's pier; then wind down dale and up hill in sight of Old Rock Ferry toward the picturesque pass at Smith's Ferry.

---

[1] A sketch with illustration of the Porter-Phelps-Huntington homestead is included in Bacon's volume on *The Connecticut River*.

[2] Amherst lies also in the great basin south of Mt. Toby, together with Hadley, Leverett, and Sunderland on the east side of the Connecticut and on the west side Northampton and the three other Hamptons, Hatfield, Williamsburg, and Whately. The meadow intervals in the valley contain from 500 to 5000 acres and rise in terraces. Electric cars facilitate the pleasure of a trip through the Deerfield Valley as far north as Greenfield and Turner's Falls.

Photograph by Clifton Johnson.   "The Galloping of the Mountain."   Holyoke Range.
A load of corn homeward bound from Northampton meadows.

You are traversing "the short road" between Amherst and South Hadley, the pastoral seat of Mount Holyoke College, that inspiration of Mary Lyon. Goodenow Park within the college grounds commands the full sweep of the range. You will not forget to visit the Observatory, the Falls at Lake Nonotuck, and to stroll through the Pass of Thermopylæ, and up Granby Hill for the superb prospect.

Finally you attain the bold summit of Mt. Tom by railway from the city of Holyoke (famous for its paper-mills) seated by the Great Rapids; so plentiful were shad here that the boatmen's taverns overflowed with fishermen and fishermen's luck, with 2000 shad at a haul.

Even half-way up Mt. Tom at Mountain Park, the glorious air is a rare elixir for lungs and brain, exhilarating without oppression; as you face Mt. Holyoke the buzz of Pandora's wingéd troubles is imperceptible before the beauty of the splendid battalion of mountains on the horizon. Mt. Monadnock signalled Mt. Tom by mirror for the first time in 1898. This day is cloudless, but on the next a fog-sea fills the valley; by noon, playful clouds chase up to the summit and down on the other side, then become sullen and ragged with lightning; or the clouds are massed below like a "sea of cotton," and you, in clear air, watch the sun transform them into a "fleece of gold," the phrase of Lafcadio Hearn; now, they disperse in a gamut from orange to pink, and far below appears a white toy village, Easthampton, and the golden river, "River of Pines," flowing down from Agiochook (Mt. Washington), the Indians' Throne of the Great Spirit.

The old man of the mountain, Phœbus Pomeroy, relates the legend of how "Little Mountain" came to be: "Old Claw-foot got angry at the folks in South Hadley, and filled his leather apron with rocks to throw at them; but the apron strings broke, and the rocks fell in a heap and made Little Mountain."

Mount Tom in Winter.

From South Hadley you return to Northampton by Smith's Ferry or Lower Farms. Pascommuck was the scene of a frightful Indian raid in 1704. Here Benjamin Wright's house (afterwards the Elias Lyman place and Cargill homestead or "Old Long House") was fired by spiked arrows dipped in brimstone, and extinguished by the grit of Thomas Stebbins, who wrapped himself in a feather bed and "put for" the well.[1]

In Easthampton, Joseph Bartlett's and Major Jonathan Clapp's were fortified houses. Clapp's tavern was the famous hostelry between Connecticut and Vermont. Williston Seminary (founded by the Hon. Samuel Williston)

[1] The Indians escaped over Pomeroy Mountain after having killed or taken captive the families of John Webb, John Searl, Benoni Jones, and Benjamin and Samuel Janes.

From a Painting by Elbridge Kingsley

Spectres of French and Indian Wars—only too real to village folk on the New England border.

recalls Easthampton's first minister, Rev. Payson Williston, whose beautiful wife was the daughter of Rev. Nathan Birdseye.

An interesting record was made of the number of houses in each Connecticut Valley town, about the time Springfield was burned by the Indians in 1675; twenty years before the Springfield commissioners (John Pynchon, Elizur Holyoke, and Deacon Samuel Chapin[1]) laid out to the Planters, "the boundes of Nonotuck from the upper end of the little Meaddowe called by the Indians Cappawonke [Hatfield]—to the great fales [Falls] to Springfield ward." This list of houses is preserved in the British Museum[2]:

Weathersfield	150	Springfield Burnt	50	Hatfield	50
Hartford	500	Hadley	100	Northfield	30
Winsor	400	Northampton	100	Deerfield	30

During border-wars, from under every one of Northampton's roofs, men went forth on the most hazardous adventures; Captain John Parsons conducted the "Grand Scout towards West river" in Queen Anne's War; Captain Benjamin Wright and Lieutenant John King received government bounties for the Cowasset scout; Captain John Taylor was killed at Pascommuck, and Captain Thomas Baker of a long romantic history was carried captive to Canada and married Madame le Beau, a child-captive from Dover, N. H.

The veteran military commander was Colonel Samuel Partridge of Hatfield; Colonels John Worthington of Spring-

---

[1] The influential Deacon Samuel Chapin of Springfield was a founder of the church in Northampton, and the original of the statue of *The Puritan* by A. St. Gaudens; Springfield has also a statue to Sergeant Miles Morgan, a hero of 1675. The first street laid out in Springfield was named for Col. Worthington.

[2] Communicated through the courtesy of Lieut. C. D. Parkhurst of Fort Monroe. Trumbull's *History of Northampton*.

field and Israel Williams commanded the Hampshire County regiments.

By the advice of Colonel John Stoddard—in charge of general defence and commissioned to snatch back our captive people from the reluctant French—large dogs were trained to ferret out trails in service of the scouting parties ranging from fort to fort; from Fort Dummer to Pittsfield and Hoosac. Lieut. Timothy Dwight of Northampton was first commander of Fort Dummer near Brattleborough, Vt.

Mere statistics which concern the daring Rangers, inured to greatest fatigue and danger, recall Cooper's romances. A letter of instruction to Captain Caleb Lyman dated Boston, June 19, 1755, runs:

> "You must perform a scout of at least thirty days upon every marching. . . . And before you receive the bounty for any Indian killed or captured, you must deliver up the person captivated, or scalps of those you kill. PHIPPS."

> Marching forces were allowed for rations by the Commissary General, John Wheelwright: 1 *lb. of bread*, 1 *lb. of pork*, 1 *gill of rum, per day.*

> The load of the ranging corps alone was no sinecure, carrying thirty days' provisions with muskets; now camping under brush, now marching on snowshoes or lying in ambuscade by a wilderness trail; in combat generally superior to the Indian, in finesse little inferior.

Troublous times are depicted in the letters of Colonel Seth Pomeroy to his wife[1]; he was ever at the front, Ensign in 1743, Brigadier-General in 1775. One letter is written after "a warm engagement" before Louisburg, others from Fort Massachusetts, and from Albany in 1755 where 5000 troops assembled under Sir William Johnson for the expedition against Crown Point.

---

[1] The letters of Gen. Pomeroy are quoted by the courtesy of Mrs. William Francis Bartlett (née Pomeroy) of Pittsfield.

MAJOR SETH POMEROY TO HIS WIFE.

"Monday Morning 4 o'clock. *Fort Massachusetts, Aug. 3rd, 1747.*
"MY DEAR AND BELOVED WIFE,
    "I have not time with ink and pen to say much but hope
to have an opportunity in a little time to speak face to face.
. . . We live at the Fort, well; my dinner yesterday
was buiscake, suet, Whortleberry pudding and a good piece
of corned beef with squashes and turnips—no cider, but
a good appetite . . . last Friday night the Indians
were about the Fort. . . ."
                                    "Boston, Oct. 22, 1747.
    "No longer than I have business shall I stay, for it is
no delightsome place. I have bought an English girl's time
for five years I hope will prove well, for I know I gave price
enough for her. If you have an opportunity to send me
a horse and bridle I should be glad to have it done (saddle
I can have here). If no other way I design to buy a horse
and bring her up, for I am determined if it is in my power
that you shall have help by a maid to ease you of some
of your hard labor."

    The Major sent the maid to Mrs. Pomeroy by land with
the following letter (the supplies being sent around by
Long Island Sound to Warehouse Point, were poled in
flatboats to the "Landing" below Northampton and loaded
on wood-sleds. "Jed Day's Landing" was long famous:)
                                    " *Boston, Nov. 7.*
    "The Thanksgiving I hear is week after next, but I hope
to keep one next week at my own house. I send a receipt
of things I have sent by water, . . . Let one of the
boatmen go directly after them. Elisha and Mr. Wright
have things in the same vessel."
                                    " *Albany, July 15th, 1755.*
    "MY DEAR—I have slipt several opportunities hoping
soon to be able to Inform you more Particularly how things
occur than I now can—in general the army are well and

in high spirits but not without some fears what may have happened to Col. Titcomb. By whom our stores were expected, he not yet heard of. . . . I know of nothing now to hinder our marching but for want of Stores.

" Governor Shirley is here General Johnson is also here. . . . We have frequent news from ye Ohio by Indians that Mr. Johnson hath sent some time ago to Gen. Braddock. . . .

A Mt. Tom Brook.

w Across the Connecticut River from Holyoke, ith Mt. Holyoke Range and Old Boatmen's ʼavern.

I think there is ye greatest Probability that General Braddock is master of Ohio—Before this time. . . . The People in this place are kind and seem to be hasty to put forward the Expedition. . . . What he [Governor Shirley] designs this Day I can't tell, he sent a Sergt this morning Desiring

me to dine with him and I suppose ye rest of ye Field
officers are invited also.   .   .   .

"SETH POMEROY."

In '75, as he was returning for a rest, Colonel Pomeroy
received the news that the army had left Cambridge; in
spite of his threescore years and ten he unhitched his horse
from the wagon, mounted, and arrived at Bunker Hill amid
roar of cannon.   General Putnam wrung his hand: "Pomeroy, you here!"   As the ammunition gave out, he walked
backward from the field, saying, "No enemy shall ever
say he saw the back of Seth Pomeroy."   On his way to
join Washington at the front, he died at Peekskill.[1]

Colonel Seth Pomeroy was of a race of noted gunsmiths
and used the anvil said to have been brought over to Windsor, Conn., by Eltweed Pomeroy: his family traditions run
back to Sir Ralph de Pomeroy who accompanied William
the Conqueror to England; ponderous horseshoes were
invented by Pomeroys for Tudors and Plantagenets.   To
induce Eltweed Pomeroy to found an armory in this country, the Colony granted him 1000 acres on the Connecticut
River.   Even fifty years after the death of Col. Seth, Canada
Indians boasted of his guns as masterpieces for a long and
unerring shot.   Col. Seth was a blacksmith in all its branches
employing people to make his guns: *Seth Pomeroy's Account
Book* is a replica of pioneer times (each man then being
compelled to be a Jack of many trades, from "taking care
of Ye clock, making a pair of tongs," to "puling a tooth"
and "carrying a warrant to Noah S.").   The accounts are

---

[1] At the dedication of the monument to General Seth Pomeroy un-
veiled at Peekskill-on-Hudson, by the Sons of the Revolution of the
State of New York on the anniversary of Bunker Hill, 1898, the address
was by George E. Pomeroy of Toledo.   Present were delegates from the
Order of the Cincinnati, Society of the War of 1813, Society of Foreign
Wars, Society of Colonial Wars, Society of the Colonial Dames of America,
Daughters of the Cincinnati, and Daughters of the Revolution.

ady for the Colonial Ball in Grandmother's Wedding-veil, on the 250th
Anniversary of Northampton, Mass.

to familiar Northampton names: "Caleb Strong Dr. 1739,"
Sam Kingsley, Deacon Allin, Phinehas King, Preserved
Bartlett, Sam'l Wait.[1]

In spite of the raging of the heathen roundabout pioneer
hearthstones, Rev. Solomon Stoddard (whom the Indians
refrained from firing upon because they believed him "the
Englishman's god") was so much concerned about his
people's domestic extravagances that he begged the Rev.
Increase Mather to mention it to the Governor for refor-
mation: "many sins are grown so in fashion, that it becomes
a question whether it be sins or not . . . especially
. . . that intolerable pride in clothes and hair." Soon
after, "for wearing silk and in flaunting manner," Hannah
Lyman [2] and two daughters of the honored Elder John
Strong were presented at the court; also several young
men "for wearing long hair, greate bootes and gold and
silver lace."

A typical courtship of ye olden time was that of the Rev.
Mr. Mix. He journeyed from Wethersfield to Northampton,
called on Mr. Stoddard, and asked to see his five daughters.
After a few minutes' conversation, he offered Mary his hand
and heart, saying he would smoke a pipe with her father
while she made up her mind. The pipe was not long enough,
however, and Mr. Mix returned to Wethersfield, receiving
shortly the following:

"Northampton, March 169-.

"Rev. Mr. Mix:—Yes.

"Mary Stoddard."

[1] *Seth Pomeroy's Account Book* and his anvil are the property of
Mrs. Edward Pomeroy of Pittsfield; his tortoise-shell tobacco box
and drinking-glass, a gift of the French officer Dieskau, of Edward Van
S. Pomeroy, Esq. A Pomeroy musket is owned by S. Harris Pomeroy,
Esq., of New York.

[2] Land in the centre of Northampton was held by the Strong family for
103 years. Elder John Strong came over on the *Mary and John* with the

Rebekah Stoddard married Lieutenant Joseph Hawley of Northampton, their son being the distinguished statesman, Major Joseph Hawley. The beautiful Esther Stoddard became the wife of the Rev. Timothy Edwards and her son Jonathan Edwards [1] was born in the year of the Sack of Deerfield, when Mrs. Eunice Mather Williams, their half-sister, perished.

The postscript of a remarkable letter of Mrs. Stoddard to her daughter at South Windsor on the birth of Jonathan is very practical:

" I would have sent you half a thousand of pins and a porrenger of marmalat if I had an opportunity: If any of your town come up and call here, I would send it.   Give my love to son Edwards and the children."[2]

This custom of sending packages by kind neighbors continued until the day of railroads.   The note-book of Schoolmaster Joseph Hawley of Pudding Lane (Hawley St.) when starting on a trip to Boston was filled with such varied items as: "Capt. Partridge, a dial and a dish kettle"— son Joseph, speckled red ribbon, whistles, buckles and

---

Rev. John Warham and William Clark, a Planter and one of the seven pillars of Northampton Church.   Among the unusually large families in Northampton Elder Strong's was the largest with eighteen children. His purchase included John Webb's home-lot, corner of Main and South Sts., the late Enos Parsons house, extending westerly to the Academy of Music, the gift of E. H. R. Lyman to the city.

[1] Little Jonathan Edwards was born in a clerical atmosphere; his Aunts Stoddard had married famous preachers, and in those days the minister was the head of the town.   His sisters also married leaders in the Province, so that, counting the "in-laws," the Warham-Mather-Stoddard-Edwards-Pierpont connection were an influential clan and a positive factor in any undertaking in New England.

[2] This eminent woman, Esther Mather Stoddard, was the daughter of the Rev. John Warham, founder of Windsor.   Of her other daughters, Christian married the Rev. William Williams of Hatfield, Sarah, the Rev. Samuel Whitman of Farmington, and Hannah, the Rev. William Williams of Weston.

fish hooks"—"a shilling worth of plumb and spice"—"2 psalters a bason and a quart pot"—" a place for Mary Holton."

It was the same even as late as Judge Lyman's day; his daughter Mrs. Lesley writes in her delightful *Recollections of My Mother:*

"There were no expresses then, and so when it was known in the village of Northampton that Judge and Mrs. Lyman were going to Boston (and they always took pains to make it known) a throng of neighbors were coming in the whole evening before; not only to take an affectionate leave but to bring parcels of every size and shape, and commissions of every variety. One came with a dress she wanted to send to a daughter at school;—one brought patterns of dry goods, with a request that Mrs. Lyman would purchase and bring home dresses for a family of five. And would she go to the orphan asylum and see if a good child of ten could be bound out to another neighbor? . . . Would Mrs. Lyman bring the child back with her? . . . The neighbors walked into the library where the packing was going on, and when all the family trunks were filled my father called out heartily, 'Here, Hiram, bring down another trunk from the garret, the largest you can find, to hold all these parcels.' . . . A little boy came timidly in with a bundle nearly as large as himself, and 'would this be too large for Mrs. Lyman to carry to grandmother?'—'No, indeed, tell your mother I'll carry anything short of a cooking stove.' 'Another trunk, Hiram,' said my father; 'and ask the driver to wait five minutes.' Those were the times when people could wait five minutes for a family so well known and beloved. . . . our driver had only to whip up his horses a little faster before he came to the Belchertown hills; and when he came to those the elders got out and lightened the load."[1] At Belchertown, a few

[1] *Recollections of My Mother Mrs. Anne Jean Lyman, of Northampton. Being a Picture of Domestic and Social Life in New England.* Houghton, Mifflin and Company.

miles from Amherst, lived for a time J. G. Holland and Eugene Field.

In Southampton, one Sabbath during the sermon the audience of the Rev. Jonathan Judd suddenly left him at the sound of a gunshot at a "bare." Also, by Parson Judd's Diary, we find that he, at least, stood by Jonathan Edwards on his melancholy departure, after being deposed from Northampton Church: "Oct. 16—Met Mr. Edwards and family at Bartlett's Mills and rid some miles."

The Northampton Octogenarian has a reminiscence of one who was a leetle nigh: "so penurious was Old Lick Sheldon, that it was said whenever he went down to the meadow to work, he would stop his clock from running, thinking it would last longer."[1]

There is a tradition in the Strong family that when the Rev. John Hooker, the fourth minister of Northampton, was married to the sister of Colonel Worthington at Springfield in 1755 his bride, according to the etiquette of the period, rode to her new home on a pillion behind one of Mr. Hooker's deacons.

The first tea ever seen in Northampton was sent to Colonel Timothy Dwight in 1746 and called "bohea." The family steeped it all up at once as an herb drink, and finding it bitter, threw it away in disgust. The delightful New

[1] The *Hampshire Gazette* was founded in 1786 by William Butler, who married a daughter of Colonel John Brown of Pittsfield, and built on Hawley Street, where also stands the old Clark tavern, the Washburn residence.   Ezra Clark built his homestead near the toll gate on Bridge street.   Lieutenant William Clark, the pioneer, moved from Dorchester in 1659 to Northampton.   His wife rode on horseback, with panniers, carrying one boy in each basket and one in her lap, her husband proceeding on foot.   *Antiquities of Northampton* by Rev. Solomon Clark.

Anniversary edition of the *Hampshire Gazette*.   Its present editor, Henry S. Gere, author of *Reminiscences of Old Northampton, 1840 to 1850*, is the senior editor of Western Massachusetts.

The Connecticut River, Great Bend at Holyoke.

"*Rivers must have been the guides which conducted the footsteps of the first travellers. They are the constant lure . . . to distant enterprise and adventure . . . They are the natural highways of all nations . . . and where the animal and vegetable kingdoms attain their greatest perfection.*"—Thoreau.

211

England homestead built by Colonel Dwight (the father of the first President Dwight of Yale), afterwards occupied by Nathan Storrs and by Dr. Charles Walker, stands on King Street in company with the Hopkins and Judge William A. Allen homestead; also the Josiah Dwight Whitney house built on the site of the home of Jonathan Edwards. A remarkable photograph is extant of the distinguished Whitney family, under the "Jonathan Edwards Elm."

King Street recalls Captain John King, who named Northampton in honor of his native town in England. An Indian war-club captured by his son Lieutenant John King is in the possession of his descendants.

At Florence, the village created by the silk industry, the oldest inhabitants are the Warner family near the fork of the road to "great bridge."

The Parsons homestead (1755) on South Street, or "Lickingwater," together with the famous Parsons Elm, brought up by Noah Parsons from the meadows on horseback, make a charming picture near the centre of a busy city. The Clapp homestead has always been proud of its grand staircase. On old South Street at the corner of Mill Lane lived the organist of the "Old Church" and director of the singing school,—Professor George Kingsley. On Elm Street is the gambrel roof of the Judge Samuel Henshaw house for a time occupied by Sidney E. Bridgman, later owned by Bishop Huntington.

At 13 Main Street the hospitable and charming Miss Polly Pomeroy entertained her friends. She is said to have borne a striking resemblance to Adelaide, the Queen of Louis Philippe. The six sons and six daughters of the Jonathan Lyman family were remarkable for rare beauty. Other hostesses of Mrs. Judge Lyman's day were Mrs. Isaac Bates, Mrs. Thomas Shepherd, Mrs. Judge Dewey,

Mrs. Hopkins, Mrs. Sam'l Wells, and the Misses Cochrane.

On Pleasant Street, or "Bartlett's Lane," so-called from the gate-keeper, is the house of Hon. Eli P. Ashmun, member of Congress, later occupied by Dr. Sylvester Graham. Bridge Street has a wonderful elm which stood in front of the house of Hon. Isaac Chapman Bates, removed to North Street. The Isaac Parsons homestead of 1744 on Bridge Street faces the common, and stands on the farm purchased by Cornet Joseph Parsons in 1674. The house of Governor Caleb Strong, one of the framers of the Constitution, was removed to Pleasant Street from Main.

A picturesque house with colonial door-knockers on Bridge Street was built by Asahel Pomeroy for his daughter Hannah. The portrait of Mrs. Levi Shepherd, a daughter of Gen. Seth, hangs in this house, the residence of Thomas H. Shepherd, Esq.

The famous Round Hill School, founded by the historian Bancroft and Dr. J. G. Cogswell, was housed in the early homes of three brothers—Levi, Colonel James, and Thomas Shepherd, who built the "Soapstone House" in 1810; this is now one of the halls of Clarke Institute for the Deaf.

On present College Hill was the home of Judge Charles A. Dewey, now "Dewey House," one of the Smith College dormitories; on its old site that of the Clark homestead of four generations stands the home of President L. Clark Seelye. The Hillyer Art Building and the campus of Smith College were comprised formerly in the home-lots of the Planters, Lieut. William Clark and Henry Woodward. The Administration Building is on the site of the Judge Samuel F. Lyman house.

The Mary A. Burnham Classical School occupies the old Thomas Napier and Judge Samuel Howe houses and the Talbot residence, now the Çapen house.

Jenny Lind passed her honeymoon on Round Hill and

named the beautiful region below near Mill River, "Paradise." Scenes of J. G. Holland's *Kathrina* were laid here. "Tarryawhile," the home of George Cable, is on Paradise Road, a spot of lovely seclusion, yet Elm Street with its incessant clatter and hum is but four hundred yards away. The bluffs in "Paradise," Mr. Cable writes, "suddenly sink to the river seventy feet below, canopied and curtained by a dense foliage of pine and hemlocks. . . . the sounds of nature alone fill the air; song of birds, chirp of insects, the rattle of the kingfisher, the soft scamper of the chipmunk, the drone of the bees, or the pretty scoldings of the red squirrel. A boat rowed by college girls may pass in silence, or with a song: . . . Of trees and perennial shrubs and vines alone, I have counted in 'Paradise' more than seventy species."[1]

A beautiful view of Paradise Lake with the mountain range beyond is obtained from the Kneeland garden with its border of wild-wood carpeted with marvellous ferns.

At "Tarryawhile," Mr Cable wrote *The Cavalier* and other works. He is a moving spirit in the great and successful undertakings of the Home Culture Clubs of Northampton. Mr. Carnegie also has put his shoulder to this wheel of Progress.

The traditional literary atmosphere has never waned since a pioneer wearing the graduate's magic "H. C., 1656," knocked at Northampton's gate. The Clark and Forbes libraries are great acquisitions; and Northampton is the home of Jeannette Lee, Ruth Huntington Sessions, and the Rev. George Gilbert. The *Mount Tom* magazine comes to us from the pen of Gerald Stanley Lee, and Mrs. Lee is one of the Contributors' Club of *The Atlantic;* Dr. Lyman Powell, Professor Joseph Johnson, and Mrs. Cochran are

---

[1] "Paradise Woods," a sketch in *Northampton, The Meadow City,* edited by F. N. Kneeland and L. P. Bryant.

associated with Northampton as well as the historian
Charles D. Hazen, Miss Mary Jordan, Elizabeth Hanscom,
and others of the Smith College Faculty. A picturesque
literary pilgrimage is to mount to Williamsburg and follow
the footsteps of Matthew Arnold and many another philosopher to Ashfield among the hills, the summer home of

The Students' Building, Smith College.

Charles Eliot Norton. Charles Goodrich Whiting is our
guide on inspired *Walks In New England*.

J. G. Holland's confrère of Springfield Samuel Bowles
moulded much of the spirit of letters in Western New
England, his Journal being notable as closed except to

facts and honorable retort. Holland's *Bay Path* is a picture of the colonist's life at Agawam and bittersweet is ever kept on the grave of him who loved the rural scene in the Valley of Nonotuck:

> " *The old red farm-house, dim and dun to-night,*
>   *Save where the ruddy firelight from the hearth——.*"

STOCKBRIDGE (INDIAN TOWN), 1737-9

"Are they not sweet,
These chimes that come to us on western air ?"
Evening Chimes, CROWNINSHIELD.

ON the border of the Province of Massachusetts Bay there
lies a gentle valley indented by low, wooded mountains,
each of a contour strikingly unlike its neighbor. The river
of this "Happy Valley" hesitates and lingers on the edge
of that luminous, green bowl of forest and meadow, meanwhile changes her accustomed dancing, vivacious step, and
walks serenely in a curvéd path west and north across the
lovely plain of Stockbridge, tracing a double, willow-
fringed ox-bow, on which the birch canoe must travel five
times as far as the horseman who rides from bridge to
bridge.

This Taconic-Hoosac bowl in which Stockbridge lies was
a home of the Mohekanew or Muh-he-ka-nuk, the people
of the continually flowing waters, who, in past unknown
suns, ranged far northwest. Here 'mid the softer hills of
the Green Mountain range the tribe told the hours of the
day by mountain shadows, the sundial of the savage.
Wnau-ti-kook is the first to become wrapped in shade as
the sun falls below her summit. Above Rattlesnake or
Deowkook—*Hill of the Wolves*—stands the north star,
their compass of the night, whilst Orion served as their
clock. Captain Konkapot's name for Rattlesnake Mountain was Mau-ska-fee-haunk when he indicated the north
boundary of the tribe's lands of "Housatonack [1]—allias

---

[1] The territory of Housatonic, comprising parts of Stockbridge,
Lee, and Great Barrington, Mount Washington, Egremont, and Alford,
was conveyed to the committee appointed by the General Court, to

Westonhook"—deeded to the whites "in consideration of
Four Hundred and Sixty Pounds, Three barrels of Sider
and thirty quarts of Rum." The north line of Westenhook
patent probably ran within half a league of the enchanting
wild-wood park on Mr. Daniel French's estate at Glendale.

*Lake Makheenac or Stockbridge Bowl; here burned the council fires of the
Mohekanew.*

On the banks of Lake Makheenac or the Great Pond
(afterwards the Stockbridge Bowl of Mrs. Sigourney's
poem) burned the council fires of the River Indians; here
treaties were sealed, but a runner's message without belts
of wampum was set aside as "an empty word."

admit settlers to this region west of the Connecticut, hotly disputed
by New York and Massachusetts. The Committee were Col. John Stoddard, Capt. Henry Dwight of Northampton, Capt. Luke Hitchcock of
Springfield, Capt. John Ashley of Westfield, Samuel Porter of Hadley,
and Capt. Ebenezer Pomroy.

Monument Mountain.

Well-beaten trails criss-crossed Stockbridge like the spokes of a wheel. One twisted westward toward the ancient council fire of the tribe at Eswatak or Schodack (now Castleton, N. Y.) where Henry Hudson once visited the Chief of the Mohicans. Another trail ran to the Sugar Bush at Tyringham, another followed the Housatonic south past the "Great Wigwam" and Weatogue village in Salisbury, Conn., to the meadow of the Schaghticoke Indians in Kent. Judge Church says that the first settlers could accurately trace this Indian path by the apple-trees sprung up on its course from the seeds scattered after their repast on our "national fruit," as Emerson calls the apple. The most intimate trail of the Stockbridge tribe mounts the shoulder of Prospect Hill, crossing the garden of the Dr. Henry M. Field place with its ever bubbling spring, and runs on past "Windymore" (where the Williams garrison stood) to an Indian village on Rattlesnake.

Hunting was good on Beartown hills,—so-called, tradition says, because a pioneer of Lee killed a bear in the forest depths with a knotted rope's end. A story handed down at Beartown is of a circuit preacher, who remarked after a scanty contribution: "It is as hard to convert one of ye Beartown sinners as it is for a shad to climb an apple-tree—yea, tail foremost." The river washes the fore-feet of the Bear at Ice Glen before it leaves Stockbridge meadows to leap southward toward the Great Wigwam "in a place called Ousetonuck" (Great Barrington). On its path thither the river passes below the face of the sacred crag of Maris-nos-see-klu,[1]—the *Fisher's Nest*,—on whose proud summit no Indian treads without first casting his reverential tribute of a stone upon the monumental cone on its southern slope.

---

[1] According to other authorities the Indian name for Monument Mountain is Mas-wa-se-hi, signifying *a nest standing up*, as appears in the form of its topmost boulders.

This pile of stones on Monument is one of the mysterious shrines[1] of the aborigine, of whose import no Indian will speak.

Many believe that it may be a memorial to that gentle and sorrowful maid who threw herself over the white precipice to assuage a despairing love, having been forbidden to marry her warrior-cousin through the unchanging law of the forefathers. To Bryant was related by a squaw the romance of the Indian maid of Monument Mountain:

> *"It was a summer morning, and they went*
> *To this old precipice. About the cliffs*
> *Lay garlands, ears of maize, and shaggy skins*
> *Of wolf and bear, the offerings of the tribe*
> *Here made to the Great Spirit, for they deemed,*
> *Like worshipers of the elder time, that God*
> *Doth walk on the high places. . . .*
> *Below her—waters resting in the embrace*
> *Of the wide forest. . . .*
> *She gazed upon it long, and at the sight*
> *Of her own village peeping through the trees,*
> *And her own dwelling, and the calm roof*
> *Of him she loved. . . . She threw herself*
> *From the steep rock and perished."*

LANDMARKS: The First Church (1824) Memorial Tablets. Henry Williams Dwight homestead. Stockbridge Cemetery. Indians' graves in southwest corner; they asked to be buried near Dr. Sergeant that they might rise with him. In the Sedgwick lot is a tribute to the faithful Mumbet, the first slave given freedom in Massachusetts and through the

The wild legendary existence of the Indians of the Housatonic merged into the celebrated Stockbridge Mission. The silent fishing-grounds at the double Ox-Bow —whose beauty aroused such

[1] Such commemorative heaps of stones are found always near a beaten trail, or a spring or stream. The cone mentioned in a deed given by four Indians to Stephen Van Cortland in 1682 now marks an angle of the boundary between Claverack and Taghanick townships, New York, standing within the ancient bounds of Claverack Manor.

efforts of Judge Theodore Sedgwick. Edwards monument. Miss Nancy Hoxey house, residence of Mrs. Thomas H. Rodman, Jr. Captain John Whiton house (about 1812), the Rectory; residence of Dr. Arthur Lawrence. Rectory Cottage; one end built without windows because the owner said he would not be indebted to his Federalist neighbor for light and air. Site of schoolhouse in which taught Theodore Dwight, John Kirkland, afterwards President of Harvard, Dr. Joseph Catlin, and Ma'am Pynchon, strict in spelling and politeness. St. Paul's Church, a church of memorials (key at Red Lion Inn). The Red Lion Inn stands on site of the Red Lion built by Silas Pepoon, 1773; Plumb collection of antiques, illustrated pamphlet on, by Allen E. Treadway. Jackson Library contains Jonathan Edwards's desk. St. Joseph's Church. Interior ornaments gift of Charles Astor Bristed. Williams Academy, endowed by Cyrus Williams (Major Jared Curtis first preceptor followed by Jonathan Cutler, Mark Hopkins, Elijah Whitney, Rufus Townsend, Edward W. B. Canning) Laurel Hill or Little Hill; Sedgwick gift to Stockbridge. Laurel Cottage built by Jahleel Woodbridge. Here David Dudley Field entertained Hawthorne and other distinguished people. Burrall house, summer residence of Judge Byington Brownell. "The Nunnery," residence of Miss Virginia Butler, on site of Henry Dwight Sedgwick house. Rev. Josiah Brewer homestead, boyhood home of Chief-Justice Brewer, residence of Miss M. Adele Brewer. General William Williams house on road to Lenox, property of

enthusiasm in the gentle soul of Dean Stanley — became their school-ground.

In those days *The Hill*[1] and *The Plain* were the two parts of Stockbridge, and you might have stood with Missionary John Sergeant in the doorway of his Mission House on the Hill— already famous in Great Britain —and listened to a conch-shell's blast drowning the song of the bobolinks, whereby David Naunau-ka-nuk, the tithing-man, summoned Mohican and Mohawk chiefs and men of the Six Nations into the little church on the Plain; hence now, from vine-clad bell-tower, the Children's Chimes chant softly to the valley that day is done. Presently from the line of wigwams on Stockbridge Street you perceived Indian converts appear with tools and set to building or planting after the English manner. Konkapot, commissioned as Captain by Gov. Belcher, built and shingled his barn on the brook[2] named in his

[1] "The Hill," as the oldest families like to call it, has been variously designated as Sergeant's Hill, Field Hill, Choate Hill, and Prospect Hill. The sinuosity of the Housatonic is remarkable, circling twenty-seven miles in going eight.

[2] Konkapot or Konk's brook crosses the Crowninshield place, in Stockbridge; in Great Barrington it is Muddy Brook. Tradition says

Charles Whitney. The Hill or Prospect Hill. Dr. Lucius Adams house, owned by Hon. Joseph H. Choate. "Sunset," residence Mrs. Henry M. Field. "Windymore," on site of Williams Garrison; here Dean Stanley and distinguished men from "foreign parts" entertained by Dr. Henry M. Field. "Clovercroft," residence of Mrs. Oscar Iasigi. "Council Grove," formerly the Cone estate, present summer residence of Charles S. Mellen, Esq. Judge Ezekiel Bacon-Palmer house, residence of Mrs. J. F. Pitkin, boyhood home of Wm. Pitt Palmer; mountain spring which turned Judge Bacon's grist and cider mills. Frederick Perry homestead, property Mr. Edward M. Teall. Cyrus Field Park, old site of the First Church. Old Lynch house, West Stockbridge Road, mentioned in Life of Miss Sedgwick—built in 1777, was home of Deacon Charles Lynch: Judge Sedgwick suggested to Mr. Larry Lynch that he should call the road "Larry's Walk," hence the Larawaug district. Ice Glen; south entrance is near "Glenburnie," the Dr. Henry C. Haven estate. Frederick Crowninshield residence, Konkapot Brook. Luke Ashburner

honor. The schoolmaster and first magistrate was the Rev. Timothy Woodbridge.

The Indians in their turn introduced the English to the squash, as Ku-tu-squash, or Vine-Apple, and impressed the whites with the dignity of their ancient laws of hospitality. A Muh-he-ka-neuw who enters the home of a neighbor says nothing until he has eaten, and no one speaks whilst the squaw hastens to set forth food.[1]

The Stockbridge Mission was sought eagerly by the Iroquois and the astute Mohawk Chief, Hendrick, sent his grandson thither to be educated.

that Captain Konkapot lived not far from Agrippa's little weather-beaten cottage on the old County Road (Goodrich Street). Agrippa, the colored body-servant of Kosciusko, and his wife were "characters" in Stockbridge. No one could make such gingerbread and root-beer as Black Peggy. "Grippy" was sexton; it is said that one evening when the church members were dilatory in arriving, Grippy opened the prayer-meeting himself: "O Lord, Thou knowest how I comes here and rings de bell and rings de bell, and Thy disciples halt by de way, paying no 'tention to its solemn warning sound."

[1] Other interesting customs of the ancestors of the Stockbridge tribe are included in Jones's *History of Stockbridge*, edited by E. W. B. Canning; Mr. Canning's sketch of the Indian Mission is included in the Berkshire Historical Society Papers. The hut of Kokkewenaunaunt, "King Ben" occupied the site of "Cherry Cottage," the birth-place of Mark Hopkins. Ten years previous to his death (1781) at the age of 104, he resigned to "King Solomon."

Parkman says that this tribe was in many respects the most remarkable

Housatonic, River of the Hills.

"Contented river! in thy dreamy realm—
The cloudy willow and the plumy elm:

The Old Mission House on the Hill.

Built by the Commonweatlh of Massachusetts for John Sergeant the Missionary. Owned by Mr. S. H. Woodward. The oldest house in Stockbridge.

house (1823), residence James D. Hague, home of G. P. R. James for two years. Old County Road. Goodrich Street. William Goodrich married a daughter of Hon. Timothy Woodbridge. " Ox-Bow meadow," surveyed 1829 by Samuel Goodrich. David Goodrich house. Isaiah Byington homestead. Timothy Woodbridge-Baldwin homestead. Enoch Willard-Seymour house, residence Jonathan E. Field. Severus Fairman-Tracy house, birthplace of

Great was the romantic interest of the Old World in the heathen savages " who dwelt in the midst of Nature." Dr. Ayscourt, Chaplain to the Prince of Wales, sent over a Bible filled with fine engravings, inscribed: *presented to Rev. John Sergeant, Missionary*

of our country. Captain Hendrick Aupaumet, their historian, was, like Cornplanter and Redjacket of the Six Nations, statesman and leader of his people. "According to the peculiar ethnology of our aborigines," the Delawares were the grandfathers, the Suawanees and Oneidas the younger brothers, the Mohawks, Onondagas, Cayugas, and Senecas the uncles of the Muh-he-ka-neew."

15

Maria Fairman, a writer for *Godey's Magazine* and *Youth's Companion.* Mark Hopkins's birthplace on the " Cherry Farm" of Dr. Charles McBurney. The Golf Meadows, once owned by Oliver Partridge, afterward known as Hunt Meadows and Choate Golf Grounds.

GLENDALE : House of Daniel C. French, James Dresser house (1800). " The Knoll," residence Richard P. Bowker.

Interlaken or Curtisville: Curtis homestead, Dr. Vassall White house. The old hotel is now St. Helen's Home, for " Fresh Air Children," founded by the Hon. John E. Parsons, as a memorial to his daughter.

DRIVES: Curtisville—*3* miles; Curtisville (by turnpike, return base West Stockbridge mountain, Lake Averic) —*7;* Fernside—*6,* Glendale—*1½*; Glendale (by Butler estate)—*3*; Great Barrington—*7½*; " Highlawn" —*5;* Housatonic—*4*; Lake Buel—*10;* Lake Makheenac—*3;* Lee (over hill)—*4;* Lenox—*6;* Lenox by Makheenac—*7;* Long Lake (by Glendale, Housatonic, Williamsville, return by Van Deusenville Monument)—*16;* Monterey (by Monument Valley, Blue Hill, return by Beartown)—*18;* Monument Mt., summit—*5;* Monument, around—*10;* Perry's Peak (by West Stockbridge and Richmond) —*24;* Pittsfield—*12;* Tyringham, Hop Brook Road—*8;* Warren's Woods (view Tyringham Valley) —*12;* W. Stockbridge, by Williams River, Fuary's Quarries, Glendale —*12.*

to the Stockbridge Indians, *in the vast wilderness called New England.* Sergeant was ordained Missionary with impressive ceremonies at Deerfield before the Governor, Council, and Indian Delegates. The occasion was marked by one of the famous ordination addresses of the Rev. William Williams of Hatfield, a cousin of the "Redeemed Captive," and a son of the cordwayner Robert of Norwich, who crossed in the *Rose of Yarmouth* and settled in Roxbury.

Nobles and poets alike contributed on the Indians' behalf, in gold or literature: Lord Gower, Charles, Landgrave of Hesse, Pope, Rousseau, Addison, and Steele. This came about after the audience granted by Queen Anne to chiefs of the Six Nations —the "Four Kings"—who were conducted to London by Colonel Schuyler and Ex-Governor Nicholson of Maryland. After presenting their petitions to the Queen that she should send an army against the French, they were returned to their apartments in her Majesty's coach. Ballads were written in their honor, portraits were painted of "the Emperor of the Mohawks, wampum in hand," and his three royal companions by Verelst, who "engrossed the fashion "; after their departure, their characters were assumed at masquerades.

Addison's version of what the Indians thought in their turn of the Court in wigs, powder, and patches is excessively pertinent and amusing. The "odd observations" of King Sa Ga Yean Qua Rash on English manners are presented by *The Spectator*.

"Their dress likewise is very barbarous, for they almost strangle themselves about the neck.   .   .   . Instead of t h o s e b e a u t i f u l feathers with which we adorn our heads, they often buy up a monstrous brush of hair, which .   .   . falls down in a large fleece . .   . and are as proud of it as if it w e r e t h e i r o w n growth. .   .   . The women look like angels, and would be more beautiful than the sun, were it not for little black spots that are apt to break out on their faces, and sometimes rise in very odd figures. .   .   . When they

Drawn from Life by G. Catlin

The Mohegan, Psalm Book in hand.

*"A nobler task was theirs who strove
    to win
The blood-stained heathen to the
    Christian fold."*
—Memorial to Francis Parkman by
                    HOLMES.

disappear in one part of the face, they are apt to break out in another, insomuch that I have seen a spot upon the forehead in the afternoon which was upon the chin in the morning." [1]

---

[1] *The Spectator*, No. 50.   The portraits of the "Four Kings" are in

The Valley Indians' dearest foe was, first, the Dutch trader from across the New York border, balancing his saddle-bags with evil fire-water; secondly, the French, who sent Indian viceroys to entice their young men from an English alliance, by holding orgies in the Taghonic woods. The Stockbridge tribe proved difficult to proselyte, and forthwith French and Indians prudently omitted Housatonic towns in their war programme of pillage and massacre.

REVOLUTIONARY DAYS

At the opening of the Revolution, Stockbridge Indians strung anew their faithful bows, and, as minute-men, marched to join the camp on Cambridge Common and await orders from a great new chief—General Washington. On June 30, 1776, General Washington, speaking of the arrival of the Caughnawaga friends and other tribes, says, " They honored me with a talk to-day." John Logan says:

> *"But just believe me, onst for all,*
> *To them that treat him fair,*
> *The Injun mostly alluz, wuz,*
> *And is and will be, square."*

The County Congress[1] met in 1774 at Stockbridge Tavern,

---

the British Museum. Mezzotint copies are in the John Carter Brown Library, Providence. These Mohawk kings were of the race of unswerving British alliance, whose courage was a factor in deciding the predominance of the Anglo-Saxon in America. They produced Brant and Tecumseh. The poet E. Pauline Johnson of "Chiefswood" is a daughter of the head chief of the Mohawks and his wife Emily S. Howells of Bristol, England.

[1] The Berkshire Convention appointed Mark Hopkins, Theodore Sedgwick John Brown of Pittsfield, Peter Curtis of Lanesboro, a committee to take into consideration the acts of Parliament made for the purpose of collecting revenue in America. *The non-consumption of British manufacturers* League or Covenant, a crusade against the Tories, was drawn up by Timothy Edwards, Esq., Dr. Erastus Sergeant, Dr. Lemuel Barnard of Sheffield, Deacon James Easton of Pittsfield, and Dr. William Whiting.

under the sign of the shiny Red Lion[1] with a green tail, to storm against all things British. Captain Solomon Wahauwanwaumet or "King Solomon," chief sachem at Stockbridge, journeyed to Boston by the old Bay Path to pledge the fealty of his tribe in an eloquent and rhythmic oration. In a moth-eaten hair trunk in a New York house, among certain other cherished papers of the color of the weather, belonging to the Andrews family of Farmington, Conn., is a document[2] which appears to be the proceedings of this remarkable conference at Boston. Its sentences vibrate with the passions and strange, picturesque customs of a unique seat of war, in wilds of the New World, wherein a hatchet expresses more than words. The white commissioners speak first:

"Uncles the Six Nations, attend.

"At our late interview with you at place you told us that you took the hatchet from our hands, that you pulled up

---

[1] The Red Lion Inn, Stockbridge, is the lineal descendant of this "Stage Tavern." At the Red Lion is the Plumb collection of Colonial china and pewter.

[2] Inherited by Mrs. Alfred Whitman. Among the contents are a newspaper account of King George's coronation, printed on cotton in order to avoid the paper tax: a deed of the "Shuttle Meadow" at Farmington "in the year 9 of His Majesty's Reign," and "Polly Bissell's Book," being an illuminated writing-book of the dreary sentiments then considered proper for the edification of beautiful young ladies. Examples of Mistress Polly's copy: "Rural Meditations: Beauty is a flower that fadeth in an hour without virtue is of small estimation."

ALL IS VANITY.

"The active youth a lifeless lump shall be,
The laced lord shall leave his pageantry,
The carcass of the King the worms shall eat,
. . . .
And all on earth is fading Vanity."

a large pine-tree, which made a great hole in the ground, through which you ran a current of water, in which you told us you flung our hatchet, covered the hole with a rock, and set on it the tree again in the same place.

"Uncles, attend: possess your mind in peace. Let not our present declaration offend you. Uncles, we have taken up the hatchet to defend our rights and properties which are taken from us by the king, and cannot deliver it up and tamely see our property possessed by others. No, Uncles, we have taken up the hatchet with our Brothers and neighbors, the white people, and with them will fight in defence of our just possessions (etc.).

"Uncles, this is all we have to say."

"Brothers, the commissioners appointed by the twelve United Colonies, attend. We your Brothers, the Stockbridge Indians, take this opportunity most heartily to thank you our brethren . . . for the care you have taken of us since we have been at this place . . . and we beg that you use your influence in our favor that we may have a minister to teach and instruct our old men, women, and children while our young men go to the war; and should a kind Providence crown our united efforts with success, we hope that our Brothers the Colonists will restore us to the peaceable possession of all these lands of which we are at present so unjustly deprived; . . . and be assured, Brothers, of our most entire friendship. *Wherever your armies go, there we will go; you shall always find us by your side; and if providence calls us to sacrifice our Lives in the field of battle, we will fall where you fall, and lay our bones by yours. Nor shall peace ever be made between our nation and the Red-Coats until our brothers the white people lead the way.*

"This, Brothers, is all we have to say."

"[The Reply of the Commissioners]: Brothers of the Stockbridge Tribe, attend: We heartily thank you for the kind assurances of your unalterable attachment to us. We

assure you, Brothers, that we will use our utmost influence
that you shall have a minister to instruct you, [etc.].
"This, Brothers, is all we have to say."

To each Stockbridge Indian enlisted under Jehoiakim
Mtohskin, selectman, the Provincial Congress at Concord
sent a blanket, a yard of ribbon, and an address, through
Colonel John Paterson of Lenox and Captain William
Goodrich.

This remarkable tribe kept faith and celebrated the
Declaration of Independence on Laurel Hill in Stockbridge.
Washington presented them with an ox for a barbecue,
whereupon they buried the hatchet on the hill-slope near
King Solomon's house, not far from the old fording-place
crossed by the graceful Memorial bridge,[1] in an hilarious
powwow, adding a sombre, savage postscript by scalping
the effigy of the traitor Arnold.

Certain of these Stockbridge warriors distinguished themselves as scouts, and it must have been an extraordinary
scene when Captain Ezra Whittlesey's dark-skinned
company marched to their post at the "Ty" Saw Mills by
General Gates's orders, wearing blue and red caps to distinguish them from Burgoyne's Indians.

Stockbridge "smelt powder" more than once during the
heat of the Revolution. One peaceful Sabbath morning
a messenger roused Deacon Timothy Edwards to say that
the army was at Berkshire's very door, for Burgoyne had
sent a detachment to capture Bennington's supplies. Dea-

[1] Memorial bridge was erected by a bequest of Mrs. Mary Hopkins
Goodrich, granddaughter of Colonel Mark Hopkins and Electa Sargeant,
the first white child born in Stockbridge. Mrs. Goodrich was the moving
spirit of the far-famed Laurel Hill Association, the parent of Village
Improvement Societies. Even a crumpled leaf seems a blot on the
shining grass borders of the swept and garnished Stockbridge street
and close-cropped exquisite hedges of this model town.

con Edwards fired his gun in the street three times to call out the Stockbridge militia, who arrived too late for action, but Dr. Partridge aided friend and foe alike, attending the unfortunate English commander Colonel Baum.

After the dramatic surrender of the battle of Saratoga (pictured by Colonel Trumbull in the rotunda of the Capital), marking the first surprised failure of the British to cut our army in twain, a detachment of Burgoyne's crestfallen troops passed through Stockbridge en route to the seaboard, where transports were to receive them "whenever General Howe shall so order." Colonel Prentice Williams as a boy remembered seeing "the Hessians smoking their pipes on Laurel Hill." Burgoyne's Pass, over which they marched, is the grass-grown road which throws itself over a spur of Bear Mountain near "Bowlder Farm," the estate of Professor Henry W. Farnam of Yale.

Beautiful Laurel Hill is a "Sedgwick Gift" to the town; in that delightful season of the year when every copse in Berkshire is veined with gold and violet, the people of Stockbridge assemble on the grass arena for the delectable feast of wit and philosophy set before them by the Laurel Hill Association.

Sergeant's mission idea being somewhat after the fashion of modern University settlements, several white families volunteered to settle in Indian Town: the Ephraim Browns, Josiah Joneses, Woodbridges, and—most conspicuous in his fortified house on The Hill—Colonel Ephraim Williams,[1] Esq., deferred to in vexatious boundary disputes. They looked daily for Indians from the hostile north, and at

---

[1] Stephen W. Jones said that the Williams house (built in 1750) had clapboards 3½ feet long and 5 inches wide, lasting one hundred years. It was subsequently occupied by Dr. Stephen West, who married a daughter of Col. Williams. The old "Fort" well is still under the present house "Windymore," owned by Dr. Henry M. Field.

*Monument to the Housatonic Indians, "the
Friends of our Fathers."*
[*The natural shaft is from Ice Glen.*]
*"It is the spot—I know it well—
Of which our old traditions tell."*
—Indian at the Burial-place of his Fathers.

Great Barrington and Sheffield, Conrad Burghardt's and
Elisha Noble's houses were garrisons. The Williams house,
an almost impregnable fortress, was planked with black
oak and surrounded by a moat.

Between Stockbridge and the St. Lawrence lay a sea of
forest broken only by Fort Massachusetts and a few farms
at Pittsfield and Lanesboro'; these and the one settler
at Lenox were called into Stockbridge by mounted mes-
sengers when the tocsin was sounded at Dutch Hoosac

on its destruction by 500 Canada Indians. Terror seized the upper Housatonic and Connecticut River settlers, the equal of which the veteran commander of the Indian fighting militia, Colonel Israel Williams of Hatfield, said he had never seen. Jonathan Edwards dipped his philosophical quill to ask aid from the province and to keep Sir William Pepperrell at Kittery advised of western perils, (amazingly far west was Stockbridge—her first newspaper being entitled *The Western Star*), and of the crucial moment to engage the friendship of the Six Nations.

To light signal fires of danger on these western mountains, spread out "as thick as hasty puddin' " along New York's border, gallant Ephraim Williams, Jr.,[1] rode in hot haste from Newton, and was placed in command of a line of frontier posts established by the Province beyon necticut River, from above Northfield to Hoo Old French War Major Williams successfully Fort Massachusetts, the Night Watch ⸴f that menac in our nor'west corner, at present Williamsto by the old Mohawk trail; their Eastern war like a deadly rattlesnake within thirty miles of S —out from the scenes of crafty moonlit war-da Mohawk; forded the Hudson, and stole onwa tow Deerfield River by the "Dugway" at Pownal, and g Hoosac Plain east of Florida Mountain; the finish being in rocky passes on Hoosac Mountain where a moccasin leaves no scent; regard how the trail always sheers off from the Hoosac River bank, because the Indians disliked wet ground.

---

[1] Ordered to the front, Colonel Ephraim Williams fell on the "bloody morning scout" of September 8, 1755. Dr. Thomas Williams of Deerfield was surgeon of his brother's regiment and attended Dieskau, the captured commander of the French. Dr. Williams's son, the Hon. Ephraim Williams, studied law with Judge Theodore Sedgwick; his son was Bishop John Williams of Connecticut and President of Trinity College.

Over this fateful Indian path through Williamstown
Valley, Mohawks stealthily hurried eastward to attack the
Deerfield River tribe in 1662. Haughty Greylock, king of
Saddle-back Mountain and monarch of Massachusetts,
towers two thousand and eight feet above the trail and
appears to quarrel with Vermont's hoary Green Hills for
standing room. Up this same "Hoosac Road" (as Chaplain Norton calls the Mohawk path) merciless French and
Indians carried their captives northwestward to thraldom
in Canada, after the siege of Fort Massachusetts, the most
notable in the war except Louisburg.

The traveller need not search the north bank of Hoosac
River for the site of Fort Massachusetts; as he rides between
North Adams and Williamstown, he will perceive a lofty
ᵣᵢₑd ᵇy men of Williams College as an appreciation
commander and their benefactor—Ephraim
all fellows still pledge loyalty to the hero:

" ᴼᵗ, here's to the health of Eph Williams,
    ₙₒ founded a school in Bill-ville."

            .   . ₐ⸍ .   .   .   .   .

And here's to old Fort Massachusetts,
And here's to the old Mohawk trail,
Ar⸱ ₗᵤre's to historical Pe-ri[1]
Who grinds out his sorrowful tale."

At the head of Stockbridge affairs during these troublous
times, Jonathan Edwards showed judgment in things martial
as well as spiritual, for his mother, the wise Esther Stoddard
of Northampton, left a broad and splendid inheritance to
her eleven children.

---

[1] "Historical Pe-ri" refers to the historian of Williamstown, Arthur
Latham Perry, to whom Williams men were particularly devoted. His
son is Bliss Perry.

236 Old Paths of the New England Border

Dr. Edwards's letters to the Rev. John Erskine of Cul-
ross are filled with our political problems. After General
Braddock's defeat he writes:

. . . "It is apparent that the ministry at home miss
it very much, in sending over British officers to have the
command of our British forces. Let them send us arms,
ammunition, money, and shipping: and let New England
men manage the business in their own way, who alone
understand it. . . . All the Provinces in America seem
to be fully sensible that New England men are the only
men to be employed against Canada. . . . However,
we ought to remember that neither New England men
nor any other are anything unless God be with us."

Jonathan Edwards, in the frontier parsonage built by
Sergeant on The Plain, doubtless found sermonizing to the
Indians an awkward task, and spent far more congenial
hours on *Original Sin* than expostulating through his interpreter, John Wouwanonpequunount, to a people of
"barbarous and barren tongue." Edwards's heart was
bound up in marvellous metaphysics which he squared and
multiplied in Stockbridge's laurel-lined forest lanes, subsequently pouring out his soul on paper in his famous
little room, measuring scarcely a man's length, but broad
enough to hold *Freedom of the Will*. The Doctor's study[1]
is marked by a sun-dial on the present Caldwell[2] estate on
Stockbridge Street.

The Edwardses rejoiced in living "in peace," after unhappy controversies which had driven them from Northampton, and Dr. Edwards writes to his father at East
Windsor, "The Indians are very much pleased with my
family, especially with my wife" (the beautiful Sarah

---

[1] Dr. Edwards's study-table may be seen at the Jackson Library;
also the Indian's conch-shell antedating the church bell. "Edwards
Hall" was for some years the Reid and Hoffman School.

[2] An unusual Whistler collection is hung in the house of John Caldwell, Esq.

The Owen house. Elm, one of four planted in 1786 by Col. W. M. Edwards, a grandson of President Jonathan Edwards. Soldiers' Monument. St. Paul's Church. The Chancel Memorial window is by La Farge.

237

Pierpont of New Haven, great-great-granddaughter of Thomas Hooker).

The daughters eked out the pastor's salary (£6, 3s. 4d. "lawful money," and twenty-five loads of wood from his white congregation, also eighty sleigh-loads of wood from the Indians) by embroidering and painting fans for Boston dames; thus Esther Edwards earned her wedding outfit, and the village was in a buzz of excitement when the rather elderly Rev. Aaron Burr arrived to carry away his youthful and lovely bride. On the Thanksgiving Day when the first grandchild, Aaron, was brought home there was unusual festivity at the Edwards house. As a lad, Aaron often tarried in Stockbridge at the home of his uncle, Deacon Timothy Edwards.

The fascinating and wayward blade Colonel Aaron Burr, who would fain conquer every feminine heart, even daring to coquette with Dorothy Q., after she was promised to John Hancock, was of a fibre unlike his grandfather's household. Our well-beloved Donald Mitchell has flung the high lights of a sweet humor across that gray homespun age when the rod was not spared, and domestic life ran by rule at the homestead on Stockbridge Street. Jonathan Edwards was "rigid with the Westminster Assembly's Shorter Catechism on every Saturday evening, never allowing his boys out of doors after nine o'clock at night: and if any suitor of his daughters tarried beyond that hour he was mildly but peremptorily informed that it was time to lock up the house. Among those suitors . . . was a Mr. Burr, who came to be President of the College of New Jersey at Princeton, and whose son, Aaron Burr—grandson of the Doctor—had, in later days, a way of staying out—after nine." [1]

Dr. Stephen West, the patriot parson, was held in great

---

[1] *American Lands and Letters* by Donald G. Mitchell. Charles Scribner's Sons.

reverence. One of the good dames of his parish, being much frightened at passing alone at dusk the huts of Great Moon and Half Moon, murmured very fast under her breath as a talisman to protect herself from harm, "Stephen West—Stephen West—West—West!" [These Indian huts stood on the site purchased by Nathan Appleton, "Oak Grove," presented to Longfellow, but never occupied by him. Afterwards it became the estate of Charles F. South-mayd, Esq.] The Rev. Dr. Kirkland, who succeeded Dr. West, lived on the Tuckerman estate, "Ingleside Hall." It is said that he had a passion for the "cup that cheers," and was partaking out of the forbidden Revolutionary tea-chest, with curtains drawn, when startled by a knock. He sprang to hide the urn in anything but a clerical manner, and opened the door, only to find one of his Indians wondering over his prolonged wait.

Next to the minister, Deacon Timothy Edwards and Squire Jahleel Woodbridge were the "great men" of the town. At the funeral of Madame Woodbridge, Bellamy says in his *Duke of Stockbridge*, there was a notable gathering of the gentry: the Stoddards, Littles, and Wendells of Pittsfield, Colonel Ashley was there from Sheffield, Justices Dwight and Whiting from Great Barrington, and Barker from Lanesboro. The carriages, some of them bearing coats of arms upon their panels, made a fine array; the six pall-bearers were Chief-Justice Dwight, Colonel Elijah Williams, the founder of the iron-works on old Saw Mill Brook or Williams River at West Stockbridge (Queensborough 1767), Captain Solomon Stoddard, commander of the Stockbridge militia, Oliver Wendell, and Henry W. Dwight, the county treasurer.

In the days of Shays's Rebellion the dreaded hemlock bough of the insurgents waved above the heads of innocent citizens, who had not rebelled openly against grinding taxes; even magistrates were not respected, and the malcontents gave Judge Sedgwick little quarter, pillaging his house. As a member of the old Continental Congress and a leader in politics his correspondence with the brothers Van Schaick, Ames, King, Pinckney, Charles Carroll of Carrollton, and others, is a replica of the times. The last letter written by Alexander Hamilton was to him.

The Hon. Theodore Sedgwick, Federalist, was much of an autocrat, yet most benevolent, possessing a tender heart, which he bequeathed to his daughter Catherine, the champion of the cause of letters in early Berkshire.

To visit the author of *Hope Leslie*, and the glorious country pictured therein, literati of the Old World crossed the Atlantic, and the home of Miss Sedgwick [1] on the Housatonic became to the Massachusetts border that which Concord on the Musketaquid is to the Eastern coast.

In her garden by the river flowing behind the homestead, Miss Sedgwick, the priestess of good things for all people, encouraged flowers and shrubs new to Berkshire, much as we have seen the stately Susan Coolidge bending over her Spring blossoms at Newport: "all these are early blooms of June," said Miss Woolsey, " for we like to see the shrubs in flower before we flit to Onteora at midsummer. "

A characteristic little note of our early novelist is written to her friend Mrs. Richard Goodman at Lenox (hitherto unpublished):

" MY DEAR MRS. GOODMAN,

" I have to-day—according to my promise to you— potted three or four plants for your daughter—the pots are too large to be either convenient or seemly, but the roots had so spread in the ground that I feared to contract

---

[1] The mother of Catherine Maria Sedgwick was Pamela, daughter of Brigadier-General Joseph Dwight, the military officer of highest rank in western Massachusetts, who commanded the Massachusetts artillery before Louisburg. When trustee of the Indian schools, he married the lovely Mistress Abigail Williams, widow of John Sergeant, one of the best-known of the ante-Revolutionary women.

The Sedgwick Homestead, 1785.

"The Old House" built on The Plain of Stockbridge by Judge Theodore Sedgwick, one of the "Republican Court," and a friend of Washington. Residence of Mr. Alexander Sedgwick. The garden sloping to the Housatonic was cultivated in the old days by Catherine Sedgwick.

them into a smaller space. I have trimmed them into
rather a forlorn condition—they may lose the few leaves
they have, but I hope they will survive and look better.
Would that we could see with the clear eye of perfect faith
the unfolding of those clip'd lives removed beyond our
sight!   Yours aff'n'y,

                                      " C. M. SEDGWICK."

Some ninety years ago, a humble cavalcade entered
Stockbridge Street after a stony scramble up and down
dale from old Haddam on the Connecticut: one lumber-
ing wagon carried valuable luggage—priceless, indeed, as it
turned out, for, on top of family bales and books, bobbed
the six children of the new minister—David Dudley Field
—enchanted like all children to be on a journey, and such
an eventful journey![1] It came to a happy end, after crossing
Little Plain [2] (the Dwight meadows), at their new home " on
the rise." ("Linwood," the present Butler estate.)

Here Cyrus, Henry, and Mary were born, nigh the roof-
trees of Mark Hopkins and Miss Sedgwick, all cradled under
the benign inspiration of the great stone face of Monument
Mountain, whose mystic moods Hawthorne affectionately
tallied up in the little red house on Makheenac.

From his far-away window to the north the face was

---

[1] Dr. Henry M. Field says in *The Field Family* book: "As my
eldest brother and I took our morning ride on horseback over the hills
of Stockbridge, we passed a farmer's door. . . . He had still one of
the old wagons that had taken part in this memorable exodus." For
more than fifty years its tough timber frames had held together.

[2] The fine pollard willows on Little Plain were planted to absorb water
in the spring floods, by Colonel Henry Williams Dwight. The Dwight
homestead of 1790, "The Old Place," stands next the Indian Memorial.
When Colonel Dwight was a member of Congress he used to travel in
his carriage to Washington. Governor Christopher Gore's appointment of
Henry W. Dwight, Esq., as aid-de-camp to Major-General Joseph Whiton
is in the collection of Berkshire Historical MSS. gathered by R. Henry
W. Dwight, Esq.

not visible, and Monument frequently appears to him as a "headless sphinx," this morning wrapped in October's "rich Persian shawl" and again—under magnificent sun gleams aslant the valley mist—shining as "burnished copper." Just as in Hawthorne's tale of the Great Stone Face of the White Hills, may there not also have been a prophecy concerning some noble soul born here in Stockbridge vale under the influence of the wondrous Titanic visage of Monument?—some long-forgotten legend, so very old that it "had been murmured by the mountain streams, and whispered by the winds among the tree-tops" to the forefathers of the Indian inhabitants.

It would appear that the famous Fields were much like other boys, in that when the parsonage caught fire several packs of playing-cards scattered from the good Doctor's desk, much to his horror and glee of the mischievous ones deprived of them. A barrel of sermons burned furiously —"they give more light to the world than if I had preached them," said Dr. Field. When he went to Curtisville to preach, he would take two of his boys into the pulpit, and Mrs. Field two with her; during the "lastly" and the "long prayer"[1] he would pray with a hand on each boy's head "to be sure they were there."

Stockbridge and Williamstown are rich in gifts of the Fields and the world in their deeds. Indomitable Cyrus

---

[1] Dr. Field's "long prayer" was short by comparison with the Colonial parsons' of the Connecticut Valley; the four-hours sermon with its twenty-seventhlies manifested the minister's godliness and endurance, and the prayer lasted one hour, all standing. Although Stockbridge was born after the Blue Law period, yet her town records reveal that on account of Puritan discipline pretty piquant Sylvia Morgan suffered. She was complained of at church meeting in 1782 for associating with "vain, light, and airy company, and joining with them in dances and frolicking and by companying with a man on Saturday night, which she professedly considers a holy time." (The Sabbath began at sun-setting on Saturday.) Sylvia bore social ostracism bravely for eight long years, but finally confessed her innocently wicked deeds, and was taken back into the fold.

devoted his all that the Old and New World might converse by cable.   Living side by side in Gramercy Park, David Dudley Field and Cyrus counselled together, and to the unfaltering courage of the elder brother the Atlantic telegraph is greatly indebted, says Dr. Henry M. Field in his romantic chapters on Cyrus Field's twelve years' struggle to bridge the mountains beneath the Atlantic.   The first through message was sent by England's Queen to President Buchanan, accomplishing one of those costly first strides in modern history by which the United States entered the charmed circle of world-powers.   A star has been added to the family escutcheon by Stephen D. Field, Esq. (a nephew of Cyrus West Field), in whose electrical workshop in Stockbridge wireless telegraphy first wrote her message for us in Morse characters on paper ribbon [1905].

In the little red schoolhouse, Judge Stephen J. Field wrestled with the three "R's", and Dr. Field preached at early candle-lighting in spite of driving snows.   (The schoolhouse stands on the estate of Mrs. Bernard Hoffman, on the road to Interlaken.)   This was the stage of *The Smack at School*, once as much quoted as *Nothing to Wear*.   Wm. Pitt Palmer, the author, lived hard by on Prospect Hill, and this ambitious boy—with 31 cents in his pocket—walked to Albany that he might touch the hand of his hero Lafayette.

On the hill-slope at the picturesque Perry homestead one discovers another charming view of Stockbridge vale: from the windows facing west Susan Teall Perry writes:

> "*I can see the pleasant valley
> See the mountain's woody crest.*"

Mrs. Perry recalls many a piquant *quart d'heure* when her mother entertained Charlotte Cushman on the stoop with caraway cookies and a glass of milk, as she lingered

Aspiration

" *Ye spell me, O, ye tree-tops, thrusting high*
 Your darksome domes and pinnacles that pale
 The enameled vault."

—From *A Painter's Moods*, by FREDERIC CROWNINSHIELD.

for a chat on her way into Stockbridge from Curtisville, where she was staying on the Beckwith place.

And Fanny Kemble would often dash by before breakfast on her big black horse, or jog along on a charcoal cart, enjoying a lively spar with the smudgy and witty Irish driver. The country was quite shocked at her independent ways and dress, but they soon came to admire her and she was dubbed simply as "very peculiar." Not a whit cared she; Fanny Kemble dressed, as she said, "for the occasion," whether in bloomers to "go a-fishing" or in splendid attire for one of her unrivalled scenes in Macbeth's castle. She adored the "Happy Valley," and when far away refers again and again to the "dear hill-country."

She writes to Mrs. Jameson when visiting at the Sedgwick homestead, in 1837: "I think the scenery and people you are now amongst fit to renovate a sick body and soothe a sore mind. Catherine Sedgwick is my best friend in this country, but the whole family here bestowed more kindness upon me than I now can sufficiently acknowledge. The place of their dwelling combines for me the charms of a great natural beauty with the associations that belong to the intellect and affections." [1]

Longfellow was told on a drive to Stockbridge that the very grasshoppers of the valley chirped "Sedgwick, Sedgwick."

Among the delightful stories of distinguished visitors at old Stockbridge, related by Henry Dwight Sedgwick, is one of Longfellow:

"About 1840 the Misses Appleton, daughters of Mr. Nathan Appleton of Boston, passed the summer at Stockbridge. . . . Mr. Longfellow, who in 1843 married Miss Fanny Appleton, visited Stockbridge in his courtship. . . . I was then a student at Harvard and was repeatedly called

---

[1] *Records of a Later Life*, by Frances Ann Kemble.   Henry Holt & Co.

on by him at recition as 'Stockbridge.' When this first occurred, a titter ran through the division; the second time the titter developed into a loud giggle, which led him to remonstrate mildly. . . . Suddenly his mistake flashed upon him, and he joined himself in the laugh, though with a little embarrassment. Many years after, in meeting him at Newport, I introduced myself, 'Mr. Longfellow, you don't remember me?' 'Yes, indeed I do,' he said. 'To my dying day I shall never forget calling you Stockbridge.' "[1]

Of Washington Irving's visit " I recall nothing but the thrill of awful interest with which I saw him seated on a sofa in the parlor talking with Miss Sedgwick"; and the " small country boy" was much impressed by Macready's daily appearing in a different-colored dress-coat, black, blue, or claret. Others were Mrs. Martineau, the Hon. Miss Augusta Murray, Frederika Bremer, William M. Evarts, the genial General S. C. Armstrong.

Hawthorne and James T. Fields were caught in a sharp and never-to-be-forgotten thunder-shower on Monument; they had been invited by Mr. Field of Stockbridge to make the ascent with Dr. Holmes, Mr. Duycinck, Henry D. Sedgwick, Cornelius Matthews, and Herman Melville.

> " *To the north a path*
> *Conducted you up the narrow battlement*
> *Steep on the western side, shaggy and wild.* "

It was a stifling August morning and our delightful party of parts fled to shelter before the ominous yet refreshing storm-cloud. Hawthorne and Herman Melville were blown into so narrow a crevice that shy reserve retreated and perforce they became fast friends. Hitherto the sensitive man of letters had held aloof, although Melville's appre-

---

[1] " Reminiscences of Literary Berkshire," by Henry Dwight Sedgwick. *The Century*, vol. xxviii.

The Charcoal Cart on an Old Path of Berkshire.

ciation of the *Scarlet Letter* in the *Literary World*—edited by mutual friends, the Duycincks—was known to Hawthorne. Three days later Hawthorne wrote to Horatio Bridge: "I met Melville the other day, and liked him so much that I have asked him to spend a few days with me." Melville speaks of "tumbling down in my pine-board chariot" from Pittsfield to see Hawthorne.

As they crossed the valley on the return, looking back at that mighty height where they had felt the tumult of shrieking wind and thunder-bolt, the elect sympathized vividly with Bryant, that

> "*It is a fearful thing*
> *To stand upon the beetling verge, and see*
> *Where storm and lightning, from that huge gray wall,*
> *Have tumbled down vast blocks.*"

A brilliant dinner followed at Mr. Field's, and simple withal, for such creative minds sought with avidity the Berkshire hills because "the comparatively small society was noted for its simple mode of living, for its intelligence, and its culture." Fanny Kemble from "on top" of Lenox Hill describes to Mrs. Jameson the good old times: "You

Studio of Daniel Chester French, Glendale.

The famous equestrian statue of Washington, presented by the "Society of American Women" to France, was created here, groups for the New York Custom-House, and other statues. "Newchester" the home of Mr. French has a superb prospect across the Housatonic valley. Its parlor is a copy of that in the Daniel French homestead at Chester, N. H. "Newchester" was earlier the Marshall Warner farm.

know the sort of life is lived here: the absence of form, ceremony, or inconvenient conventionality whatever; we laugh and we talk, sing, play, dance, and discuss; we ride, drive, walk, run, scramble, and saunter, and amuse ourselves extremely with little materials." The frolicsome winter party is not entirely a thing of the past.   How the Sedgwick homestead has rung with merry shouts of old and young playing together in hide-and-seek from garret to cellar. Those were incomparable winter evenings of fun with the beloved host and hostess Mr. and Mrs. Charles Sedgwick, who delighted in the informal hospitality traditional in the Sedgwick family.

Hawthorne's final note on this memorable August 4, 1850, reads: "Afternoon, under the guidance of J. T. Headley, the party scrambled through the Ice-Glen." A lively and weird scramble indeed.   If Ice-Glen and Laurel Hill had kept a sentimental guest-book, then ingenious visitors might have left us a legacy of individual impressions of this most curious fissure in all Berkshire, lying concealed between Bear and Little Mountain.   Veritable moss castles of gnomes and elves seem the tumbled boulders in the twilight of the gorge: all too sunless here for lovers' tryst— not even golden Queen Summer succeeds in erasing the chill of his majesty the Frost-King's footsteps, yet by her commands beautiful fern-clusters line the yawning black rock caverns.

> *"Away to the Ice-Glen,*
> *The night dews are falling,"*

calls blithe Fanny Kemble, and inaugurates the Stock-bridge custom of startling the dryads of Ice-Glen once a year by a gay invasion of humans in fantastic masquerade with ghostly torch.

The first torch-light party was arranged by Dr. S. P. Parker for the amusement of his pupils.   Dr. Parker was the first rector of St. Paul's, Stockbridge's beautiful Church of memorials, founded at the house of Dr. Caleb Hyde, now Laurel Cottage.[1]

---

[1] The story of St. Paul's Church and an account of the growth of the church in Berkshire may be found in the anniversary sermon by Dr.

"Windswept Snow," Stockbridge.

From the painting by Walter Nettleton, S.A.A., A.N.A. In the Collection of Peter A. Schemm, Philadelphia.

251

At Laurel Cottage David Dudley Field entertained Hawthorne and other distinguished people visiting Stockbridge in that day, a hospitality which he continued later in his house on The Hill. His daughter Lady Musgrave of London sold Laurel Cottage, only on condition that two trees planted by Matthew Arnold during his residence should never be cut down. The acacia was brought from a tree on the grave of Napoleon Bonaparte in 1886.

Matthew Arnold was at first very much put out with the climate of Berkshire, finding it first too hot, then excessively cold; but after his return to his beloved English hedgerows and nightingales he writes to his daughter: "You cannot think how often Stockbridge and its landscape come to my mind. None of the cities could attach me, not even Boston, but I could get fond of Stockbridge."

From Laurel Cottage Arnold wrote to Sir Mountstuart Grant Duff:

. . . "What would I give to go in your company for even one mile on any of the roads out of Stockbridge! The trees, too, delight me. I had no notion what maples really were."

Again to his sister from Stockbridge: "I see at last what the American autumn which they so praise is. . . . Day after day perfectly fine. . . . I wish you could have been with us yesterday, that is, if you are not nervous in a carriage, for the . . . hills are awful. But the

---

Arthur Lawrence, rector at Stockbridge. St. Paul's grew out of the efforts of the church in Otis, and Trinity Church, Lenox. The first building was designed by Upjohn; the present building by McKim, and is a memorial to Susan Ridley Sedgwick Butler by her husband Charles E. Butler. The baptistery is designed by St. Gaudens. The pulpit is Florentine; one lovely memorial window is to the son of Ambassador Choate, the clock and bell, gift of G. P. R. James, the English author, and Maunsell B. Field. The mission chapel of St. Paul's at South Lee—the Church of the Good Shepherd—was made possible through the energy of the Rev. Sidney Hubbell Treat.

horses are the best tempered and cleverest in the world; the drivers understand them perfectly. . . . We were per-petually stopping the carriage in the woods . . . the flowers are so attractive. . . . You have no notion how beautiful the asters are till you see them; I remember the great purple one (*A. patens*, I think) grows wild about Yar-mouth and the Isle of Wight. There is a nice youth here, a German called Hoffman, who is an enthusiastic botanist.[1]

The autumn of 1905 was unusually splendid in riotous color. That year Stockbridge saw herself in a mirror, as it were, in the *Outdoor Studies* of Frederic Crowninshield, who painted Stockbridge in varied moods, from the yellow-ing of her pollard willows to the November browns of pasture and hill—an historic procession of the Months from the Moon of Blossoms to the Moon of Snows, typical of all Berkshire; yet the artist set up his easel within a stone's throw of his own door.

Here is the harrowed field and Monument; there rises Tom Ball, beyond a blue abundance of larkspur in the garden; of a shaggy richness is August's hedge of golden-rod and aster; September has stencilled a Venetian border of red and gold (maples) across the olive-green skirts of Bear Mountain; in late September the close-cut hedge is smothered in fallen leaves of the sort which little Julian Hawthorne picked up so joyously—"Look, papa, here's a bunch of fire!" Most splendid is October's sentinel-tree in full flame at the turn of a mountain road. "If but only my cousins in Norway could see these views of Stockbridge, then they would understand what our American autumn really is," said a transplanted Norwegian.

The mirror of our Stockbridge year is complete with the painting *Wind-Swept Snow* of Walter Nettleton; Berkshire's

[1] *Letters of Matthew Arnold*, arranged by George W. E. Russell. Macmillan & Co.

"winter veil of maiden white" in which the artist sees the reflection of Puritan character.

Robert Reid is a native of Stockbridge, and one may well believe that his boyhood's unconscious feasts of line and color in mountain lanes and meadow are infused in his mural paintings in our Statehouse and the Library of Congress.

The Children's Chimes on site of the first Church which the Indians attended. Erected by David Dudley Field as a memorial to his little granddaughter. The chimes ring every day at sunset.

TYRINGHAM, 1739–1762

"In the elms and maples the robins call,
And the great black crow sails over all
In Tyringham, Tyringham Valley."

GILDER.

IF you would visit a celestial valley in Berkshire, take the road out of Stockbridge to the pleasant village of South Lee with its artistic chapel; cross the Housatonic, and follow up the wild-wood mountain way toward Fernside, and you find yourself in old Tyringham-Township "No. 1" of four elderly townships—(Tyringham, New Marlborough, Sandisfield, and Becket) purchased by Colonel Ephraim Williams and Nahum Ward of the Stockbridge Indians in 1735; this in order that a proper road might be thrown across the Green Mountains between Westfield and Sheffield, for "his Majestie's subjects" who found it "utterly impossible to provide themselves with foreign commodities" in this wilderness almost impassable even on horseback, and with blazed trees.

What a prospect is this! "a sight to hanker arter," as David Harum would say: up and down reaches a marvellous valley—long and narrow; the converging hills seem almost to swallow up the sweet meadows of the plain, through which Hop Brook leaps toward the Housatonic, half concealed by willows and cat-o'-nine-tails, the white ribbon of the Lee and Tyringham stage-road following through the village in its wake. No railroad has impertinently thrust itself here, and the bark of a dog with the haymakers a mile distant, echoes as a sharp intrusion on the imperative stillness. At the smaller apex of the valley the setting sun casts a tender pink glow over all.

Who might fancy that this rich intervale was known as "Bear Swamp" to the plucky ox-cart pioneers, Captain John Brewer, Isaac Garfield, Thomas Steadman, John Chadwick, Thomas Slaton, and also Deacon Orton, first to venture over the mountains from the "Old Center" at Monterey, to found a village at Hopbrook, now Tyringham village. Your path climbs more than 1000 feet above tide-water into Fernside; here on Mount Horeb, for nearly a century, away from the world's people, the Shakers of the Upper and Lower Family swayed in their peculiar religious dances, described by Fanny Kemble in a vivacious and somewhat irreverent manner.

Enchantingly picturesque are the old roads hereabouts. A wild country way it is from Jerusalem to the deserted village of Beartown, nigh on a thousand feet up toward the blue.

Into Jerusalem from the "Old Center" was cut the Royal Hemlock road in 1743. Through Otis and old Tyringham, now Monterey, ran the King's highway, the "great road" across the Hoosac from Westfield, over which Lord Viscount Howe travelled to Ticonderoga by way of Great Barrington and Albany. It is said that Lord Howe fell in love with the beauty of these forest-lined lakes and hills, and named the region Tyringham, for his favorite country seat in England. At "Old Center" the Rev. John Cotton [1] of Boston owned lot No. 1, on which the church [2] was built, and many settlers came out from The Bay. The first settler of Old Tyringham was Lieutenant

----

[1] Other proprietors of Old Tyringham were the Rev. Jonathan Townsend of Needham, the Rev. William Williams of Weston, and the Rev. Warham Williams of Waltham, who owned the Jonas Brewer lot.

[2] The first minister, Rev. Adonijah Bidwell, a Yale graduate, was chaplain under Sir William Pepperrell at Cape Breton. The Rev. Joseph Warren Dow preached twenty-five years.

Squire Thomas Garfield house (1794) "Cobble Hill Farm," from the bridge across Hop Brook dam. Residence of De Witt C. Heath, Esq.

Isaac Garfield. His silver-coin snuff-box, marked *I. G.* 1793, is in possession of a descendant here.

At the turn of the road is an embowered mill; on the brow of the hill, passing the Deacon Cyrus Heath[1] house of the odd ox-door, you draw rein to drink in a wide reach of upland fields, flaked with the brilliant orange of black-eyed Susans, extending from Cobble Hill to Sodom, where Long Mountain appears to meet Smith Hill, and abruptly terminates the line of pretty white farms "strung all along down thro' the holler."

Nigh the "great bridge" at Hop Brook dam is the "post-office store" and Tyringham Library of rare-built rubble stone contributed by the citizens from their mountain farms. Just over "little bridge" is the house of Elder Hall, founder of the Baptist society; his mischievous son was found plunging his wee cosset-lamb in the brook, asserting, "I 'm goin' to make a Baptist of him!" Beyond are the Steadman saw-mill and Riverside Inn, the early Justin Battles [Battell] place. The old-fashioned loom is seen in the village weaving a "hit-or-miss rug" of rags.

Your waking dreams are of the Austrian Tyrol, being attended by the tinkling of cow-bells on Cobble Hill, and the chattering of Hop Brook, fed by a thousand new rills out of the rain-cloud over night.

Whither?—ever the traveller's interrogation in Berkshire, where each path has twenty rivals in charm and beauty.

---

[1] The Deacon Heath house, Shaker Pond, and the Arthur Cannon corner are a part of 150 acres in Jerusalem owned by Mrs. Emma Andrews of Newport. The Slaters of the long lean-to in Jerusalem came from Old Rehoboth, a branch of the family who founded the first cotton-mill in America.

The barn-yard at "Riverside Farm," the Justin Battles house built 179–, residence of Mr. L. B. Moore; one summer the home of ex-President Cleveland.

LANDMARKS—Jerusalem district:
Fernside. once home of Shakers,
property of John B. H. Dingnell.
Deacon Cyrus Heath house (1811).
Sergeant Solomon Heath farm,
Jerusalem Road. Heman Sweet-
William Heath house. residence
Wallace Johnson; oldest house built
before a road ran through the
valley. Brewer house (1799) "stands
plumb north and south." Solomon
Slater homestead, residence E. H.
Slater. Gideon Hale house (1783).
John Hale farm (1762) residence
Charles H. Hale; Deacon William
Hale of Tyringham came from
Suffield, Conn. Clark-Hubbard
house (about 1796) residence Wil-
liam Bliss. The Elijah Garfield
house, Crittenden, Fenn, Daniel
Clark and Solomon Garfield-Beach
farms (1776) included in Ashintully
Farm, property of Robb dePeyster
Tytus. Daniel Clark house. Old-
Mill Farm, summer home of R. C.
Fordham. Snow-Cannon House,
residence George Cannon. Stedman
house. residence of Marshall W.
Stedman, built from timbers hewn
in the forest. Stedman saw-mill.
Reference: "Tyringham Old and
New," Old Home Week Souvenir by
John A. Scott. Tyringham by
O. C. Bidwell, in Beers's *Berkshire
County.*

MONTEREY.

Monterey was named in honor
of General Taylor's victory, Mexico,
1846. Alvah Smith house, Smith
Hill, residence of Mrs. Edward R.
Ward, near boundary of Monterey
and Tyringham. Major Allen-
Colonel Daniel A. Garfield house
(1796). Morse farm, residence
George Whitfield Morse, at the
cross-roads. Huckleberry Hill. Dea-

To the heights of Monterey and
Sandisfield [1] and "The Specta-
cles," or to the famous Otis ponds?
To romantic Becket by way of
Goose Ponds, or by the lower
or upper road to busy Lee, with
its paper-mills and granite quarries, Fern Cliff, and Laurel Lake?
Or shall it be Lake Buel and the
homesteads of New Marlborough?
But we'll none of these to-day, for
Tyringham river—as Mr. Gilder
delights to call Hop Brook—summons you to the wild, where its
waters "head up," the undiluted
fastnesses of Berkshire.

The Hop Brook highway is
lined with pleasant farms laid
out on "squadron lines." Near
Camp Brook, you cross a trail
entering the sugar-bush, a mag-
net to Stockbridge Indians; tapping the trees, they caught the
delectable sap in birchbark buck-
ets, and invited Sergeant the
missionary to his first "sugaring
off." This historic grove of sugar maples is on the Ashintully
Farm of Robb dePeyster Tytus,

[1] Sandisfield is the birthplace of president Jeremiah Atwater and
of Colonel John Brown, distinguished in the Revolution. a prominent
citizen of Pittsfield. His daughter Huldah—a lady of the old school
after the pattern of Madame Dwight—married William Butler of Northampton, who established the veteran *Hampshire Gazette.*

con Thomas Hale farm. Amos Langdon house. Traces of the Captain John Brewer house, fortified in French and Indian wars, seen near Frances G. Heath residence. Rev. Adonijah Bidwell parsonage, residence Elihu Harmon. Bidwell homestead, "Lake Farm." Orton house, property of George W. Eggan. Parson Miner house, oldest in Monterey. Luther Marcy house. Old Thompson farm, just over Sandisfield line, now "Lost Lake Farm," property of R. W. Gilder. the Egyptian archæologist,[1] who bought up five old farms under Long Mountain. Far above, the denizens of Wild-Cat Ledge still shriek o' nights. "A piece beyond," your road runs up against the house of Daniel Clark in Sodom, who was well known for his fine mineral collection of this region. Muir "went wild" over the Valley's "quite wonderful glacial deposit." [2]

At the divide, one road takes a climb ("Steep!" said a Yankee stage-driver. "Steep! Chain lightning could n't go down it 'thout puttin' the shoe on!") into Monterey by Smith's Hill and Four Corners, passing the Colonel Daniel Garfield,[3] Morse, and Hale places and on to Twelve-Mile Pond. Here courageous Captain John Brewer,[4] who slept

---

[1] Mr. Tytus's *Preliminary Report on the Re-excavation of the Palace of Amenhotep III.* is a fascinating monograph with remarkable color plates of the ceilings of the palace.

[2] The Clark list of minerals is in Field's *Berkshire County.* Professor Benjamin K. Emerson of Amherst describes the rock formations of Tyringham in his "Geology of Eastern Berkshire" Bulletin, 126 and 159 U. S. Geological Survey.

[3] Colonel Daniel Garfield was the son of Lieutenant Isaac Garfield of Weston and Tyringham. The first Garfield came over with Winthrop and possessed forty acres of the Rev. George Phillips grant at Watertown. Solomon Garfield of Weston, a nephew of Lieutenant Isaac Garfield, moved westward; his grandson Abraham was the father of President Garfield; when a student at Williams College, the future General spent a vacation in Monterey at the Colonel Daniel Garfield house. The visit at his Berkshire cousin's came about through Colonel Garfield's sister, who settled in Ohio, where her son went to school with the President. President Garfield always looked back with pleasure to his years in Berkshire. He was starting to attend commencement at Williamstown when he was shot, and he was also expected at Monterey.

[4] The Rev. Josiah Brewer, missionary to the Greeks, was a native of Tyringham, and married Emilia, daughter of Rev. David Field.

under his ox-cart, pioneer fashion, built Tyringham's first saw- and grist-mills.

The other road, on a level with Hop Brook, enters a deep

The Mountain Path.

Sweets of mid-summer.

cuplike vale of indescribable beauty, enhanced by the picturesque log house of "Old-Mill Farm" and the Steadman rake-mill of 1820. A cart-path beyond a pair of bars leads into high wood-lots. Leave this breezy pasture and plunge into dim and breathless forest depths, home of the crystal

Lake Garfield, Monterey; of old Twelve-Mile or Brewer's Pond.   Renamed in honor of President Garfield, July 4, 1881.

stream, running down over its rock-bed at the foot of a cliff, caverned for wolf and bear and sheer as a castle-wall. Under a huge boulder, mid-stream, trout play in a pool turned emerald under the canopy of leaves; on top, a marooned flower opens its heart to catch a few stray rays of sun.   Up and up for a mile and a half all is coated with glistening moss, and you turn your ankle on Time's dense carpet of decay.   Under mossed arms of fallen trees are hollows of long-forgotten cellars and stone walls which fenced the "clearing" made by the settler's axe; a bent sapling indicates a fox-snare.   At last, amid the generous sunshine of an open woodland, you may pick giant blueberries by the handful along Hayes's Pond in West Otis, the source of Hop Brook.

The present town of Otis was granted to Old Tyringham as an "equivalent" for the acreage lost under Twelve-Mile and Six-Mile Ponds (Lake Garfield and Lake Buel), being twelve and six miles respectively from Sheffield); it was called the *Tyringham Equivalent*.   In colonial days, Otis was on the King's highway between Springfield and Albany; they used to "slaughter a whole ox" between her two rival hotels; now the breezy and hospitable village possesses secluded charms, and is somewhat bereft of man, the officers of the Episcopal church being women.   Otis is famous for the wild beauty of unmatched fishing ponds, and the Farmington River, called "the Rivulet" by Governor Winslow's Plymouth Company.   The district is almost as deliciously rugged as in 1817, when Professor Silliman and Daniel Wadsworth, following the river road, crossed the Farmington sixteen times between New Hartford and its source: "We passed almost the whole distance [forty miles] between a vast defile of forest, which everywhere hung around us in gloomy grandeur, presenting lofty trees rising in verdant ridges, but occasionally scorched and blackened by fire, even to their very tops."

A wagon waits at Hayes's Pond to carry you back to Tyringham across the rough ridge of Long Mountain.   The views are constantly superb; from the highest elevation, see the blue line of the Catskills.   Long ago the Battells or Battles and other farmers lived on Tyringham Mountain, later moving down into the valley.

Captain Thomas Steadman planted here, having deserted his coasting-trade out of Narragansett in Rhode Island, because he did not wish his boys to be sailors; he arrived on horseback with "Aunt Sally" Steadman, his youngest, in a silk handkerchief slung around his neck.   Captain Steadman voted for Washington for President.   He lived to walk to Goose Ponds at 92, but was once supposed to be drowned in a heavy gale off Po nt Judith, when commanding a Narragansett Pier boat, and his cousin, a Baptist minister on Block Island, preached his funeral sermon.

On the mountain's face is the summer home of Francis E. Leupp, our Indian Commissioner; it would seem that just as the colonist built high in Lanesboro and Tyringham to avoid Indian trails, so does the builder of a country house to escape the highway's dust and to take part in the play of storm and sunlight.

The "one-hoss shay" was long the sole conveyance; the

Elephant Rock, Monterey, Lake Garfield in the background; the sandstone shows the effect of frost and storm. The fisherman's grain-sack is full of fish.

first four-wheeler driven through town caused so much excitement that people were late to church. Deacon B. was remonstrated with, and allowed to use his carriage on Sunday only on condition that he should drive slow .

Tales have been handed down of an elder who was a "leetle nigh" on a trade. To a would-be purchaser said he,

"Waal, I 'll allow that you 'll be pleased to see that horse go up hill." The man bought the horse, soon returning. "The pesky critter balked at the first rise; tho't you sed she was a prime goer!" "Not jes' so," answered the elder, "I said you 'd be pleased to see her go up hill: naow would n 't you ? "

Expecting a customer for a cow, and wishing to keep the

"Four Brooks Farm," of old the Elder Sweet place, summer residence of Richard Watson Gilder.

bargain on his side, Elder C. selected the most undesirable cow and placed her in his best stall; the farmer was affably told that he might choose any from the herd except Mammy's pet butter cow. "Could n't part with her no ways." The customer got the pet cow. There is a saying in New England, "All deacons are good, but there 's odds in deacons."

The old Elder Sweet farm, now called "Four Brooks," on which a Battell built his log hut, is the home of Richard Watson Gilder, who with Mr. Leupp and the late John R. Procter, president of the national Civil Service Commission, have long been identified with village interests. These have drawn kindred spirits in art and letters to Tyringham. Cecilia Beaux painted in a studio made in one end of an old barn at Four Brooks *The Dancing Lesson, or Dorothea and Francesca;* Mr. Okakura Kakuso completed in Tyringham a book on Japan's extraordinary awakening; ex-President Cleveland and Mrs. Cleveland enjoyed visits and one whole season here, Mark Twain a summer at "Glencote"; the place has been visited by John Burroughs, Thompson-Seton, Jacob Riis, Edith M. Thomas, Thomas Bailey Aldrich, Robert Underwood Johnson, Mary Hallock Foote, Anne Douglas Sedgwick, Alice Hegan Rice, Adele Aus der Ohe, Hamilton Mabie, and other writers.

Stroll up the winding mountain lane of Four Brooks Farm, up from Willow Glen, a feathery forest of willows, half-concealing the shining river, up to maples, laurels, pine, and pastures, where flickers nest in high holes. Lean on the bars and listen to Mr. Gilder's prose-poem, *The Night Pasture.* No language can more happily touch the matchless charm of Tyringham Valley.

"In a starry night in June, before the moon had come over into our valley from the high valley beyond, . . .

Terrace on terrace rises the farm, from meadow and winding river to forest of chestnut and pine;

There by the high-road, among the embowering maples, nestles the ancient homestead;

From each new point of vantage lovelier seems the valley, and the hill-framed sunset ever more and more moving and glorious;

But when in the thunderous city I think of the mountain

*farm, nothing so sweet of remembrance,—holding me as in
a dream,—*
　*As the silver note of the unseen brook, and the clanging of
the cow-bells fitfully in the dark, and the deep breathing of
the cows*
　　In the night pasture." [1]

[1] *Poems and Inscriptions* also contains "Autumn at Four Brooks
Farm" and other poems of Tyringham. Mr. Gilder's poem on "The
Pine" (included in *Songs of Nature*, edited by John Burroughs) is luminous with the atmosphere of their literary camp among the hills.　It is
interesting to contrast a sea poem, *The Tent on the Beach*, inspired likewise at a poetical picnic of kindred spirits on a sand spit at Old
Hampton.　Page 243, Vol. I., of *Old Paths and Legends of New England.*

LENOX (YOKUNTOWN) 1739–1767

"There is an eminence—of these our hills
The last that parleys with the setting sun:
We can behold it from our orchard seat;
And when at evening we pursue our walk
Along the public way, this peak, so high
Above us, and so distant in its height,
Is visible, and often seems to send
Its own deep quiet to restore our hearts."

WORDSWORTH.

LENOX, "on top of the hill," has long been a "Land of
Heart's Desire" to one and another of the world's gifted.
No great upheaval in war or peace has fretted the Happy
Valley's mirror lakes, the intervals of sunny meadow, or
superb Lenox range, crowned by dark forests and Yokun's
Seat.

You may, nevertheless, distinguish four marked periods
in Lenox history: first the half-legendary reign of the Indian
Chiefs Yokun and Ephraim; to the second period belong the
colonial proprietorship of the Quincys, and the 4000-acre
grant to Ephraim Williams and those ministers who gave
up their lands in Stockbridge to the Indian mission. These
sold their claims, and in the middle of the century the
settler's axe rang through the woods, lilac and syringa
blossomed at their hearthstones; in snapping cold weather,
oxen drew into the kitchen back-logs of such length, that
as the sap ran it froze into an icicle at the other end. The
patriot yeomanry of Yokuntown and Mount Ephraim,
separated only by the lofty Lenox spur of the Taconics,
christened their new villages after the English nobleman
of proverbial good-will to Americans—Charles Lenox, Duke
of Richmond, the friend of Horace Walpole.

Scintillating years of literary proprietorship opened the

third period in Lenox with the advent of the county judges to the shire town; the hospitable board of Major Egleston —a founder of the Society of the Cincinnati—and the Berkshire Coffee House rang with toasts and repartee. In the early twenties arrived, as clerk of the courts, the love-compelling Charles Sedgwick—his delightful humor equalled that of his sister's stories—followed by his life-long friend the incomparable Judge Henry W. Bishop, who purchased the Egleston house.[1]

Miss Sedgwick could not be separated from her favorite brother, and left Stockbridge to occupy the "wing" of his Lenox house, and literary pilgrims flocked around her: among them Harriet Martineau and the noted Italian exiles, Confallieri and others, released from imprisonment at Speilberg. (Castillia spent a year in Berkshire, and after his emancipation became a *senatore del regno*. "A lovelier nature than his was never given to mortal man," says Mr. Henry Sedgwick.)

In 1846 Mr. Samuel Gray Ward of Washington, the friend of Emerson, and the American representative of Baring Bros., took a fancy to the farms at the head of Stockbridge Bowl, and built High-Wood, a forerunner of the summer homes at Lenox; his farm included beautiful "Shadow Brook," recently the estate of Anson Phelps Stokes, and the namesake of the favorite rivulet of the children of Hawthorne's *Wonder Book*.

In the heat of the day at mid-summer Hawthorne used to gather his children and their playmates together at Shadow Brook,—the talking brook, where overreaching

---

[1] Major Egleston fought at Valley Forge and on the staff of General John Paterson, who built the house in 1783. It was occupied for some years by Judge Samuel Dana and by Thomas Egleston, LL.D., the biographer of General Paterson, and is standing on Monument Square. It was recently remodelled by Mrs. Alfred Edwards.

Photograph by Mr. Wm. Radford

Catherine Sedgwick.

From a crayon portrait made by Seth Cheney in Lenox sixty years ago, and recently presented by his Niece, Miss Lilian Goodman, to the Sedgwick Library, Lenox.

271

branches created noontide twilight; then Sweet Fern, Periwinkle, Cowslip, and all the rest would beg for the story
of brave Perseus, with his winged slippers and enchanted
wallet, and of the mysterious friend Quicksilver who helped
him to cut off the Gorgon's head.   When the leaves over
the brook changed to gold, "Cousin Eustace" told the
children the story of King Midas and the Golden Touch.
Thus, before this book of exquisite humor and simplicity
was in the printer's hands (the only one of Hawthorne's
without a sad page in it) his children could repeat it by
heart.

From Mr. Ward's house, Jenny Lind was married, and it
was Mr. Ward who induced Hawthorne to come to Lenox
and occupy a tiny house near Lake Makheenac just over
the Stockbridge line; "all literary persons seem settling
around us" writes Mrs. Hawthorne from her "little Red
Shanty," as she calls it.

Horatio Bridge, Hawthorne's college-mate, assisted them
in establishing their household gods at Lenox.   Mr. Bridge
writes to his wife:

" *La Maison Rouge,*
" *July* 18, 1850.

" CARA MIA . . .
    " Be it known, then, that Hawthorne occupies a house
painted red, like some old-fashioned farm-houses you have
seen.   It is owned by Mr. Tappan, who lived in it awhile;
but he is now at High-Wood, the beautiful place of Mr.
Ward [Samuel Gray Ward].   . . . The view of the lake
is lovely: I have seldom seen one so beautiful." [1]

Lenox's fourth period of distinction belongs to the makers
of modern history, the *Now*, all too close to be chronicled:
a brilliant train of diplomatists, financiers, scientists, dis-

---

[1] *Personal Recollections of Nathaniel Hawthorne*, by Horatio Bridge.
Copyright by Harper & Brothers.

coverers, seeking a *dolce far niente* after the exacting and complex winter of the city. The register books of the Berkshire Coffee House, Fanny Kemble's "Old Red Inn," and its successor of to-day, are classic in autographs, and become historical, sociological, or genealogical to the reader according to his penchant.

That is a curious silver thread which links one thousand

The Old Saw-Mill, Lenox.

acres in the heart of Lenox to a Latin inscription at Bun-hill Fields, London, whereby Dorothy Q. came into landed possessions in the domain of Yokun, sachem.

It happened in this wise: Judge Edmund Quincy, when on a mission to the English government, fell a victim to a direful small-pox epidemic in London, and a memorial

was erected to him in Bunhill Fields, the resting-place of
Bunyan, and the Puritans; the Great and General Court of
the Province of Massachusetts Bay granted to his heirs,
for the great loss sustained in the death of their father while
in the agency of the province, 1000 acres on the west side
of the Housatonnuck River "between Stockbridge and a

A Deserted Quarry, Lee in Berkshire.
*Lee is celebrated for its marble, such as is used in the newer portions of
the National Capitol.*

township laid out to the Honble. Jacob Wendell, Esq., and
others." (Wendell's Town or Pittsfield.)

Wherefore in 1739 out of Northampton town rode Sur-
veyor Timothy Dwight[1] across the wilderness trails and
down over the bridle-path through Pontoosuck, *Field of the*

[1] Timothy Dwight, born in Hatfield in 1694, son of Nathaniel Dwight
and Mehitable Partridge, was a great-grandson of Judge John Dwight of
Dedham; his son married a daughter of Jonathan Edwards and their
son was the first President Dwight of Yale College.

Winter Deer, to lay out the Quincy grant. The dainty maid of Braintree, "Damsel Dorothy, Dorothy Q.," in hanging "sleeves of stiff brocade," probably never saw how lovely an inheritance was her portion of Lenox, threaded by little Yokun River, its north bound marked by a great oak tree on the Pittsfield road, and scarcely more than a league from "Canoe Meadows," where her irreverent great-grandson Oliver Wendell Holmes was destined to dwell "seven sweet summers" on the land-grant of his distinguished forbear Jacob Wendell, colonel of the "Ancient and Honorables."

The Quincys' north bound ran across the main road between Lenox and Pittsfield to the foot of the west mountain range. Yokun Mountain has been chosen latterly as a picturesque background for the "Fernbrook" of Thomas Shields Clarke; the house is Tyrolean Gothic and the lines of the hills are repeated in the roof lines. Mr. Clarke's studio is fashioned after the refectory of an ancient monastery at Ragusa, Sicily.

The south bound of the grant to Josiah Quincy crosses the present estate of Mrs. Richard T. Auchmuty; there a house was built by his grandson Samuel Quincy (registrar of deeds at Lenox), the father of the beloved "Miss Debby." Except for the occasional transfer of a lot on the "Quincy Grant Line,"[1] this episode of Lenox history is forgotten.

DRIVES: Adams—*20* miles; Around Lake Makheenac—*10*; Bashbish—*27*; Chatham by West Stockbridge —*20*; Cheshire—*16*; Curtisville (Interlaken)—*4½*; Dalton (Station) —*12*; Fernside—*9*; Fernside return by Lee—*19*, Glendale by Stockbridge return—*16*; Great Barrington by new road—*15*; Higginson's Corner, "Highwood" return—*4½*; "Highland Farm"—*4*; Housatonic

We feel "marvellous well acquaint" with Lenox life in the middle of the eighteenth century; the merry enthusiasms of "our Fanny" over her beloved Happy Valley, where she would live alway, crop out in letters to Mrs.

[1] "The Quincy Grant Line," by Robert C. Rockwell, *Springfield Republican*, Oct. 11, 1897.

—*10;* Lake Makheenac—*2½*; Laurel Lake—*3;* Lebanon Road, by Happy Valley, return—*5½*; Lebanon Springs —*12;* Lee—*6;* Lee return by Lenox Furnace—*10;* Lee return by "Highland Farm"—*10;* Lily Pond—*1½*; Stockbridge, return by lake road—*13,* Stockbridge, return by Interlaken —*14;* Over Bald Head, return—*7;* Pittsfield—*6;* Pittsfield, return by mountain road, New Lenox—*16;* Richmond Hill—*9;* Richmond, Barkerville, Pittsfield, return—*16;* Tyringham by Lee, return by South Lee—*20;* Under West Mountain—*5;* Washington Mountain, by Lenox Furnace, return by New Lenox—*18;* West Stockbridge, Williamsville, Housatonic, return—*22;* West Mountain drive—*10;* West Stockbridge —*6;* Williamstown—*26.*

Jameson, and we have the letters of Miss Sedgwick edited by Miss Dewey, and not least the *Note-Book* and letters of the Hawthornes and reminiscences of Lenox days by his children,—by his college-mate Horatio Bridge, and by Mr. and Mrs. Fields. Moreover, Hermann Melville and Charles Sumner and other delightful letter-writers were among the elect recuperating in Berkshire in the fifties. The following is an unpublished memory of James Russell Lowell:

"Elmwood, 23 May, 1875.

"To Richard Goodman, jr., Esq.,

"Lenox, Mass.

"My dear Mr. Goodman:

"I know Berkshire tolerably well for one born among loving and placid landscapes. I once spent a summer— (1847, I think, at any rate it was while Hawthorne was there) partly in Stockbridge and partly at Mr. Palmer's, whose farm if I remember rightly lay within your boundaries. I have spent a summer day alone on the mossy top of Deowgkook (pardon my phonetic spelling—being interpreted, it means Rattlesnake Mountain). I know Monument Mountain and Taghkonic well; had a distant acquaintance with the Pittsfield Elm, though I can't say he ever returned my visits. Above all, I had the pleasure of knowing those two admirable persons Mr. and Mrs. Charles Sedgwick. My friend Ward lived at the head of the Lake. You see I am not altogether a barbarian." [Dr. Holmes spoke of the Pittsfield Elm as "sorely in need of a wig of green leaves."]

Mr. Lowell's day in solitude on Rattlesnake was prac-

tical illustration of his thoughts of the blithe season when
" 't is good to lie beneath a tree."

> . . . *"What a day*
> *To sun me and do nothing! Nay, I think*
> *Merely to bask and ripen is sometimes*
> *The student's wiser business; the brain*
>
> . . . .
>
> *Will not distil the juices it has sucked*
> *To the sweet substance of pellucid thought,*
> *Except for him who hath the secret learned*
> *To mix his blood with sunshine, and to take*
> *The winds into his pulses."*

The accomplished Mrs. Elizabeth Dwight Sedgwick,[1] to
whom Mr. Lowell refers, kept a famous young ladies'
school, a "character-factory," she called it. One of her
pupils living in New Orleans says: "The girls all adored
Mrs. Sedgwick, she was so good to us; she was far ahead
of her time in Greek, Latin, and Hygiene. Hawthorne
used to bring little Una to see us, and one of her pretty
childish phrases was, 'I don't memory that.' Fanny
Kemble was a household word, and the girls counted as
the great intellectual event of their lives the delineation
of Shakespeare's men and women by the 'tragedy queen'
(as Dr. Holmes calls her) on Mrs. Sedgwick's piazza, where
visitors and neighbors gathered around, every one electrified
by that wonderful voice."

With the proceeds of a single night's reading Fanny
Kemble gave a clock to the Church on the Hill, and planned
one "for the poor"; finding there were no poor in Lenox

---

[1] Mrs. Sedgwick was a Dwight of Northampton. Her son Major-
General William Dwight Sedgwick, killed at Antietam, was born in
Lenox. Pupils of note at Mrs. Sedgwick's school were Charlotte Cushman,
Harriet G. Hosmer, Maria Cummings, author of *The Lamplighter*, Miss
Jerome of New York (Lady Churchill), Lucy Marcy, daughter of the
Governor and wife of Chief Justice Brigham.

she gave a reading for that historic institution the Lenox Library.

> The Library of Lenox was founded as a Social Library in 1797, through the Rev. John Hotchkin, a prominent educator. (The old Hotchkin house stands on Cliffwood Street, the residence of Miss Anna Shaw.) The home of the Charles Sedgwick Library is in the second courthouse, purchased and presented to the trustees by Mrs. Adeline E. Schermerhorn "to exhibit her affection for the beautiful town in which she had so long passed her summer days." A fund was the gift of Ammi Robbins of New York, a native of Lenox. Its first treasurer and librarian was Elijah Brewer. The treasurer for twenty-two years was the Hon. Richard Goodman, and the Hon. John E. Parsons of New York is the president. In 1874 the trustees were Judge Julius Rockwell,[1] Charles Kneeland, Richard Goodman, Richard T. Auchmuty, and F. Augustus Schermerhorn. Among interesting documents preserved at the library are a letter of General Washington to the Hon. Jonathan Williams, Esq., Egleston Collection, and the non-importation agreement signed by the Inhabitants of Lenox 1774.

Frances Anne Kemble is still the best remembered of the sojourners in her beloved Happy Valley, because, like the adorable Dolly Madison, she never scorned the least of the charming amenities of life.[2] Even Hawthorne, the

---

[1] "The old home of Judge Julius Rockwell on Walker Street, of the Georgian ("Colonial") period, stands on the grant to Jonathan Edwards, his portion of the Minister's Grant. The house was built by Judge Walker for his son. An illustration of its beautiful porch is included among the admirable plates of *The Georgian Period*, edited by William Rotch Ware.

[2] Fanny Kemble to Lady Dacre from Berkshire, 1839:
"You know I do not value very highly the artificial civilities which half-strangle half the world with a sort of floss-silk insincerity; and the longer I live the more convinced I am that real tenderness to others is quite compatible with the truth that is due to them and one's self."

Kemble Street, Lenox.

"silent man" as he spoke of himself, delighted to see her
come flying down on a large black horse — sometimes
she would snatch up little Julian for a gallop; and the
cynical Charles Sumner confessed to the piquant pleasure
of her company on a ride to Pittsfield, and begged this
"sympathetic, noble, and unaccommodating" woman to
be his cicerone over the beautiful lanes and wild paths
of Berkshire.

As early as 1838 Fanny Kemble writes at the "Old Red
Inn": "The village hostelry was never so graced before;

it is having a blossoming time with sweet young faces shining about it in every direction, looking out upon that prospect from the hill-top." She speaks of "making common cause in the eating and living way" with Mary and Fanny Appleton, at the hotel for a week. (Mary married Robert, son of Sir James Mackintosh, and the lamented Fanny the poet Longfellow.)

Many stories are told of Fanny Kemble during her various sojourns at the "Old Red Inn" and the Curtis Hotel, planted on the site of the tavern of 1773. She did not purchase her cottage, "The Perch," until 1850, the year Hawthorne arrived.

One day Mrs. Kemble, while waiting for her "spachcock" to be served, following an ante-breakfast canter over hill and dale, gave some directions at the desk about her favorite horse, and added, "You should remove your hat; gentlemen always remove their hats in my presence." "But I am not a gentleman, ma'am, I'm a butcher." This pleased her so much that she was his friend forever afterward.

Mrs. Kemble annotated a volume of her poems for Mr. William O. Curtis; the blanks of dedication are filled in "To Mrs. St. Leger," "To Mrs. Norton," etc. A sonnet to her aunt Mrs. Siddons finishes:

" *Think only that I loved ye passing well*
And let my follies slumber in the past."

The remarkable portrait of Mrs. Siddons and Mrs. Kemble by Briggs hangs in the Boston Athenæum. The distinction which Mrs. Kemble's grandson Owen Wister has achieved in the literary world revives anew the interest in her life and letters.

The old paths around Lake Makheenac, Shadow Brook, and Tanglewood will ever be associated with the second of Hawthorne's great romances—*The House of Seven Gables;*

written during that first happy autumn at Lenox, it followed closely on the publication of the *Scarlet Letter*, composed during the dark, pinched days after the author's dismissal from the Salem custom-house.

Possessing Hawthorne's journal and letters, one may follow him down through his apple-orchard to the pretty glen between the house and the lake. Picture "the silent

The Apple-Orchard of the Little Red House Slopes toward Lake Makheenac.

"I shook our summer apple-tree, and ate the golden apple which fell from it. Methinks these early apples, which come as a golden promise before the treasures of autumnal fruit, are always more delicious than anything that comes afterward."—HAWTHORNE.

man" walking along the twilight road each evening to a neighbor's, carrying a tin pail for milk, the boy Julian darting across the "milky way" like a humming-bird, and little Una trudging after; or ascending Bald-Summit with the children for a frolic and a wonder-story.

Hawthorne writes:

"Una and Julian grow apace, and so do our chickens.
. . . There is a difficulty about these chickens, as well
as about the old fowls. We have become so intimately
acquainted with every individual of them that it really
seems like cannibalism to think of eating them. What is
to be done?" It is quite probable that fowls, flowers,
and vegetables of the Red-house establishment were studies for Phoebe's garden favorites in *The House of Seven
Gables*.[1]

Here at last, Hawthorne came into his own in spite of
himself. Fame knocked at the door of the little red house
by the lake, and the author mails a jubilant letter to his
publisher, James T. Fields: "Mrs. Kemble writes very
good accounts from London of the reception my two romances have met with there. She says they have made a
greater sensation than any book since *Jane Eyre;* but
probably she is a good deal too emphatic."[2]

Hawthorne, after a year, began to weary of the hills,
which he says stereotype themselves on the brain; the secret of his discontent was a hunger for the placid slopes and
a glimpse of the beseeching sea, his birthright. Neither
Longfellow, Hawthorne, nor Aldrich, each born in an
old town by the sea, could allow himself to be far
from the salt tang, the flavor of boyish dreams; in his
native port, at each lane's ending, is the white-winged
fleet, whose pinions would take far man's "restless fancy."
Aldrich voices the long, long thoughts of the youth of all
three:

---

[1] Henry James speaks of *The House of Seven Gables* as "pervaded
with that vague hum, that indefinable echo, of the whole multitudinous
life of man, which is the real sign of a great work of fiction."

[2] Hawthorne acquired that year the wherewithal for material com-
forts for his family; he says: "The only sensible ends of literature
are, first the pleasurable toil of writing, second, the gratification of one's
family and friends, and, lastly, the solid cash."

The Church on the Hill, Lenox.

"When the bells of Rylestone played
Their sabbath music—'God us ayde!'"—WORDSWORTH.

283

"I leave behind me the elm-shadowed square
And carven portals of the silent street,
And wander on with listless, vagrant feet,
Through seaward-leading alleys, till the air
Smells of the sea, and straightway then the care
Slips from my heart, and life once more is sweet."

It is the glory of Massachusetts that her children do not need to step without her borders to know the charms of wooded crags and the boundless sea, of both old King Greylock and rock-bound Nahant.

Perhaps the last pages Hawthorne wrote on the shores of the lake were his luminous Dedication to the *Twice-Told Tales* (dated at Lenox, November 1, 1851).

In that deliciously personal and shyly characteristic epistle to "My Dedicatee" Horatio Bridge, Esq., U. S. N. (afterward Paymaster-general), Hawthorne recalls to his college-mate that they were once two idle lads at a country college, gathering blueberries, in study hours, under those tall academic pines, or watching great logs as they tumbled along the current of the Androscoggin; and says: "If anybody is responsible for my being at this day an author, it is yourself." The near-by pines at High-Wood no doubt recalled those at Bowdoin. These "Hawthorne Pines," as beautiful as any in the world, belonged to the Sergeant family of Stockbridge.

Twenty days later, in a storm of snow and sleet, Hawthorne left Lenox. It must indeed have been a droll emigration; Una, Julian, and Rose waved a lingering good-bye to their hens with the Christian names, while five pet cats trailed behind the farmer's wagon as it clattered down the road.

Lenox Church on the Hill-top commands eighteen miles of valley in middle Berkshire; its burnished tower serves

as a beacon to strangers.   Mounted therein, the imaginative
pilgrim may fancy that he is in a lookout-tower on an
island's wooded height, and misty mountain ranges rolling like billows of the sea on toward the horizon.

The ground on which the church stands was a gift in
1770 of the children of the Rev. Peter Reynolds of En-
field, Conn.   'Neath the quaintly carven cherubim on the
churchyard slates you trace sweet and stern old-time
sentiments and warnings to the thoughtless.

> Close at hand rise the magnificent wooded heights of
> the old Woolsey and Aspinwall estates, now Aspinwall
> Hill, whence the horizon broadens to the Catskills. You may
> drive a dozen miles over the roads of this natural park,
> and cross Lenox range by the West Mountain road: so
> dense are the hemlocks that after dark the path is shrouded
> in an intense witching blackness, and the belated traveller
> is fain to loosen rein, and allow his horse to pick his own
> road.   Deer were so plentiful on these heights that Lenox
> annually elected officers called "deer-reeves."

For more than fifty years the Rev. Samuel Shepard
preached in Lenox church to all the countryside.   "His
Lenox was not the Lenox of to-day.   On every southern
hillside, with protecting walls of forest to the north, stood
ample farmhouses.   The valleys were luxuriant with corn
and waving grain.   Town meeting day found the old town
house—which is still standing and still in use—full of as fine
a set of New England farmers as any town could boast.
Eloquence was the rule."[1]

Familiar figures of old days in Lenox were Major Caleb
Hyde, Samuel Collins, and Colonel Elijah Northrup (his

---

[1] "The Church on Lenox Hill-Top and round about It," by the Rev.
Frederick Lynch of Pilgrim Church, New York.   *New England Magazine*,
October, 1900.   The house of the first minister, the Rev. Samuel Munson,
stood on the site of the house of the Hon. John E. Parsons, "Stonover."

house of 1778 is still standing on Main Street, the residence
of Henry Sedgwick), also Representatives Asher Sedgwick,
Oliver Belden, and William O. Curtis, Senator Charles
Mattoon, County Treasurer Joseph Tucker, James Robbins,
and Judge William Walker who came from old Rehoboth
in 1770, and purchased some 200 acres on Walker Hill (now
Lanier Hill). Judge Walker always drove four horses
or four oxen; in his house, Yokun farm, remain still the
huge chimney, and exquisite French wall-paper laid on in

*"Yokun Farm," the Judge Walker house, as it looked
in 1865, when the Hon. Richard Goodman purchased it of Judge Edwards Pierrepont, minister to
England under Grant.*

sheets, and the room in the "L," where Madame Walker
directed her maidens at their spinning. "Yokun" has
been the home for many years of the family of the Hon.
Richard Goodman.

Judge Walker raised his gambrel-roof on a most attractive
height, whence may be observed the clear waters of three embowered ponds—Makheenac, Lily, and Laurel Lakes; the
latter is literally a "mountain mirror." Seated beneath
"Yokun's" honeysuckle summer-house on the west knoll,

one becomes the guest of the clouds, the cirrus trains which float or scud across Bald Head and Monument, to be finally drowned in the azure distance of Sheffield's proud Dome. One of the prettiest of days is when "the clouds are slicking across,"—as the daughter of a Cape Cod fisherman expressed it, her weather eye unconsciously alert for the smacks outside the bar.

On the hither side of Laurel Lake is the broad sweep of "Erskine Park," the summer home of the inventor George Westinghouse; thence you may command, set in sublime scenery, "Yokun" and the "Allen Winden" of Charles Lanier, Esq., on this Walker's or Lanier's Hill.

"The Perch" of Fanny Kemble also overlooks Laurel Lake, on which she spent long days fishing for pickerel, "the most patient fisherman hereabouts."

Where willows dip, by the western shore of Laurel Lake, the close-cropped upland rises to the terraces of "The Mount," the home of Edith Wharton. Simplicity is the accent of this estate by the author's preference, and the house is a copy of Beton, the seat of Lord Brownlow in Lincolnshire. June is full of invitations to the outdoor revel of bird-folk and flowers; quite equal here to the scene at Elvetham in Hampshire, poetized by Peter Lylly, for the occasion of "The Honorable Entertainment given by the Queen's Majestie in Progress" by the right Honorable the Earle of Hertford. Thus runs the *Dittie of the Six Virgins' Song*:

> "*Now birds record new harmonie,*
> *And trees doe whistle melodie!*
> *Now everie thing that nature breeds*
> *Doth clad itself in pleasant weeds.*
> *O beauteous Queene of second Troy,*
> *Accept of our unfained joy!*" [1]

---

[1] *At Elvetham*, by Peter Lylly. "To bee sold at the little Shop over against the great South dore of Paules. 1591."

Still another estate in the literary annals of Lenox touches Laurel Lake—"Wyndhurst," originally the "Blossom Farm" of the Rev. John Hotchkin, principal of the celebrated Lenox Academy.[1] Henry Ward Beecher wrote *Star Papers* here and the height is known as "Beecher's Hill." Gen. John F. Rathbone christened the place "Wyndhurst"; it looks out upon bewitching October Mountain, and the Housatonic Valley. The ivy-mantled tower of the "Tudor" mansion of the present owner, John Sloane, Esq., commands a sweep of sixty miles across Berkshire from Greylock to the Dome.

In the appropriate landscape setting of "Wyndhurst" yearly blooms the memory of the power and charm of Charles Eliot and Olmsted the elder.

Adjoining the Beecher farm is "Coldbrooke," the estate of Captain John S. Barnes, who has an unusual collection of war-relics of 1812. Coldbrooke is the summer home of James Barnes the author.

The early estate of Mrs. Dorr, a sister of Samuel Gray Ward, is now part of "Blantyre," the present estate of Robert W. Paterson, Esq. His collection of paintings includes the signatures of Meissonier, Romney, Bridgman, Henner, and Lembach. The furniture is modelled after Hatfield House, and includes pieces from the Marquand collection. The old Albany post-road used to run through the Paterson and Barnes places.

The Elizabethan villa built by George H. Morgan, Esq., on the old Ogden Hagerty estate and designed by Arthur

---

[1] Lenox Academy, founded in 1803, had many distinguished associates: Matthew Buckham, President of Vermont University, Levi Glezen and Professor H. H. Ballard, now of the Pittsfield Athenæum, who founded the Agassiz Association in connection with the Lenox High School. Among the pupils of Lenox Academy were Mark Hopkins, Governor Yancy of South Carolina, the Hon. David Davis, and Anson Jones, president of Texas.

"Yokun" to-day; built by Judge Willaim Walker in 1794, and remodelled; residence of Mr. Richard Goodman.

Rotch, well becomes its setting of magnificent old pines. Mrs. Hagerty held the earliest salon in Lenox, and among other interesting events Christine Nilsson sang in her drawing-room. Miss Hagerty became the wife of the gallant Robert Gould Shaw.

The foundation of the Parish of Trinity Church was begun as early as 1771: its fine group of buildings of Berkshire limestone are largely memorials. The parish house is a gift of the Hon. John E. Parsons, the chimes, of George H. Morgan, Esq., the chancel, of the Kneeland family, the campanile tower of Mrs. R. T. Auchmuty and F. Augustus Schemerhorn. Tablets have been placed to Chester Alan Arthur, twenty-first President of the United States, Major-General Paterson, Debby Hewes Quincy, Wm. Ellery Sedgwick, Richard Goodman, Mrs. John E. Parsons, Miss Sarah Schermerhorn.

"Sunnyridge," the old Brevoort place, is the house of George Winthrop Folsom, Esq.

Between the Lanier and Goodman estates is that of Cortlandt Field Bishop, Esq., the president of the Aero Club of America. one of the new marvels applying science to sport, combined with valuable explorations of earth and air; the earliest ascensions were made in Pittsfield.

Through the pines of Lover's Lane one may enter "Wheatleigh," overlooking Lily Pond, the estate of Henry H. Cook, Esq.[1]

This was the farm of a determined loyalist, Gideon Smith, an early settler of Stockbridge, when Captain Biddle led out the Lenox Minute-men after Lexington. He was a special thorn in the side of the patriots, who had many Tories to deal with, and lay concealed in his own house for weeks. It is said he required his children to pass before

---

[1] A capital history of this country in detail is *Lenox and the Berkshire Highlands*, by Rev. R. De Witt Mallary.

a certain crevice every day, that he might see that they were safe and well.   Discovered in harboring a British prisoner-of-war, he fled to Tory Glen, a wild gorge on October Mountain.   Indian friends protected him from the vigi-

" Shadows of the silver birch," "Stonover,"
at the Lenox Estate of Hon. John E. Parsons.

lance committee, and brought food to his rocky cavern, over which dashed Roaring Brook.

An enchanting road to Tory Glen winds through New Lenox of rich farm lands past the Gothic St. Helena Chapel, set in this lovely spot at the foot of Washington Mountain by the Hon. John E. Parsons in memory of his daughter.   One lingers beneath the grateful shade of roadside elms to drink in the glorious outline of the Saddle of noble Greylock, across checkered fields of waving grain.

Berkshire is famous for its rural festivals; the Ice-Glen Procession at Stockbridge and the Tub Parade at Lenox may claim first place in point of seniority over our American rural pageants, says Mrs. Burton Harrison.

The Gymkhana of 1904, arranged by the Berkshire Hunt and held on the green arena of "Tanglewood" (the Tappan-Richard E. Dixey estate), was an international play-day at Lenox. Among those participating in the brilliant games on horseback were Sir Mortimer Durand, members of his suite, and Baron von dem Bussche.

The gay Tub Parade has been displaced by the run of the Berkshire Hunt, and the horse-show at "Highlawn Farm." When the first frost sets the blood racing, and the fox-hounds and pink coats are out, snatches of an old hunting ballad on the Greenwood dance in the brain, as sung at West Riding in Yorkshire:

> " ' Let 's go to the greenwood,' said Robin a Bobbin,
> ' Let 's go to the greenwood,' said Richard a Robin . . .' "

The refrain runs thus in Derbyshire:

> " ' Let 's go a-hunting,' says Robin to Bobbin,
> ' Let 's go a-hunting,' says Richard to Robin,
> ' Let 's go a-hunting,' says Little John,
> ' Let 's go a-hunting,' says everyone "

PITTSFIELD (PONTOOSUCK), 1752

"How I sometimes long for a sight of Saddle-mountain! but then I would have to go down to our old Place, and I could not make up my mind to do it. I should (want to) cry so as to make Sackett's Brook run over its banks and there would be danger of a freshet in the Housatonic."—Dr. Holmes in Boston to Mrs. Kellogg, Pittsfield.

THE boundary line between New York State and Berkshire, our western border-land, rests on the summits of the Taconics for fifty-one miles; Berkshire's bounds north and east touch here and there the ragged Hoosacs, whilst Pittsfield, the county-seat, is seated, in high state between, one thousand and thirteen feet above tide-water—commanding a marvellous perspective of a thousand hills. Six lakes smile in the arena of this splendid mountain amphitheatre, and two little rivers join forces in the centre of the city, flowing to the sea as the powerful Housatonic.

The discriminating eye of Colonel Stoddard in his diplomatic journeys to Albany and Sheffield saw the luxuriant Pontoosuc meadows and fine water privilege of the upper Housatonic; therefore he chose six miles square of these ancient hunting-grounds of the Mohicans and Schaghticokes as the patent which he received as a grant from the province, in return for his "great services and sufferings on divers journeys to Canada and Albany," and his entertainment of the Indians at his own house.

There was difficulty in settlement with Indian claimants and others, and finally, by purchases and amicable exchange of deeds, Colonel Stoddard and two other distinguished men held equal divisions of the region extending from a point at sixteen miles north of Captain Konkapot's house in Stockbridge. The others were kinsmen: one, Colonel

Jacob Wendell, a rich Boston merchant, born in Albany and of Dutch descent, the ancestor of Wendell Phillips and Oliver Wendell Holmes; the other, Philip Livingston, Lord of Livingston Manor, the father of Philip the Signer. Dr. Holmes wrote Mr. Holker Abbott: "All of the present town of Pittsfield except 1000 acres was the property of my great-grandfather, whose deed used to hang in the entry of my house. It was dated 1738." A deed in which the land is "farm-letten" to Colonel Stoddard reveals a curious mixture of Dutch and Mohican names, and confirms the fact of their immigration from the Hudson "over the mountain" into the Housatonic Valley.

> "*To all People to whom these shall come.* Greeting: Know Ye, That We, Jacobus Coh-qua-he-ga-meek, Mateakim, and Wampenum, formerly of Menanoke, or the island in the Hudson below Albany, now planters in the Indian town [Stockbridge] on Housatonic River, have demised, granted and to-farm-letten, and by these presents do farm-let unto John Stoddard . . . land of six miles square lying . . . about sixteen miles northward of the place where Concupot [Konkapot] now dwells, and at the place where Unkamet's Road, so-called, that leads from Albany to Northampton crosseth said branch of the Houseaatunnick . . . executed in the eleventh year of our sovereign Lord, King George the II., and *Anno Domini* 1737, . . . in presence of Timothy Woodbridge," etc.[1]

The Unkamet road was the lone trail from Northampton trodden out a bit by the pack-horses of soldiers and surveyors. Unkamet was the sobriquet of a Mohican guide, who used to point out the *Old Path-over-Yonder*, that is, Unkamet.　Pittsfield keeps the name still in street,

---

[1] "Preserved in the collection of the Hon. Thos. Colt." Smith's *History of Pittsfield.*

*Sentinel Poplars on Pittsfield's " old road to Lenox."   There are none equal
to these in all Berkshire.*

meadow, and brook, and an important house (Fort Anson remodelled) at Unkamet Crossing in 1761 was that of Lieutenant Graves, where the county courts held quarterly terms.

A few years pass and the pioneer ventures over the Hoosacs, hewing the way for his ox-team. What huge problems confronted courageous Berkshire pioneers! Glance on the map, at the contrasting halves of the Old Bay State: a comparatively smooth surface on the east, and the west's curling waves of brown, spilling over a bit into Vermont and New York, retreating down the Housatonic toward New Milford, Conn.; marvel once again at the sand of the English race who chose to defy such obstacles for the love of land. How tenacious a love is this which impels him to scale these stiff passes with a household wagon, plant his field of corn and potatoes, and pasture a lonely cow or sheep on the heights. If you have been rolled about in the comfortable Deerfield stage of the old days across grim and glorious Hoosac's ledge—Hoosac to the Indians was the *Forbidden Mountain*—or climbed a thousand feet or more from the valley and come upon the little village clustered about Florida church, snow-bound above that "tenth wonder"—Hoosac Tunnel[1] (projected by Colonel Loammi Baldwin when the canal was found impossible); if you have listened to the snorting of the Albany engine east of Pittsfield as it strains every muscle to carry you over Washington Mountain on Unkamet's Path, the old trail east; if you have driven, or rather slid, down the precipitous three miles on table rocks into forest-lined, enchanting Tyringham Valley from Monterey's sunny plateau, your horse on his haunches most of the time, and your heart in your mouth—you can partially appreciate

---

[1] Hoosac Tunnel next to that under Mont Cenis is the largest tunnel in the world, being very nearly five miles long and twenty-six feet wide.

Clifton Johnson

God's Acre, a family burial-ground among the Green Mountains near the birthplace of Charles Dudley Warner; the lad is reading inscriptions to those killed in a struggle with the Indians.

the problem of the rude forties. An Irishman at first sight of the hills, so luxuriant in Berkshire, exclaimed, " Bedad! the land is so plenty they had to sthack it ! "

On Washington Mountain,[1] there is a veritable banquet of the giants, one outlook in which every glimpse of the

---

[1] Washington Mountain, to whose fastnesses fled the defeated insurgents of Shays's Rebellion, was of old called most appropriately "Rock Mountain," being of adamantine quartzite, quarried for flagstone. It is defiant to the chisel, and the ancient stones in "Pilgrim's Rest," "Pittsfield, are as if cut yesterday. In Cheshire, and Lanesboro, along the Hoosac range, the valuable bed of quartzite furnished silicious material for the once-famous glass-works at Lenox Furnace and those near Cheshire and Lanesboro. Washington Center is the birthplace of former Governor Edwin D. Morgan of New York.

valley is cut off: "On the north and on the south   .   .   .
extended the long, rolling, billowy swells of the Hoosacs.
On the west, the ever beautiful Taconics; and looming
far beyond them the shadowy Catskills, looking like huge
ghosts of perished mountains."

> "Among those misty hills," said Eustace Bright as he
> pointed out the Catskills to the children on Bald-Summit,
> "was a spot where some Dutchmen were playing an ever-
> lasting game of ninepins, and where an idle fellow, whose
> name was Rip Van Winkle, had fallen asleep, and slept
> twenty years at a stretch." The children eagerly besought
> Eustace to tell them all about this wonderful affair. But
> the student replied that the story had been told once al-
> ready, and better than it ever could be told again.

Pittsfield's first settler, Solomon Deming, came over the
hills from Wethersfield with his wife on a pillion. Others
came from Westfield, driving their cattle before them, as
did Thomas Hooker from Cambridge to Hartford. Nathaniel Fairfield was obliged to lie in a hollow log for three
days with savages about, whilst his companion Dan Cad-
well returned to Westfield for provisions. After making
a clearing in Pittsfield near Captain Bush, and building a
log hut, he returned for his bride; it was a somewhat intri-
cate and dangerous wedding journey through beautiful
green woods, yet these made merry over the passing of
each blazed tree—the guide-board at the thousand cross-
ways of the forest—which set them on the right track.

Bancroft describes Hooker's journey as "a wearisome
way," but a New England journey in June has compen-
sations. Richard Burton writes:

> "Now say,
> What month is more beauteous in beauties, in balms,
> In lyrics, in psalms,

In gold-heart fair fancies of sunset, and calms
Of twilight, or after-glows wondrously clear ? "

Charles Goodrich—who later owned some 6000 acres in
Hancock, and other outlying towns, including the mineral
springs of Lebanon, N. Y.—hewed a way for his cart and
pair, the first in Pittsfield; at night, for fear of wild beasts,
he tied his horses to a tree and stood guard all night munch-
ing apples to keep awake. Often the wolves drove the
sheep "clean up" to the stoop, and then it was discovered
that Mrs. Judith Fairfield and Mrs. Seth Janes and other
pioneer wives were excellent shots.

Wendell Square was the point selected to make a centre
by four men, Charles Goodrich, Eli Root, Elisha Jones, and
Colonel William Williams, who agreed to build houses
where their settling lots joined, but the ledges of rock
prevented sinking wells. Colonel Williams built the "Long
House" in Honasada Street, and into the "long room"
guests were ushered through doors of twenty-six panels
each, by a colored servant—very grand state for those days.

The first road in Pittsfield was "chopped" through native
forests from Park Square to the present House of Mercy
Hospital[1] and thence through Waconah Street over the old
highway to Hancock. The first town meeting was held
in 1761 at Deacon Stephen Crofoot's on Elm Street: the se-
lectmen elected were David Bush, William Williams,
Josiah Wright; constable, Jacob Ensign; wardens, Solomon
Deming and David Noble; fence-viewers, William Francis,
Nath'l Fairfield; deer-reeves,[2] John Remington and Reuben
Gunn.

---

[1] The House of Mercy Hospital, which stands near the cross-roads to
Dalton and Lanesboro, has grown from a single cottage opened some
thirty-three years ago by a charity bazaar, into its present splendid
equipment. It was established and has been conducted entirely by
women.

[2] Smith, the historian, says, in 1867, that the last deer known in Pitts-

A " Wine-Glass " Elm.

Savage Mt. (*in the foreground*) and Greylock.　The pasture is near the once famous Berkshire Glass-works at Lanesboro.

As the Revolution approached, patriotic feeling ran high in Pittsfield. The Rev. Thomas Allen, the "Fighting Parson" who served as a private under Stark at Bennington, and whose *Diary* tells us the story of White Plains and other events, writes in 1775 to General Seth Pomeroy: "Our militia this way, sir, are vigorously preparing . . . the spirit of Liberty runs high at Albany . . . I have exerted myself to spread the same spirit in the King's District which has, of late, taken surprising effect. The poor Tories at Kinderhook are mortified and grieved, are wheeling about, and begin to take quick-step."

Two leading men charged with disaffection in 1774, Woodbridge Little, Esq., and Major Israel Stoddard, and other Tories were obliged to prepare hiding-places: the former in his old-fashioned spacious chimney, and another in the Diamond cave at the base of the Taconics. After Lexington, Little and Stoddard fled, and an advertisement was inserted in the *Hartford Courant* addressed to the friends of liberty (by the Committee of Inspection of Pittsfield, Richmond, and Lenox, signed John Brown), asking them

DRIVES : North Adams—*20* miles; Adams, by Cheshire—*15;* Becket—*16;* Barkerville—*3;* Balance Rock—*5;* Coltsville—*3;* Cheshire—*10;* Dalton, Village—*5½*; Dalton, Carsons'—*4½*; Greylock Mountain—*16;* Hancock—*8;* Hinsdale—*8,* Hinsdale, by back road—*12;* Lanesborough—*5;* Lenox—*6;* Lake Pontoosuc—*2¼*; Lake Onota—*2;* Lake Ashley—*7;* Lebanon Spring—*7;* Lebanon Shakers—*8;* Lulu Cascade—*5;* New Lenox—*4;* New Ashford—*11;* Peru—*12;* Queechy Lake—*11;* Richmond—*8;* Roaring Brook—*5;* Savoy—*17;* The Gulf and Wizard's Glen—*4;* Washington—*9;* Weststreet, Stearnsville and return—*5;* West Stockbridge by Barkerville and Richmond—*11;* Washington east to Station, return by Ashley Lake—*22;* Windsor—*12;* Waconah Falls—*8*;

The drives and walks about Pittsfield in detail have been published by the Berkshire Life Insurance Company. Also a map of Berkshire County, which can be had free on application. Many Berkshire points may be reached by electric cars and a short walk additional. These cars now extend from Pittsfield and Williamstown to Great Barrington, also to Bennington, Vt., and will shortly reach Canaan, Conn.

---

field were seen in 1780, when the snow-drifts were so high that the hunters killed them without possibility of escape from the yards the deer had beat out for themselves; there was a great need of buckskins that year for the military. Deer are frequently seen in New England of late years.

to take into custody these incurable enemies, and clap them into His Majesty's jails until the war be ended. These very men, however, soon pledged allegiance and served as privates in Lieutenant Hubbard's detachment at Bennington.

Captain David Noble fitted out his company of minutemen by sacrificing several of his farms, and with the gold —which was quilted into his garments—proceeded to Philadelphia to obtain the blue and white for the "regimentals," and engaged a breeches-maker to come to Pittsfield and make up the buckskins. And there were spinning matches and clothing bees for the army by the daughters of Pittsfield.

Pittsfield was closely in touch with the capture of Ticonderoga, a consultation being held by Captain Edward Mott and others of Connecticut with John Brown[1] and Colonel James Easton on the proposed action, at the tavern of Colonel Easton, which stood south of Park Square. Captain Mott and Colonel James Easton took the road over the mountains through Hancock and Williamstown to meet Colonel Ethan Allen, the commander of the expedition, and his Green Mountain Boys, picking up volunteers on the way. Major John Brown was appointed to announce the surrender of Ticonderoga of May 10th, 1775, to the Continental Congress, and Colonel James Easton to the Provincial Congress.

Stark's[2] messenger from headquarters, with the news

---

[1] Early in "'75," John Brown, on a mission to Canada for the Provincial Congress, met Ethan Allen on the shores of Lake Champlain, it is believed by chance, which resulted in an important close to John Brown's report to Warren and Adams. "One thing I must mention as a professed secret: The Fort at Ticonderoga must be seized as soon as possible, should hostilities be committed by the King's troops! The people on New Hampshire Grants have engaged to do this business," etc.

[1] The hero of Bennington, General John Stark, had an eventful and romantic history. He was at one time taken prisoner by St. Francis

The John Chandler Williams-Edward A. Newton House (1773–) Pittsfield. Now the Rectory, Residence of the Rev. Thomas W. Nickerson, Jr.

Miss Bessie Newton bequeathed her home to St. Stephen's Parish on condition that it never be removed, and always inhabited by gentlefolk. At the famous Peace Party here a roasted ox was served with platoons of geese and turkeys. The house contains interesting heirlooms. and an Innes of Susan Matilda Gouverneur (Mrs. Garrett Storm).

303

that Colonel Baum, by General Burgoyne's order, had advanced to seize Bennington's fabled supplies, reached Pittsfield on Thursday, August 14th, and the patriots hastened to the usual rallying-place, the Meeting-house; a company under Captain William Ford was enrolled and every man in hot haste got to Bennington as best he could. With him served the veteran Colonel Easton, Rev. Mr. Allen, Captains Goodrich, James Noble, and William Francis, Lieutenant Joseph Allen Wright, and Rufus Allen. Drs. Timothy Childs and Jonathan Lee went as surgeons. With Lieutenant Hubbard were Captains Israel Dickinson, John Strong, and Lieutenant Oliver Root. Colonel Symonds, for whom Mount Symonds is named, marched with a full regiment; a detachment of the middle district was commanded with spirit and skill by Lieutenant-Colonel David Rossiter of Richmond.

After a powerful address, Parson Allen started out for the field of action in his sulky, as Mrs. Plunkett says, "wisely conserving his forces for combat"; the sulky was "an important adjunct to the pastoral work of a minister whose parish was six miles square."

The English did not at all realize the concentrated power of the farmers. When Colonel Baum first saw, at the rear of his camp, small bands of men in shirt-sleeves carrying fowling-pieces without bayonets, he thought them to be country people "placing themselves where he could protect them," says Bancroft; it was the yeomen of Vermont, western Massachusetts, and New Hampshire, who gradually hemmed him in and gained the victory. Lafayette said to Napoleon, who, being accustomed to sway hundreds of thousands of troops, spoke slightingly of the scanty armies

---

. Indians and carried over several portages to Memphremagog, and at first treated with great severity; subsequently he was adopted by the tribe and much caressed. He, however, escaped.

of the American Revolution, "Sire, it was the grandest of causes won by skirmishes of sentinels and outposts."

That which has been in "Wendell's Town" shall be, in that the human eye ever seeks unconsciously one object on the north horizon—the serene summit of Greylock. At this range of sixteen miles, peak and saddle are of heaven's own blue unless cloud-capped; at "Greylock's nightcap" the Vermont farmer shakes his head, discovering a "weather breeder," and fierce becomes the rage of the northern gale when concentrated in the Hopper and savage Notch of Greylock. Beneath the wild storm the Indian hears the voice of the Great Spirit speaking in anger on the wings of the wind, as it roars through the "Bellows Pipe," smothering the more gentle voice in the rushing crystal waters of Money Brook.

Where did King Greylock find his distinctive name? Was it acquired from the crafty Warranoke chief of the Gray Lock, who dwelt aforetime on the Agawam, near Westfield? Gray Lock took sides with the French and was as great a pest to this English countryside as the chimæra in the dark ages. Many like to attribute the name of Greylock, our tallest citizen of the Pilgrim Commonwealth, to his appearance when the hoar frost of the aging year creeps downward, touching each patriarchal cedar and the melancholy dark sweep of hemlock with silver gray.

The Saddle of Greylock Group, formed by Mts. Williams and Prospect, is seen in perfection from Pittsfield's own South Mountain across the meadows and lake of the historic Van Schaack mansion-house, now the Pittsfield Country Club.

Again is Greylock enchanting with green Constitution Hill in Lanesboro as a foreground, from the waters of Shoon-keek-moon-keek (Pontoosuc) Lake at twilight, haunted by the shadowy boatman and mysterious voices.

Swept along in the moonlight you may perhaps see a misty
canoe or hear the plaintive death-song of Moon-keek, the
Indian maid deprived of her devoted one, Shoon-keek, by
the arrow of the jealous Nockawando.

> " But oft from the Indian hunter's camp
> This lover and maid so true
> Are seen, the hour of midnight damp,
> To cross the lake by a firefly lamp,
> And paddle their white canoe." [1]

Easy and of a delightful winding ascent is South Mountain, by some believed to be the " Elsie Venner mountain,"
for rumor has said that the charmer of rattlesnakes lived
near South Mountain on the old Britton place, a house
haunted at midnight by ghostly visitors. The key-note for
the romance of *Elsie Venner* was given to Holmes by Professor Alonzo Clark when at Williams College. " He it was,"
said Dr. Holmes, " who told me of the woman bringing the
rattlers to him in her apron, which story you find trans-
ferred to my true narrative."

On your road to view Greylock from beautiful Lake
Onota, you climb Jubilee Hill and ride past the Dr. Timothy
Childs homestead, and the Governor George N. Briggs
place. Our old friend Godfrey Greylock [2] invites us to his
favorite elevation, on Onota's southwest shore, the site of
the old French and Indian fort. Here one may drink in
the mountain vistas across the mirror lake whilst he relates
the legend of the White Deer with hoofs so dainty as to
scarce disturb the masses of blue gentian and the stately
cardinal flower when she returned at intervals to drink
at her clear Fountain of Pirene. One of the dwellers on
the shore told his grandchildren that he once saw a fine

---

[1] Moore's ballad of " The Lake of the Dismal Swamp."

[2] *Taghonic, The Romance and Beauty of the Hills*, by Godfrey Greylock
(J. E. A. Smith).

Greylock or Saddle Mountain, from South Mountain, Pittsfield; between lie the golf-links of The Country Club, of old the Van Schaack estate. South Mountain is said to be the Elsie Venner Mountain of Dr. Holmes.

white deer stooping to drink, but before he could pull the trigger of his rifle his dog howled and the deer faded away.

Then he remembered the Mohicans' tale of the deer of spotless white who came with the opening of the cherry blossoms to drink at Onota. At this gentle creature no arrow was ever pointed, for she brought good fortune. "So long as the snow-white doe comes to drink at Onota, so long famine shall not blight the Indians' harvest, nor pestilence come nigh, nor foeman lay waste his country." When war broke out, the French sent an ambassador to induce the Housatonic tribe to become their allies. He was welcomed to their council fire and heard the tale of the marvellous white deer. Ambitious, like the other adventurers in the new West, it was his passion to carry home some unique trophy of the forests: if he could but lay the skin of the white deer at the feet of his sovereign he would receive favor. Montalbert's proffered rewards to the red hunter who should bring home the skin of their sacred deer were scorned in horror. But he so debased the warrior Wondo with fire-water that he slew the gentle animal. Immediately that the prize was Montalbert's he set out for Montreal but never reached the French border alive. Then the frightened Indians sent up prayers to Manito to arrest punishment, but prosperity returned not, and the red men became less in the valley.

Hawthorne once wished for a winged horse that he might take a gallop from Lenox to see his neighbor-authors: he would begin with Dr. Dewey at the foot of the Taconics, and finally alight on the hither side of Pittsfield, where sits Herman Melville at Arrow-Head, "shaping out the gigantic conception of the White Whale, while the gigantic shape of Greylock looms upon him from his study-window." Another bound of his flying steed would bring him to the door of Holmes, "whom I mention last," he says, "because

Pegasus would certainly unseat me the next minute, and claim the poet as his rider."

The Hawthorne children's pet name for Herman Melville was *Omoo*, meaning a rover, in the dialect of the Marquesas Islands and the title of one of his popular books of adventure in the South Seas, to which Melville shipped as a cabin-boy.   Melville is associated less with Greylock than with his charming companion in philosophy — October Mountain, which seems to stretch out an affectionate arm toward his Piazza of *The Piazza Tales*.   Melville's grandfather—the patriot Major Thomas Melvill of Green Street, Boston—was "the last of the cocked hats" of the Revolution and to the youthful eye of Holmes in 1831 his appearance had something imposing and odd about it.

> *"Not a better man was found*
> *By the Crier on his round.*
>
> .   .   .   .   .   .
>
> *But the old three-cornered hat,*
> *And the breeches, and all that,*
> *Are so queer!"*

Dr. Holmes wrote the poem of *The Last Leaf* with a smile on his lips and a tear in his eye and said, "I cannot read it without a sigh of tender remembrance."[1]

On Major Melvill's return from the Tea-Party held off Griffin's Wharf that wintry afternoon, in '73,—when Ok-wooker-tunkogog, pretender, Sachem of Narragansett and seventy of his tribe emptied 342 chests of tea in Boston Harbor—Madam Melvill shook out some tea from his shoes, but said nothing and put it carefully away in a lavender drawer.   In after years, she was obliged to seal it against

[1] Dr. Holmes wrote in an Introduction to a later edition: "Good Abraham Lincoln had a great liking for the poem, and repeated it from memory to Governor Andrew, and the Governor himself told me.   I have a copy of it made by the hand of Edgar Allan Poe."

relic hunters.   One of the family well remembers the stately Madam Melvill as she sat very straight in her arm-chair by the window and her work on the table in front of her; she wore knots of gauze ribbon under her ears attached to both capstrings and ruffs, in such a way that she could not move her head.   Whenever she rose to leave the room, the courtly Major or one of his sons would offer her his arm to the door, bowing till she had passed out.   The young people felt in the

Mansion House built by Henry Van Schaack in 1785.   Originally lot 55 assigned to one of the joint proprietors of Pittsfield and substantially intact to-day.   Now the Country Club.

presence of Madam Melvill as did the little boy of Wethersfield, who, on seeing Mistress Prudence Stoddard coming, said, "Now I must put on my manners."

Major Melville, Jr., who came to Pittsfield in 1812 as commandant of the military post, was of the same fine old school, his courtliness a little accentuated by his twenty-one years in France; he lived at the Van Schaack mansion, now the home of the Country Club, and was President of the Berkshire Agricultural Society.   Elkanah Watson, Major Melville's predecessor in the Van Schaack mansion, was its first President; he exhibited the first pair of Merino sheep seen in Berkshire under the lofty elm tree on the public square of Pittsfield, to which "novel and humble exhibition," Mr. Watson says, "many farmers and even females were attracted"; the first Cattle Show was held not long after, and the Berkshire Agricultural Society founded. On the Anniversary of 1849, Dr. Holmes was chairman of the committee on the ploughing match and read *The Ploughman*—

> "*The lord of earth,*
> *The hero of the plough.*"

On the walls of the white panelled hall in the mansion built by Henry Van Schaack, are most interesting mementoes. One portrait in " Broad Hall," which attracts the eye, is explained in Dr. Holmes's inimitable way to Judge Barker of Pittsfield.

"MY DEAR JUDGE,—

"I understand this to be a portrait of Jacob Wendell, one of the original owners of Pittsfield. The portrait was owned by Wendell Phillips and I believe that when a boy he practised at it with bows and arrows, and damaged one eye.

"Sincerely yours,
"O. W. HOLMES.

"TO JAMES M. BARKER."

Here is framed a portrait of Henry Van Schaack[1] also

---

[1] Portrait presented by Dr. Henry Colt. An extract from H. Van Schaack's letter: "The farm I live on I bought for four hundred and seventy pounds York Money, . . . with a tolerable good house, barn and a young orchard, and a pleasant lake in sight of me. In my life I never lived among a more civil and obliging people. . . . A purse of gold hung up in the public streets would be as safe from our inhabitants as it used to be in King Alfred's time. Beggars and vagrants we are strangers to, as well as to over-bearing purse-proud scoundrels."

his encomium on the charms of Pittsfield, which he refused to leave, when entreated by General Schuyler and other patriots to return to Albany, from whence as a neutral he was banished. Henry Van Schaack was Postmaster at the time of the furor over the Stamp Act, and falling under suspicion of the Sons of Liberty his house was mobbed, in spite of previous services of the Van Schaacks to the country. He fought as Lieutenant under Captain Philip Schuyler in the Crown Point expedition, and was one who went to the rescue of Colonel Ephraim Williams's regiment.

Henry Van Schaack was born in the historic mansion at Kinderhook, N. Y., of Colonel Cornelius Van Schaack, spoken of by John Jay as "the hospitable house on the hill." In those days Kinderhook was a most important point between New York and Berkshire, by the usual route of the Hudson. Mrs. Quincy, the wife of President Edward Quincy of Harvard, paid a visit in the company of the wife of Brigadier-General Dwight at the younger Van Schaack house in 1774. Madam Dwight describes Mrs. Quincy—then Miss Morton—as "a very young lady of high spirit." They left New York in a sloop and in the course of a week arrived at Kinderhook's Landing, thence overland to Kinderhook, spending several pleasant days at the Van Schaack house, thence on to Stockbridge. "At Mr. Sedgwick's [in 1792]," writes Mrs. Quincy, "I became acquainted with Mr. Henry Van Schaack of Pittsfield and visited his family at their residence. I still cherish the remembrance of Mr. and Mrs. Van Schaack's hospitable reception of me. A startling feature of their mansion was the exquisite neatness of the house and everything about it. I had never seen the floors of entries, stairs, kitchen, etc.,

---

Mr. Van Schaack's farm was originally lot 55, assigned to Colonel Elisha Jones of Westfield and the only lot of the joint proprietors substantially intact to-day. Elisha Jones, Jr., was a Tory, his confiscated lands were sold at auction to Henry Van Schaack in 1785.

painted and although brought up among natives of
Holland, who are proverbial for their neatness, this
seemed to me a stroke beyond the reach of [their] art.
Parts of the house were covered with very handsome car-
peting, manufactured, as I understood, by the Shakers." [1]

*The great pine still stands "in its solitary
beauty and grandeur" [see letter of Dr. Holmes]
at " Canoe Meadow " now " Holmesdale."*

The Van Schaack mansion with the charming "fish-pond"
passed from the hands of the Melvills to the benevolent
Mrs. Sarah Morewood and from the Morewoods to the
Country Club of Pittsfield in 1900.

[1] "An Old Kinderhook Mansion," by Henry Cruger Van Schaack,
American Magazine of History, Vol. ii.

As you walk along the old road to Lenox you will mark in a wide sweep of lawn the lone and superb pine, so much loved by Dr. Holmes. "Canoe-Meadow" was a carrying-place of the Indians, and held everything that he most delighted in. His house [1] stood on the soil owned by his great-grand-father Jacob Wendell, Colonel of the Ancient and Honorable Artillery Company. Here were half a hundred acres of forest trees, some of them probably five hundred years old; above their foliage, the Berkshire Hills reared their heads, and the Housatonic River made its course in a thousand fantastic curves though the meadows.

Dr. Holmes entered into the life at Pittsfield with great zest; he was present on that distinguished occasion in 1844, when Dr. Mark Hopkins spoke the words, "And this is the Berkshire Jubilee"; Mrs. Sigourney read "The Stockbridge Bowl," and Mrs. Kemble and Macready [2] also took part, beside the "Johnsonian Dr. Todd of Pittsfield, orthodox minister and author," whom Longfellow in *Kavanagh* sends to slay the deer. Dr. Holmes read the lines so appropriate to the Old Home Week:

"Come back to your mother, ye children, for shame,
Who have wandered like truants for riches or fame!"

. . . .

Then come from all parties and parts to one feast,
Though not at the 'Astor' we'll give you at least
A bite at an apple, a seat on the grass
And the best of cold—water—at nothing a glass."

Dr. Holmes never lost interest in Pittsfield. He writes

---

[1] "Holmesdale" is now the estate of Mr. William Pollock. Dr. Holmes's study is a part of a building on the "Meadow Farm," of the late Colonel Walter Cutting, a comrade of General Bartlett. Not far distant is "Abbey Lodge," once owned by Colonel Richard Lathers of New York.

[2] "The Literary Associations of Berkshire," by James Tucker Cutler, *New England Magazine*, 1893.

to Mrs. Kellogg of East Street, with whom he enjoyed many a spar by post: "I, and we, always like to hear about your family, . . . the Newtons . . . and the Pomeroys. We depend on you for all the news about them. . . . "; again: "When you meet any one you think remembers me, tell them I am loyal to the place where I spent seven blessed summers of my life, and that the very stones of it are precious to me."

"Boston, Jan. 1, 1885.

"A Happy New Year, my dear Mrs. Kellogg, and as many such as you can count until you reach a hundred; and then begin again, if you like the planet well enough.

" But how good you are to send me all those excellent and to me most interesting photographs [of Pittsfield]. I delighted in recalling the old scenes in this way; changed as they are I yet seem to be carried back to the broad street—East Street—down which I—we used to drive on our way to the 'four corners,' and 'Canoe Meadow' as my mother told me they used to call our old farm—I wonder that Pittsfield is not a City by this time. It seems almost too bad to take away the charming rural characteristics but such a beautiful, healthful, central situation could not resist its destiny and you must have a Mayor, I suppose, by and by, and a Common Council, and a lot of Aldermen. But you cannot lose the sight of Greylock or turn the course of the Housatonic. I can hardly believe that it is almost thirty years since I bade good-bye to the old place, expecting to return the next season. We passed through the gate under the maple which used to stand there—and is probably in its old place—took a look at the house and the great pine that stood, and I hope stands, in its solitary beauty and grandeur, rode on past the two bridges, reached the station, the old one—I think you have a little better since, and good-bye dear old town—Well that is the way—Yesterday morning I passed through Montgomery Place, and

The Home of Mrs. Ensign H. Kellogg, East Street, Pittsfield. Built by Thomas A. Gold.

315

I found workmen tearing out the inside of No. 8 where we lived for eighteen years. . . . Not a vestige is left to show where our old Cambridge house stood. We must make ourselves new habitations, that is all; and carry our remembrances, associations, affections, all that makes home, under the new roof. Once more a thousand thanks for the photographs, and with all kind remembrances, I am—we both are—

" Faithfully yours,
" O. W. Holmes."

Park Square, at the meeting of the main cross-roads of Pittsfield, has always been a place of assembly, and is surrounded by buildings of historic interest. The first which attracts the eye is the Berkshire Athenæum, the gift of Thomas Allen of Pittsfield. It contains a Public Library and Museum in which is Hawthorne's desk. The Art Gallery includes a portrait by Copley, *Mid-Ocean* by Woodbury, and paintings by Gilbert Stuart Newton. Here are held the meetings of the Berkshire Historical and Scientific Society, which has published many valuable papers. The Wednesday Morning Club, whose President is Miss Anna Laurens Dawes, the author, also assembles at the Athenæum. Another handsome building is the Museum of Natural History and Art presented to the Athenæum by the Hon. Zenas Crane; it stands on the site of the Campbell homestead, and was designed by a native of Pittsfield, George Campbell Harding.

The most important habitant of Park Square until 1864 was the Old Elm of 364 rings, which presided over all important events, even the reception of Lafayette. The sun-dial marking the spot was placed by the Peace-Party Chapter, D. A. R. The angel of the tree who stood between it and the axe in 1790 was Mrs. Lucretia, wife of the Hon. John Chandler Williams; she resided in the beautiful colonial house still

"Elm Knoll," the Thomas Gold-Appleton House built in 1790, East street; the Subject of Longfellow's Poem "The Old Clock on the Stairs." The Plunkett Residence.

"Somewhat back from the village street
Stands the old-fashioned country-seat."

317

standing on East Street, the Rectory of St. Stephen's Parish.
The cause of the proposed destruction of the Pittsfield Elm
was the erection of the second meeting-house, which the
people of the west part wished built far into the street,
that they might view it when coming into town.   In this
historic meeting-house, designed by Bulfinch, addresses of
welcome were made to Lafayette; it still exists as a part of
the Maplewood Hotel, for a time used as the gymnasium
of the famous Maplewood Young Ladies Institute.   Maplewood was originally a cantonment for troops in the war of
1812.   The corner-stone of the present First Congregational
Church (designed by Eidlitz and constructed of Pittsfield
gray limestone and Barrington bluestone) was laid by Dr.
John Todd in 1852.

St. Stephen's Church stands on the site of the old Town-
Hall.   The Rev. William Wilberforce Newton when rector
of the church originated the plan for a Congress of Churches.
Next below the Williams-Newton house, the present Rectory,
is the home of the Rt. Rev. George Worthington, Bishop of
Nebraska, and in charge of the American churches on the
Continent; "Bishopthorpe" stands on the site of the Pom-
eroy homestead.   The gun-shop of Lemuel Pomeroy, who
never laid aside the ruffled shirt and knee-buckles, was on
Gun Lane, now Pomeroy Street.   Below is the old Town-
Hall, remodelled, the residence of Mr. William G. Harding.
The two old-fashioned country seats built by the Golds
stand "somewhat back from the village street," the homes
respectively of Mrs. Ensign H. Kellogg, and the late Mrs.
Thomas F. Plunkett.

On South Street is the Berkshire Home for Aged Women
—a memorial to Zenas Marshall Crane—on the site of the
Pittsfield Female Seminary.   In the Ezekiel R. Colt homestead [1] a reception was held to Henry Clay.   The Brown

[1] Residence of Mrs. Thomas Perkins Pingree and Miss Mary Colt.

homestead, and the West homestead, and that of Colonel Clapp, built by Upjohn, are standing in Pittsfield. The Woodbridge Little place was near Peck's Bridge.

In an old chest in the Brattle house on "Court Hill" a few years ago was unearthed a rawhide wallet containing papers throwing light on what has hitherto been regarded as an absurd tradition or mysterious fact. It seems by these yellow documents that, in 1819, John Brattle was given the power of attorney to go to a certain house in a town in the north of France, where, on Casapom Street, he would discover "in N. 47 in a cellar kitchen a vault containing casks of money "Locked with a strong Lock and the Key placed behind a Loos Brick over the Dore." The sequel is wanting, for no record has appeared as to whether he was successful in this quest on which he went in 1820, as shown by his passport signed by the Mayor of Havre.

Dr. J. G. Holland was once a student at the old Berkshire Medical College. Pittsfield is the home of William Stearns Davis, the novelist, and of Harlan Hoge Ballard. Miss Anna L. Dawes (founder of the Children's Park) is devoted to letters, as was her eminent father the Hon. Henry Laurens Dawes, one of the Massachusetts Constitutional Convention in 1853, and the successor of Charles Sumner in the Senate. Mrs. Harriett M. Plunkett dedicated her timely and witty pioneer book, *Women, Plumbers, and Doctors*, "To Dr. Henry I. Bowditch, the Apostle of Sanitation in America." When the Hon. Thomas F. Plunkett intro-

---

Ezekiel Colt was the first Cashier of the Agricultural Bank, inaugurated in 1818, at Colen's Coffee-House. Even its old-style bank check was adapted to an agricultural district, engraved with oxen and a plough. A list of its Presidents includes representative men of their generation, largely with homesteads standing in Pittsfield: Thomas Gold, Henry C. Brown, Edward A. Newton, Henry Shaw, Nathan Willis, George W. Campbell, Thomas F. Plunkett, Ensign H. Kellogg, John R. Warriner, James L. Warriner, W. Murray Crane, Irving Dwight Ferry.

The William Brattle homestead, built about 1754, "Court Hill," Pittsfield, residence of General James Brattle Burbank; thence Lieutenant William Brattle went to Ticonderoga, Lexington, and Saratoga; Sackett's and Brattle brooks cross Brattle meadows.

duced a bill for a State Board of Health, the enthusiastic agitation of Dr. Bowditch aided in carrying it through. By the efforts of Lieutenant-Governor Plunkett, Pittsfield became the shire town. The house of "The Old Clock on the Stairs" was purchased by Mr. Plunkett of Nathan Appleton, but the clock was carried to the Appleton home in Boston; the old-fashioned country-seat, however, where

Longfellow found "Free-hearted Hospitality," stands to-day, as then, except for a French roof. Longfellow wrote this poem when he was revisiting with his wife—the queenly Frances Elizabeth Appleton—the home of her grandfather Mr. Thomas Gold. Their wedding-journey was to Pittsfield; on the way they visited the Springfield armory, offspring of that to which Washington refers in his *Diary;* Mrs. Longfellow compared the rows upon rows of arms to the pipes of an organ, thus inspiring the lines on *The Arsenal at Springfield.*

"Wendell Hall" was the home of General William Francis Bartlett, whose statue by French stands in the Memorial Hall of the State House. At the unveiling by his grandson James Dwight Francis, the tribute "to the advocate of peace" by General Morris Schaff was worthy both of the hero and the orator. General Henry S. Briggs and Colonel Henry H. Richardson also are claimed by Pittsfield. The history and traditions of Pittsfield and Berkshire have been preserved by J. E. A. Smith (Godfrey Greylock) and Clark W. Bryan.

DALTON

Dalton, on the east branch of the Housatonic, and the encircling region is most picturesque; it is ever up, up, up, to the well-springs of the river. At Peru you attain the highest inhabited point in the State; founded on a rock to which its steeple is tied down by cable, Peru Church is unique; if you are caught there in a shower they will tell you that the drops racing down one side of the roof run into the Connecticut, and on the other, swell the Housatonic; Peru is therefore the nearest hallooing point of the waters of these two New England rivers, first seen by the Dutch in 1614. From Peru a "sightly" road lies across the very top of the Green Mountain Range through Windsor, Savoy, and Florida to North Adams. Dalton's neighbor, Hinsdale, is also quite lofty, and an attractive walk is that from Hinsdale to Day Mountain, seven hundred feet above Dalton village.

If you are in Dalton but for a day, you will carry away a remembrance of the dark, rushing river, and the paper-mills, truly decorative. (The Carsons built the Old Defiance Mill, later owned by the Hon. Byron Weston, each playing a prominent part in town history.) Here are pleasant old-fashioned houses, that of William Williams, the first town clerk, the Deacon Abijah Parks, Brown, Nathaniel Merriam, and Crane homesteads, and fine farms on the Pittsfield border, the "Unkamet" farm of the Miltons and the Allen and Crane farms.

The settlement in 1755 was led by Dr. Perez Ward, followed by Joseph Chamberlain and Josiah Lawrence. In 1799 Zenas Crane saw in the multiple pure rills gushing from the hillsides the best of "feed" for a paper-mill[1] and erected the second in Massachusetts. The Crane mill at Coltsville now makes the bank-note paper for the government.

There are many accessible heights in the vicinity. On Mount Weston, the opening of the chalet of Lieutenant-Governor Weston was made memorable in 1885 (says Mr. Clark W. Bryan, author of the delightful *Book of Berkshire*) by the Pittsfield Monday Evening Club and "the flow of soul participated in by Senator Dawes, Pastor Jenkins,

---

[1]To this end a sprightly and fetching paragraph appeared in the *Pittsfield Sun*:

"Americans:

"Encourage your own manufactories, and they will Improve. Ladies save your Rags. As the Subscribers have it in contemplation to erect a Paper-mill in Dalton, the ensuing Spring; and the business being very beneficent to the community at large, they flatter themselves they shall meet with due encouragement etc. [Signed] Henry Marshall, Zenas Crane and John Willard."

"*Holiday Cottage,*" *Waconah Falls Road, Dalton.*

A home for the Fresh Air Children established by Mrs. Herbert S. Johnson.

"*At evening, when the earliest stars began*
To move along the edges of the hills."

THE BOY OF WINANDER.

Judge Barker, the Rev. William Wilberforce Newton, and others." On Mt. Pleasant in West Windsor is the country house of Senator Crane; from this pinnacle the Catskills are in sight. The pioneers on Mt. Pleasant, Alpheus Brown and Stephen Hume, suffered great hardships, obliged as they were to travel to Stafford's Hill in Cheshire for pork and meat.

You will not fail to see Dalton's chaotic Gulf, the Wizard's Glen, where the sweetest voice echoes and re-echoes in uncanny shrieks. One legend of the place relates to a hunter, who, while dressing his quarry, was overtaken by a thunderstorm. Lightning revealed an Indian girl with pleading eyes, about to be sacrificed on the Devil's Altar by phantoms; the hunter took out the Good Book and with a terrible crash all vanished.

A particular charm of the pastoral town of Windsor is the brook where Waconah, favorite daughter of Miahcomo, met her fate. After some successful hours of angling, she sat dreamily twining columbines in her hair by a mirror pool under the Falls; a pretty picture in her white deerskin, trimmed with oriole and bluebird feathers, thought the young brave who startled her with the words, "Hail! Bright Star!" She sprang to her feet.—"Nessacus is weary," said he, "with flying before the Long Knives, will the Bright Star's people shut their lodges against their brethren?" The maiden answered, "My father Miahcomo has gone towards the setting sun, across the Taghonics to the Mohawks, but his lodges are always open; come, my brother's people are welcome." On their path to the village, Nessacus related the fate of his chief King Philip, and Waconah told him that her people here were Pequots who escaped thither [to Dalton] after being driven from the fort at Mystic. Thereupon Nessacus, the Wampanoag, fell in love with the daughter of the Pequots. Miahcomo returning brought with him the Mohawk Yonnongah; many

Waconah Falls, Windsor.
Within walking distance of Dalton.

scalps proudly hung at his belt and he confidently asked the hand of Waconah for his fourth wife. When Nessacus declared himself also a suitor, the old warrior employed alternately threats and promises. Councils were held over the weighty matter for Waconah was the idol of the tribe. "Let the Great Spirit speak, and we will obey," said Miahcomo. Tashmu, crafty wizard or priest of the tribe, favored the Mohawk, and declared Manitou revealed to him in the Wizard's Glen that it was his will that the spirit of the stream should decide, by turning the canoe toward the worthy suitor.

After a solemn feast, the tribe assembled at Waconah's brook; the rivals Nessacus and Yonnongah were placed on opposite banks. And Tashmu was there, the hypocrite who had secretly moved the dividing rock the night before in order to favor the old warrior.

"Let Manitou speak!" and the sacred canoe, carved with mystic signs, floated on, then hung poised on the rock midstream, then seemed to incline toward the Mohawk, but the inconstant current struck it obliquely, it swung slowly around, and passed down by the feet of Nessacus. " The Great Spirit hath spoken, and it is good!" said Miahcomo, and the people shouted, "Hoh! It is good!" Tashmu and Yonnongah, discomfited, disappeared, Tashmu to betray Nessacus to the whites.

As the wedding festivities were progressing, a messenger brought news that Major Talcott, with other Long Knives had slain the sachem of Quaboag, and was at Mahaiwe on the Housatonic, and he would destroy Miahcomo's wigwams as soon as he could obtain provisions. Nessacus, taking Waconah by the hand, promised to lead them to a new prairie-home, and having executed the traitor Tashmu they took the western trail.[1]

---

[1] This legend of Waconah Falls was related to Godfrey Greylock by a young Indian of the Stockbridge tribe, who had come back from the western home of his people to be educated.

LANESBORO

In Lanesboro one may float on Poontoosuc Lake, and
visit Balance Rock, or climb the gentle slope of Constitution
Hill. From the stage-road a fascinating stretch of meadows,
broken by a rushing rivulet, meets the hills.   Here you will

*The Hubbell Homestead, Lanesboro.   Built in 1770–80 by Matthew
Hubbell of Woodbury, Conn., and his son Wolcott Hubbell.*

exclaim over the clarity of the atmosphere,—every leaf of
alder and elm is clean cut, a tree of character.   At evening
myriads of glow-worms dance in the grass.   It is said that
the Stockbridge Indians camped in these meadows in front
of the Hubbell homestead on their march to Bennington.

Captain Matthew Hubbell, a pioneer from Woodbury, now Newtown, Conn., built here about 1769; it is surmised that it may have been the property previously of Major Thaddeus Curtis, whose daughter became the wife of the Hon. Wolcott Hubbell. He served as minute-man and fought at Bennington, which General Washington said was "the turning point of the war." His son Algernon S. Hubbell was a partner of Governor Briggs. [1]

Across Hoosac Mountain came Henry Clay to visit his friend the Hon. Henry Shaw at Lanesboro. Another eminent son of the town was Jonathan Smith whose speech won the day for the Constitution of Massachusetts. The Bradley homestead stands near St. Luke's Church. Silver Street is a favorite walk. A drive to conjure with is that across Potter Mountain through Hancock, where the traveller finds the Lulu Cascade and Berry Pond on a mountain-summit; or on to Lebanon Springs, called "The Pool" by Miss Sedgwick. Horace E. Scudder wrote the *Bodley Books* in Lanesboro and Mrs. Campbell, *Prisoners of Poverty.*

From Lanesboro two roads lead toward Williamstown which are rivals in romantic beauty; the old stage-road through New Ashford and lovely valley of South Williamstown was preferred by Samuel Bowles on his annual trip to Commencement at Williams College. New Ashford lies in a picturesque gorge between Saddle Ball and the Taconics at the headwaters of the west branch of the Housatonic. For several miles a deliciously cool stream parallels the road and in the north part of the town is a wild chasm close to the highway, with the ruins of the old saw-mill, a scene for a painter. Baker's Cave is another curious abyss with a

[1] "In 1818, the Baptist church was organized through the efforts of Dr. William H. Tyler and Governor Briggs," says the Rev. C. J. Palmer in his *History of the Town of Lanesborough.*

The house of Henry W. Shaw, "Josh Billings," Lanesboro.

cold spring at the bottom.   In this fair country one recalls
Wordsworth's

> "*Up! up! my Friend and quit your books;*
>
> .   .   .   .
>
> *Books! 'tis a dull and endless strife:*
> *Come, hear the woodland linnet,*
> *How sweet his music! on my life,*
> *There's more of wisdom in it."*

ON TO WILLIAMSTOWN VIA CHESHIRE

The other Old Path to Williamstown is far more rugged;
it vaults through Cheshire and along the valley of the
Hoosac River by way of Adams to North Adams, and passes
within view of Fort Massachusetts on the Harrison flats.
Cheshire is oddly planted among the unaccountably irreg-
ular mountains of the south spur of the Greylock group.

President Jefferson's huge Cheshire cheese was created from
the curds gathered together from the mountain farms by one
of his most ardent admirers, the eccentric and celebrated
preacher, Elder Leland, who escorted it to the White House
in person.   The first Baptist church in Berkshire stood on
Stafford's Hill (of glorious views); here built the pioneers of
1766 from Warwick, Coventry, and Newport, R. I.   To the
southern part of the town came settlers from Swansea,
Mass., whose ancestors removed to Old Rehoboth from
Wales in 1663.

The saunterer through Pork Lane discovers charms which
belie its prosaic name.   A favorite road to Adams is through
the "Pumpkin Hook" neighborhood.   From Cheshire a
wood-road leads up Greylock.   Another road to the summit
is from the town of Adams to which Greylock belongs.

Adams was founded by the Uptons and other Quakers.
Familiar names are Fisk, Anthony, Richmond, and Dean.

The Thompson Memorial Chapel, and Griffin Hall, Williams College, Williamstown, Mass.

The town's fine statue of McKinley is a memory of his week's visit here. The first attempt to wrest yellow gold [1] from Greylock was made from Adams, by the historic Bowerman family.

The famous Old Notch road will carry you to North Adams. Excursions are in order to every point of the compass from the "Tunnel City"; first to obtain a bird's-eye view, at sunset, of Greylock and the inter-clustered mountains. Then a mile northeast to the Natural Bridge on Hudson Brook with its marble pool (a remarkable pot-hole) described by Hawthorne. Hudson Brook flows into the Mayunsook, or Little Deerfield, a wild highland rivulet, which endows North Adams with a wonderful water-power.

North Adams stands at the west door of Hoosac Tunnel by means of which the riches of western fields are carried direct to the Massachusetts seaboard. The Indian's Forbidden Mountain is of such a flinty heart that twenty millions of "very hard cash" was needed to pierce it effectually. An intimate book [2] of the Hoosac Valley, and a delightful companion for a tramp across the pastures of Northwestern Berkshire or by the fireside, is that by Grace Greylock Niles; she knows the secrets of marble-caverns, of sweet paths that will lead you away from the footsteps of man to Aurora's lake, under the rude brow of the Hoosac, still haunt of the pale Pink Moccasin-Flower, the wake-robin, and marsh-thrush; or, let us tramp afield and cross the border into Vermont to search for treasures in Rattlesnake Swamp, Mount Œta. You can drive up Greylock on the highway beneficently accomplished by the Greylock Park Association; but you will prefer to take fisherman's luck through The Notch, Bohemian fashion, scrambling up ragged

---

[1] "Gold-Hunting in Berkshire," a sketch in *The Berkshire Hills* of June, 1902, edited by Colonel William Phillips.

[2] *Bog-Trotting for Orchids*, G. P. Putnam's Sons.

glens of misty cascades with mural decorations of hemlocks and vine.   Is it not better—if one may—to go a-gypsying for a season, cut the wood for the camp-fire to set the pot a-boiling, rest on pine boughs, and watch the sky with a lover's look to know whether it will smile or frown, than to be merely a tame duck; or, as Dr. Van Dyke says, one of "the people who always live in houses, and sleep in beds, and walk on pavements, and buy their food of butchers and bakers,   .   .   .   boarders in the world " ?

Thoreau attained Greylock's summit and found himself " in the dazzling halls of Aurora   .   .   .   playing with the rosy fingers of the Dawn, and not a crevice through the clouds from which those trivial places of Massachusetts, Connecticut, and Vermont could be seen." Was it not the *Mist* of our Berkshire Highlands which inspired Thoreau:

> "*Low-anchored cloud,*
> *Newfoundland air,*
> *Fountain-head and source of rivers,*
> *Dew-cloth, dream drapery,*
> *And napkins spread by fays;*
> *Drifting meadow of the air.*"

"I had a view of Williamstown from Greylock summit," says Hawthorne, "a white village and a steeple in a gradual hollow with huge mountain swells heaving up like immense subsiding waves far and wide around it."

These mountains by which an ideal New England town is hemmed in, are intimately associated by name with the history and traditions of Williams College.   The twin peaks of Mount Hopkins—2790 feet high—are named for President Mark Hopkins and Professor Albert Hopkins; and Mount Fitch, Mount Griffin, and Mount Chadbourne in honor of three other Presidents of the College.   There is

The Squire Henry Peirson house, Richmond, Mass.
Built about 1787 by Joel Carpenter, purchased in 1799 by Henry Peirson of Southampton, L. I.;
residence of Mr. Joseph Josiah Peirson.

334

a choice of four passes across the Taconics into New York State, the Petersburg, Berlin, Kidder, Johnson Passes.

A monument unique is that to the memory of the Haystack, in the shade of which was founded the American Board of Foreign Missions; students' meetings were also held under an ancient willow near the old home of Professor Arthur L. Perry, for years President of the Berkshire Historical Society, and the historian of Williamstown. His son Bliss Perry was called from Williams to Princeton, and to the Editor's Chair of *The Atlantic Monthly*, and is the successor of James Russell Lowell at Harvard.

Although *Thanatopsis* was written at Cummington following Bryant's seven months at Williams College, tradition associates with Flora's Glen the lines:

" for his gayer hours
She had a voice of gladness and a smile,
And eloquence of beauty."

RICHMOND

Richmond, once known as Mount Ephraim, is famous for its boulder trains. If you will take the romantic road to Canaan Four Corners and Queechy Lake, you will note just north a mountain west of a valley; here on Fry's Hill start some remarkable boulder trains, which cross the road near the first Shaker settlement, and over Merriman's Mount, then trail across the town of Richmond into Lenox near the Stockbridge Bowl. The most interesting example of the Richmond boulders is on the top of Perry's Peak, just over the brow of the hill from the Richmond side.

Sir Charles Lyell visited Richmond in order to trace their course under the guidance of Dr. Stephen Reid, and delivered a paper on Richmond's boulder trains before the Royal Institute of Great Britain. A boulder known as

"Dr. Reid's pet" is on Snake Hill, a terrace of South Mountain. Professor James D. Dana of Yale in 1886 reported the discovery of fossils just over the Taconic range in Canaan, N. Y. He says that the Stockbridge limestone, which is also the limestone of Canaan and Williamstown, was once full of coral fossils [1] and crinoids, and but for the crystallization of the rock converting it into marble, these would be distinct in the rock now.

Richmond is also notable for its beautiful open reaches of rolling country, for as yet a superabundance of heavy foliage has not robbed her of invigorating mountain outlines and the luminous cloud-pictures of Berkshire skies, as in parts of Lenox. In her northwest corner is Perry's Peak, next in height to The Dome. Here at your feet is the Canaan Shakers' settlement and the lovely valley of Lebanon, also the Mount Lebanon Shaker village farther north, and Greylock. South are the West Stockbridge and Alford hills, and Osceola tops the Lenox range. Perry's Peak is associated with the Rev. David Perry (1784–1816). The homestead of his successor, the Rev. Edwin Welles Dwight, is now the residence of Mrs. Henry March. His son Judge Charles C. Dwight was a member of the New York Constitutional Convention and Justice of the Supreme Court. A grandson, R. Henry W. Dwight, of Boston, a past President of the Sons of the Revolution of Massachusetts, has an unusual collection of rare Berkshire manuscripts and broadsides and memorabilia of the Dwight family. The Sherrill-Jennings house, now the home of Chester Huntington, Esq., was built by Henry Sherrill, to whose fine country store on the corner of Canaan and State roads, Pittsfield people came to shop. This homestead, "Kenmore Hall" was the home of Frederick Alfred Bridgeman. One of

---

[1] The sketch by Prof. James D. Dana on *Berkshire Geology* in the Berkshire Historical Society Papers is a useful guide.

Richmond's interesting homesteads (now the Nichols residence) was the home of Miss Catherine Peirson, whose
father, Nathan Peirson, owned extensive tanneries here.
In this vicinity were built the early Rossiter, Branch, and
Cook houses. Near Stevens Corners—of old "Indian
Bread Corners"—are beautiful glens and an altogether
charming landscape.

A story of the Squire Henry Peirson homestead relates
to his son Josiah who as a youth was employed in teaming
supplies between Hudson, N. Y. and Berkshire. Belated on
his homeward road, he drove into the yard early one Sabbath
morning and unluckily was seen by two pair of bright eyes
belonging to Polly and Nabby Rossiter, the daughters of a
neighbor. All three were shortly summoned before the
court. Tradition says that Josiah was acquitted instead of
receiving a fine for breaking the Sabbath, as the judge ruled
that the two witnesses had seen him only from the inside
of the house through a closed window, and such evidence
was incompetent. He afterward married Nabby Rossiter.

22

GREAT BARRINGTON (UPPER HOUSATONNUCK)

1733–1761

"This tract of country, wild, forbidding, and destitute of roads other than the Indian trail, . . . lay in the direct route,—via Springfield, Westfield, and Kinderhook, between Boston and Albany. . . . Occasionally traversed by bodies of soldiery in the early wars, and by other parties on public business, it was better known to the neighboring New York border, whose traders were accustomed to visit it for the purpose of traffic with the Indians, than to the more remote inhabitants of Massachusetts."

History of Great Barrington by TAYLOR.

THE Valley of the great river of Berkshire was named by the Mohicans, who, leaving their ancestral holdings in the hands of the Patroons of Rensselaerwyck, Kinderhook, and Livingston, drifted over from the Hudson into the new wilderness of the Housatonic Valley; they called the valley Ou-thot-ton-nook or Housatonnuck, and the river took its name from the valley. Not many years since came a Stockbridge Indian to visit the land of his fathers, and illustrated the word by pointing to the full moon just rising over East Mountain in Great Barrington, Ou-thot-ton-nook—"over the mountain."

The settlement at Housatonnuck or Great Barrington sprang up at the principal fordway on the main trail from Fort Orange near Albany, N. Y., to Springfield and Massachusetts Bay. It was known to the Dutch as "the New England Path." Great Barrington was the "Great Wigwam" or—as the Stockbridge Indians called it—*Mahaiwe* (Nei-hai-we), the "place down-stream." (The Indian burial-ground in Great Barrington is known as Mahaiwe). Here, near the old fordway, in all probability occurred that celebrated scrimmage between King Philip's warriors flying to refuge in the West, and the gallant Major Talcott, son

The Housatonic at Great Barrington.

of the Worshipful John Talcott of Hartford, who pursued them from Westfield over the wilderness trail to the banks of the Housatonic.

As early as 1694, a party of gentlemen from Boston camped here—the Rev. Benjamin Wadsworth and other Commissioners on their way to Albany to hold a great council-fire with the "Five Nations." Mr. Wadsworth kept a journal of events:

> "With Captain Sewal and Major Townsend, being commissioned to treat with ye Mockways [Mohawks], set out from Boston about half past 12 Monday Aug. 6, 1694. . . . At Watertown, we met with Lieut. Hammond and thirty troopers, who were appointed for a guard to Springfield. . . . Mr. Dwite of Hartford did accidently fall into our company, and after the same manner, accidently he and his horse both together fell into a brook, but both rose again without damage. This day we dined in ye woods. Pleasant descants were made upon ye dining room; it was said yt it was large, high, curiously hung with green; our dining place was also accomodated with ye pleasancy of a murmuring rivulet. This day some of our company saw a bear. . . . This night we went over to Westfield, . . . thence toward Albany; the nearest way thro' ye woods, being accompanied with Collonel Pinchon, in commission with Capt. Sewal and Maj. Townsend, by ye Council of ye Province of ye Mass. Bay, and Collonel Allen and Captain Stanley, Commissioners for Connecticutt Colony. For a guard we had with us Cap. Wadsworth of Hartford, and with him 60 Dragoons. . . . took up our lodgings, about sundown in ye woods, at a place called Ousetonnuck [Great Barrington] formerly inhabited by Indians. Thro this place runs a very curious river, the same (which some say) runs thro' Stratford." (The Housatonic River at its mouth was known for a time as Stratford River.) On arriving in Albany, Mr. Wadsworth says, "The

treaty[1] was held in ye street a little above the meeting
house; Ye Sachims were attended with many other Indians . . . Ye Sachim of ye Maquas being ye leader,
. . . when we were sat down, they sang two or three
songs of peace, before they began ye treaty."

Across Pine-tops to the Dome, or Mt. Everett.

"I like Berkshire more and more.   The Dome is a really imposing and
beautiful mass; I have seen it . . . in many lights and with
ever increasing admiration.   I was shown the Green River yesterday.
the river immortalized by the American Wordsworth, i. e., Bryant."

MATTHEW ARNOLD to Charles Eliot Norton, Aug. 27,1886.

A few years after the Boston Commissioners travelled
down Three-Mile Hill (three miles it is from the top to the
Great Bridge) and passed through Housatonnuck, Captain

---

[1] At the Council were present besides the Commissioners from New
England, "His Excellency ye Governour of York with fore of his Council,
Collonel Bayard, Coll. William Smith, Coll. Stephen Van Cortland,
Chidley Brook, Esq., Major Peter Schuyler, Col. Andrew Hamilton,
Governour of New Jerseys."

Konkapot and a few Indian families were here and others at Skatekook (Sheffield) and Wnahtukook (Stockbridge). In Great Barrington a mission wigwam was built about a mile south of Maus-waw-se-ki (Monument Mt.). John Sergeant, fresh from Yale, preached here until they removed to the reservation of Indian Town.

> When Matthew Arnold visited the chosen valley of the transplanted Mohicans, did he recall his first impression of America, and his facetious little remark, apropos of the idea of many foreigners, that Indians in war-paint frequented the boulevards scarce a league from Broadway? Arnold writes: "We had crossed the bar and were inside New York Bay. . . . You may imagine I was on deck with the first light. We were lying off Staten Island, a beautiful orné landscape with spires, villas, hills, and woods. 'Just like Richmond,' I said to some one by me, 'and not a single Mohican running about.' This precious speech got into the newspapers here!"

Great Barrington was the North Parish of Sheffield from 1742–1761. Boundary disputes became hot and fierce between Patroons of the border manors and the Massachusetts settlers, over debatable land east of the Taconics. New York claimed by patent the lands east as far as the Connecticut River, and Massachusetts by right of occupation.

On the Van Rensselaer Manor in 1762, serious disturbances broke out owing to refusals to pay rent to the Manorhouse, and Robert Noble, who had been engaged with David Ingersoll and Josiah Loomis in the more peaceful occupation of establishing an Episcopal Church[1] in Great Barrington—the first in Berkshire,—"put himself at the head of an armed force, and actually defeated a strong posse headed

---

[1] The land for the church was given by John Burghardt in 1763. Rev. Gideon Bostwick was the first established minister. After the Revolution, a monument of wood with a gilded ball on top was placed to the memory of Washington near the pulpit.

Lake Mansfield.

by the sheriff of Albany who were attempting to dispossess squatters on the Van Renssalaer tract." [1]

The story of Belcher's Cave near "Bung Hill Corner" in Great Barrington is connected with these troublous times; a gang of counterfeiters is said to have had their workshop here with "Gill Belcher, Goldsmith," as leader.

Two of the most exciting events of the Revolution took place in '77. At the call for troops to resist Burgoyne, Captain William King called a town meeting and volunteers went out to Saratoga under Captain Silas Goodrich in the regiment of Colonel John Ashley, also a company from Alford under Captain Sylvanus Wilcox. Then came the

---

[1] Franklin Leonard Pope on *The Western Boundary of Massachusetts*, Berkshire Historical Papers, 1886. A map of the Housatonic Townships of 1761, drawn by Mr. Pope is included in the invaluable *History of Great Barrington* by Charles J. Taylor, to whom all Berkshire is indebted for his research on the early Patents.

news of the dramatic surrender [1] to General Gates, followed by the encampment here of the prisoners-of-war; with laggard steps the officers led the troops down over the old trail through Kinderhook into Great Barrington, wearing their side-arms according to the terms of capitulation made at this "Convention of Saratoga."

LANDMARKS: Boulder-Monument at Old Indian Fordway on the Housatonic River near the "Great Wigwam," presented to Great Barrington by the Thursday Morning Club, 1904. General Joseph Dwight-Henderson house, oldest in Great Barrington; here Bryant was married. Hopkins Memorial Manse. Hopkins house (about 1803), residence Mrs. Samuel Camp. Next stood the house (1765) of Colonel Mark Hopkins, Treasurer of the County; in his office Judge Theodore Sedgwick studied law. At the library is a photograph of Beckett House, the seat of the Viscounts Barrington, on the very ancient Manor of Beckett, at Shrivenham in the Vale of the White Horse, Berkshire, England; sent by Sir William A. C. Barrington son of the sixth Lord Barrington, to the designer of the Town Seal. Dr. William Whiting house; here the judges of the Crown took refuge when in 1774 the patriots refused to allow them to hold court. Rev. Gideon Bostwick-Burr house. Post-office on site of Major Rossiter Tavern. St. James Church; the vestibule is on site of William Cullen Bryant's law office, Tablet. Old

General Burgoyne, being indisposed, was the guest of Colonel Elijah Dwight in the quaint "Henderson house" which stands near the Berkshire Inn. This house was built by the distinguished General Joseph Dwight in 1759 and was long the finest dwelling in the township. In it William Cullen Bryant was married to Miss Lucy Fairchild. The Hessian General, Baron Riedesdel, was quartered in the old Episcopal Church.

We do not know whether the courageous and brilliant Baroness Riedesdel passed through Great Barrington on her way to Boston, after being entertained by Mrs. Schuyler during the

---

[1] The captive General admitted Gates's magnanimity and wrote to the Earl of Derby that when the British soldiers marched out of their camp to pile their arms, *not a man of the American troops was to be seen.* The English and German generals dined with Burgoyne on the day after defeat on boards laid across barrels, the Americans being accustomed to frugal meals. Burgoyne spoke flatteringly of the American dress and discipline and said: "Your funds of men are inexhaustible. Like the Hydra's head, when cut off, seven more spring up in its stead." Then he proposed a toast to General Washington, an attention that Gates returned by drinking the health of the King of England.

*A Cart-path through Winter-woods. The Searles
Estate, Great Barrington.*

"*Fill soft and deep, O winter snows!
The sweet azalia's oaken dells.*"—WHITTIER.

Rectory removed to Castle St., residence of Miss Abby Russell. George R. Ives-Ralph Taylor house (1815) residence Mrs. Charles J. Taylor. The Dr. C. T. Collins house stands on the lot of Dr. Joseph Lee. "Wainwright Hall" built by Peter Ingersoll the Tory, his confiscated house purchased by David Wainwright; his grandson, Lieutenant George Wainwright, a son of General Timothy Wainwright, distinguished

stay in Albany. But under the unexpectedly adverse circumstances of the expedition, Madam Riedesdel never parted with her rose-colored glasses or interest in all things American; for it seems the brilliant army left Canada with confidence in

himself at Palo Alto and the storming of Monterey. Leavitt estate, "Brookside." Merritt Wheeler homestead. Whitlock house. Jonathan Nash-Dearing house (1790).

DRIVES FROM GREAT BARRINGTON: Alford and return—*11* miles; Ashley Falls—*10*; Bash Bish—*11*; Bear Rock, by Mount Washington—*15*; Bear Rock, by Mount Washington, return by Sheffield—*28*; Canaan, Conn.—*12*; Clayton—*11*; Glendale, —*7*; Green River, N. Y., by Seekonk, return by North Egremont—*17*; Hudson, N. Y.—*27*; Lake Buel—*5*; "Highlawn Farm,"—*12½*; Hillsdale. N. Y.—*10*; Housatonic—*5*; Lake Garfield—*10*; Lakeville, Conn. —*17*; Lee—*11½*; Mount Washington, Whitbeck's, Sunset Mountain—*11*; Mount Washington P. O.—*10*; New Marlboro', return by Brush Hill—*22*; North Egremont—*5*; North Egremont, Prospect Lake, return by Ox Bow Summit, Baldwin Hill—*14*; Otis Reservoir—*19*; Pittsfield—*20*; Sage's Ravine—*12*; Sage's Ravine, return by Chapinville, Cooper Hill —*27*; Sheffield—*6*; Stockbridge, by Glendale—*16*; Tipping Rock, by Mill River, return by Southfield, New Marlboro', Lake Buel—*26*; The Dome Summit—*14*. Between Sheffield and Great Barrington are *7* roads, and *21* trips returning by different roads from *13* to *23* miles.

an easy victory[1] and many officers' wives attended their husbands, promising themselves an agreeable trip to New York. On the eve of surrender, the illuminated mansion of General Schuyler rang, says the *Brunswick Journal*, "with singing, laughter, and the jingling of glasses," as Burgoyne and his companions made merry over a royal supper. Outside, cold and hungry officers slept on the ground, and wet through and through by rains Baroness Riedesdel lay down with her children upon straw before an open fire. Next day General Schuyler's Saratoga mansion was burned to the ground as a military necessity, and rebuilt in fifteen days by General Gates's army with timber drawn from the forest.

The closing scene of Shays's Rebellion, that singular revolt caused by hard times after the Revolution, took place in Great Barrington. Paper money was worth nothing and the best of folks were obliged to go to jail for want of money to pay taxes. The editor of the *Worcester Spy* took subscriptions in salt pork. Captain Hamlin and other

---

[1] While Baroness Riedesdel was the guest of Mrs. Schuyler, "One of her little girls, on just coming into the house, exclaimed, 'Oh Mama! is this the palace papa was to have when he came to America?' As the Schuyler family understood German, Madam Riedesdel colored at the remark, which however was pleasantly got over."—*Life of Peter Van Schaick*.

Pond's Brook, Huntington.

Of the fraternity of hill-streams of Western Massachusetts. Here Bryant wrote "I never can Forget," a fact mentioned by him to George William Curtis.

characters in Bellamy's *Duke of Stockbridge* were real personages hereabouts.

Great Barrington is rich in rivers,—the Housatonic, the
Williams, and that loved by Bryant, the pellucid Green River,
filled with sparkles of light; the Indians called it Waum-
paniksepoot—White River,—but the Settlement Committee
changed the name of this surpassingly beautiful stream—
flowing down from Austerlitz, N. Y., through Alford and Egremont—to accord with the color of its waters. Bryant fled
from the drudgery of law to the banks of Green River seeking a lonely hour in his favorite refuge under a tree overhang-
ing the stream on the estate of the late J. Milton Mackie.
Bryant filled several town offices and Dr. Arthur Lawrence
writes: "It was Bryant's duty as town clerk to publish the
banns of marriage in the church, which was generally done
by reading them aloud; but in his own case he pinned the
required notice on the door of the vestibule, and kept carefully out of sight." [1]   As Justice of the Peace, he twice
performed the marriage ceremony, and an old gentleman
made it his boast that he was "jined to his first old woman
by Squire Bryant."

One of Nature's marvels is the sunset light flung against
East Mountain, and to me the sweetest of Bryant's verse
written here is *A Walk at Sunset*.

> *"Oh sun! that o'er the western mountains now*
> *Go'st down in glory! ever beautiful*
>
> .   .   .   .
>
> *Yet, loveliest are thy setting smiles, and fair,*
> *Fairest of all that earth beholds, the hues*
> *That live among the clouds, and flush the air,*
> *Lingering and deepening at the hour of dews."*

Every one climbs the flower-decked path of Mount Peter;

---

[1] "Bryant and the Berkshire Hills," *The Century Magazine*, July, 1895.

blue-bells and columbine find a foothold in the crevices of blue limestone. North of Mount Peter (so called for Captain Peter Ingersoll) is Kellogg Terrace, the estate of Mrs. E. F. Searles. The Hopkins Memorial Manse of solid granite was erected by Mrs. Mary Hopkins Searles for the Congregational church, in honor of its first pastor, the pupil and intimate friend of Jonathan Edwards—Rev. Samuel Hopkins, D.D. He is the hero of *The Minister's Wooing*. General Ives and the Hon. John Whiting were Major-Generals of Militia. The Hon. Increase Sumner was prominent in civic affairs for nearly fifty years.

Great Barrington was the County Seat until the courts were removed to Lenox in 1787. In that epoch the distinguished lawyer Major-General Thomas Ives was prominent in town and military affairs. Mrs. Ives was a granddaughter of General Dwight, and a daughter of the Hon. Jedediah Foster of Brookfield, Mass. The Misses Ives were great belles, and one of their ball invitations printed on the back of a playing card in 1810 is in the possession of Miss Harriet Wells.

Mr. Fuller's Public Ball
The Miss Ives
company is requested at Mr. Ruggles
ball-room on Friday Feb. 2nd, at 6 o'clock P.M.

H. D. Sedgwick ⎫
S. Jones   ⎬ *Managers*
C. Webster   ⎭

A great charm of the town is its magnificent view-points— to Prospect Rock or East Rock on Mount Bryant is a fairly hard climb, but, within half a mile of the railroad station, an easy path creeps upward through a sunshiny hill pasture bordered by a green wood; pine-needles strewn over tree-roots offer an agreeable seat in the forest balcony on the edge of the hill; across swaying tree-tops swells The Dome of the Taconics. The inspiring landscape of valley and mountain extends into three States. As evening approaches, the wood-thrush pipes in harmony with the lines of Cowper:

Morning.   The East Road to Sheffield.

"No noise is here, or one that hinders thought;
Stillness accompanied with sounds like these
Charms more than silence.   Meditation here
May think down hours to moments.   Here the heart
May give a useful lesson to the head
And learning wiser grow without his books."

The road to Alford and the East Road to Sheffield are

rivals in beauty.   The latter skirts June Mountain (named for Benjamin June who cleared it) and crosses Sheffield Plain. From Sheffield, The Dome [1] of the Taconics appears so near and so soft in its outlines that one would never dream of that ragged, precipitous Bash Bish gorge on its slope.   The famous Sage's Ravine lies between Race and Bear mountains, and the Ice Gulf west of Lake Buel.

In Sheffield is Barnard Mountain and the Barnard homestead, the home of Major-General Barnard, "the soldier-scholar of our Civil War"; Dr. Frederick A. P. Barnard, President of Columbia University, was born in Sheffield, and Daniel Dewey Barnard, minister to Prussia; also, George F. Root, the composer.   Not far from Sheffield's "Big Elm," in which "The Autocrat" delighted, lived the Rev. Orville Dewey, one of the best beloved exponents of Unitarianism. The "Friendly Union" building is a memorial to Dr. Dewey.

---

[1] The usual way of ascending The Dome from South Egremont is to ride some ten miles into the village of Mount Washington within twenty minutes of the summit.   A romantic path from South Egremont on the eastern side is described by Mr. John Coleman Adams: "Like most well-regulated mountain trails this one began in a wood-road, old and grass-grown and mossy" (*Nature Studies in Berkshire*, G. P. Putnam's Sons).

FROM GREAT BARRINGTON TO LITCHFIELD

THE UNDER MOUNTAIN ROAD

THE finest of all fine roads in Lower Berkshire is the Under Mountain Road lying between Great Barrington and Salisbury, Conn. It runs nearly parallel with the summit line of the Taconic Range—at a respectful distance, thus commanding a fine perspective. In the first miles out of Great Barrington, you pass near the scene of Shays's fight in 1787 and a corner of Bow-Wow and the Curtis homestead in its pretty green mountain frame; the road borders the lofty township of Mount Washington, the extreme southwestern corner of Berkshire. Mount Washington was long the home of the "Sky Farm poets," Elaine and Dora R. Goodale; an armful of *Apple-Blossoms* made them famous.

From the Under Mountain Road you may turn aside at the Connecticut boundary and visit Sage's Ravine, a beautiful but fearsome spot where one would not wish to lose his path with night coming on. Or you may turn east to the blue waters of Salisbury's glorious Twin Lakes—Panaheconnok and Hokonkamok, or Washining and Washinee, the "Laughing Water" and the "Smiling Water." North of the lakes rises Babes' Hill, east is Miles Mountain and bold Tom's Barack.

Washining and Washinee were the beautiful daughters of an old and tyrannical chief who claimed the land between the Housatonic and the Hudson: suitors travelled from far council-fires, but none were accepted. War was made on the chief by a hostile tribe, but the Weatogue band were crafty, and the young leader was captured and

In the Moon of Harvest, the Under Mountain Road, Salisbury, Conn.

"*Now comes the Autumn seeming not unlike the golden sheaf of its own ripened grain,*

The gentian and the aster, purple fringed . . ."

JOSEPHINE CANNING.

condemned to death by torture.   Each of the sisters secretly
fell in love with the captive brave, and brought him food.
They begged their obdurate father to set him free; finally,
wild with grief, the sisters confessed to each other their
secret.   The evening arrived before the fateful day of
torture and no reprieve.   Then the dusky maidens pushed
off their frail canoe into the moonlit waves and sprang into
the lake together.   They say that when the moon is at the
full an empty canoe is seen floating, it may be on Washining, it may be on Washinee; if you gaze long it will fade
away, and the stillness is broken only by the hoot of the
night-owl.

The Weatogue district or "wigwam place" borders the
west bank of the Housatonic in Salisbury on the early trail
joining the Stockbridge wigwams with those of the Schaghticokes below the village of Kent, traced by the apple-trees
which have sprung up in the wake of the moccasin; near
Weatogue's Council Elm many relics of the tribe have been
found.   Dutcher's Bridge spans the river between the
Russell farm and Dutcher's on the Canaan[1] side.

It was in 1720 that three men, Dutcher, Knickerbacker,

---

[1] Canaan on the Housatonic is very lovely with gentle, undulating hills
encircling its homesteads.   The Blackberry River or Bromfoxit, willow-
fringed, enhances the beauty of the pasture-lands and the railroad
follows its course, high above, on a terrace of drift.   On Canaan summit
is Lake Mangum.   On the river stands the house (1747) of an ironmaster
pioneer, Squire Samuel Forbes; it is the home of Mrs. Mary Geikie Adam,
whose illustrated Sketch of Canaan is included in *The Connecticut
Quarterly* of April, 1896.   The homestead of William Adam was built in
1808.   Canaan Falls possesses a certain grandeur; other cascades among
the Litchfield Hills are the romantic glade Kent Falls and the Maiden's
Well, the falls in Roxbury—the native town of Col. Seth Warner, who
took Crown Point,—and those at New Milford.

The hill-town of Norfolk owes much to its first minister, one of the
remarkable men in Litchfield County, and an early educator, the Rev.
Ammi Ruhamah Robbins; also to the Battells and the Eldridge family.
It is famous for its unusual privileges in music, the Library, and Eldridge
Gymnasium.

and Johannes Dyckman, Captain of the Livingston Manor company of militia, purchased land of William Gaylord and one Noble of New Milford, who possessed a grant here. The English Puritans came later from Windsor, and Swiss and Russian colliers were imported to smelt the rich iron-ore

Angoras "in Clover." Connecticut.

beds of Salisbury. There was as great excitement on the Connecticut border over Ore Hill and Mt. Riga as over the California gold-fields in '49. These early settlers have bequeathed to Salisbury a varied nomenclature—no other township in Connecticut has kept so many Indian names;

the very titles of her mountains, hollows and witching water-ways invite you to come and see and wonder, for Salisbury on the border is peculiarly beautiful and interesting, and the air pure and exhilarating.

It is still an open question as to whether unique Mount Riga was named by the Swiss colliers Mount Rhigi, or Riga by the Russians who came to work the Old Furnace (the Ball's Forge of 1781) on the mountain. Mount Riga combines the attractions of three mountains in one. The road to the Old Furnace winds four miles along a sprightly, tumbling creek—Wachocastinook or Fell Kill, haunt of speckled trout; two thirds of the distance up, the distant music of falling water entices you to the edge of the deep green ravine. Near the Old Furnace is the Pettee home-stead, built by one of the ironmasters associated with Coffing and Holley in shipping iron to the United States armories for muskets; and from Salisbury iron was made the great chain stretched across the Hudson, defying British warships.

It is surprising to find a chain of lakes high up in the air, and more surprising to see Riga Lake mountain-locked by higher peaks. From Lotus Lodge, the camp of the Hon. Donald T. Warner, the effect is startling and like artificial scenery, especially when the three encircling mountains—Brace (in Connecticut) and Buck (in New York State) and the poetical Alandar (of Massachusetts)—are decked in Autumn's scarlet and crimson and orange with a hint of olive; the pond itself, by reflection, is like a huge strawberry-colored bowl; Riga might be called the Lake of the three States. A road leads from Mount Riga to Bear Mountain, the highest peak in the State. The gilded globe on top of a monument erected by Robbins Battell of Norfolk is 2390 feet above tide-water.

As you enter the centre of Salisbury on the Under

Mountain Road, near Ball Brook is the Thomas Ball homestead of 1745, and beyond is the Scoville homestead.[1]   On
your right is the Lion's Head of the Taconic; the Clapp
house is now Maple Shade Inn.   Salisbury's log meeting-
house[2] was set so that its sill enclosed the stake driven into
the exact centre of the town.   A striking contrast in architecture is the old Bushnell Tavern and the modern
Scoville Memorial Library.   South is the John Churchill
Coffing homestead, the residence of the Hon. Donald T.
Warner.   An old saying is that the stranger who drinks of
the crystal springs which feed "The Kettle" will, without
doubt, return to Salisbury; and he must visit the Indian
Cave in the Wetauwanchu Mountain but half a mile distant.
In a house standing under bold Barack Matiff, Alexander
Hamilton studied civil engineering with Samuel Moore, the
eminent mathematician.

> In 1790 the Litchfield *Monitor* held this advertisement:
> "Salisbury Fair to be holden at the Meeting House Green
> in said Salisbury on the 13th of April inst., to begin at Sun-
> Rise and continue Three Days.   All persons inclining to
> attend may depend upon Fair Bargains and Civil Usage."

Wononscopomuc and Wononpakook welcome you at
Lakeville, formerly Salisbury Furnace; the brown hematite
is still dug out from a "live pit" in Ore Hill[3] which has been
worked for almost two centuries, and is shipped to Lime
Rock district and Canaan for smelting.   Ethan Allen had

---

[1] Residence of Mrs. Carrie Scoville Fisher.

[2] A lot for the first church was the gift of Colonel Robert Walker of
Stratford opposite the present parsonage.   Rev. Jonathan Lee's home-
lot was the present site of the Stiles house built in 1772.

[3] The story of Ore Hill and the ironmasters is included in Mr. Malcolm
Day Rudd's *Historical Sketch of Salisbury*, with an invaluable *Note on
Indian Names* by Irvin W. Sanford.   This is supplementary to Sanford's
capital Map of Salisbury.   *The Connecticut Quarterly* in 1904 published
an illustrated sketch of Lakeville, by Mr. Rudd.

iron interests here as well as Robert Livingston, who purchased the Jabez Swift house of 1773 on Old Town Hill, occupied for a time by Mrs. General Montgomery. Here was laid out a green and a market-place. From the Hotchkiss School on Old Town Hill and from Tory Hill are fine views. In Lakeville is the birthplace of Governor Alexander H.

The Governor Alexander H. Holley House; the Rudd Residence, Lakeville, Conn.

Holley and the Joshua Porter and Gen. Elisha Sterling homesteads. Between the lakes is the Warner homestead, and on Wononscopomuc is the Taconic School.

On leaving Lakeville to pursue your road southward to the home of the Schaghticokes in Kent, choose the road which enters the historic and beautiful town of Sharon [1] by

---

[1] The Governor John Cotton Smith house in Sharon is one of the finest specimens of architecture of the Georgian period. It is still perfect, having been built by skilled Italian workmen imported for the purpose. In the garret were discovered family documents interwoven recently into *Colonial Days and Ways* by Miss Helen A. Smith of Sharon.

way of Indian Pond or Wequadnach. Under Indian Mountain on the Millerton road stood an Indian village, where the Moravians established a mission, a fact well-nigh forgotten and long neglected. The story of the lake and mountain and mission has been told by the Rev. Edward Dyer of Sharon in his delightful volume on this northwestern corner of Connecticut, *Gnadensee, or the Lake of Grace*. It would be a novel adventure to ascend his "Stairs of Gnadensee," climbing mountain after mountain of Old Salisbury, a step higher each time from west to east; the first stair is Indian Mountain or Poquonnoc, "cleared land"; the next Mount Riga, then Bald Peak and Bear, and finally Berkshire's grand Dome of the Taconics.

In Northwestern Connecticut is "Hemlock Hollow," where the snow and ice rarely melt. According to a Scat-acook legend, the "Hollow" was the torture ground of the spirits of bad Indians. The soul of any one who died within its shadow could never escape their demon clutches. The fell spirits sometimes escaped for short periods and raised the fiercest storms.

THE SCHAGHTICOKES

At the point in Kent where the Housatonic swerves toward Connecticut's west boundary and turns away again, ragged Scatacook Mountain rises abruptly above a fertile interval—a green shelf as it were—on which cluster a few huts, remnant of the village of the Schaghticoke tribe, who sent out one hundred warriors to answer the call of Washington.

These organized a unique Committee of Correspondence and Safety between Stockbridge and the Sound, for it is said that they were able to communicate intelligence from the seaboard by significant Indian whoops or yells from their men stationed along the Housatonic. It is well known in Gaylordsville that the Indians often signalled members of the tribe who had gone to dig clams and oysters at Stratford by bonfires on Pickett Rocks (a high point above Ten-Mile-River) and on Straits Mountain and Candlewood.

Schaghticoke or Scatacook Mountain and The Housatonic.
Monicans from Shekomeko and Wequadnach joined the Schaghticokes just north on their Reservation.

From the huts, little paths lead to the spring and the hunting-traps. The Indians sell the skins of the rattle-snakes, which they hunt in the spring on Scatacook; Candle-wood Mountain has "rattlers" too. Scatacook is smothered in arbutus and laurel and in out-of-the way nooks you may chance on "the whippoorwill's shoe" as old Abigail says the squaws call the pink moccasin flower, because it

is as shy as the whippoorwill, of which there are many on
Scatacook. They all go down "lampereeling" for silver
eels at Eel Rocks or Great Falls at New Milford by inherited
right.

The last of the royal line was Eunice Mahwee, a grandchild of good Gideon Mahneesman, the first convert at
Pachgatgoch (1743), the Moravian Mission here. The
Indian burial-ground is north in Kent on the Raymond
farm on the old lands of the Reservation, which the Indians
sold, being indifferent to agriculture.

> Some say the Schaghticokes were Mohicans, some
> Pequots; whence they came is a mystery; these may have
> been of the Iroquois, at all events they doubtless held with
> other tribes the prehistoric tradition that mankind came
> out of caves. A Mohawk chief told a missionary that his
> people "had once dwelt in earth where it was dark and no
> sun did shine. Though they followed hunting they ate
> mice caught with their hands. Ganawagakha (one of
> them) accidently found a hole to get out of the earth;
> he went out; he found a deer which he took back with
> him, it tasted very good; he found the country above so
> beautiful that their mother brought them all out, and
> then planted corn."

The Housatonic winds with calm grace past the wild
Scatacook, then tumbles into cataracts, at Bull's Bridge
or one might say *did* tumble, for the mad and delicious
turbulence of the river here is now held in leash by a fine
exploit in engineering; the new dam compels the Housatonic
to turn far-distant wheels within wheels at Waterbury;
but alas! lost are the whirling eddies attacked by the Indian
with his spear, caused by the spirited leap upon leap between
narrow walls of the mighty stream to reach its goal—the sea.

When Ensign William Gaylord [1] was granted 1000 acres

---

[1] The first William Gaylord or Gaillard (the Gaillards were from

Whemenuck Farm or "Cross Roads."
Ebenezer Gaylord built this homestead in 1800 for his son Daniel Harvey Gaylord in the event of his marriage.   Gaylord residence.

in New Milford township (some miles south of the home of the Schaghticokes, and the meeting of the Webotuck with the Housatonic) he found Old Siacus, one of the tribe, living in a hut above The Straits, at what is now Gaylord's bridge; his beloved apple-orchard had been sold out with the township by his chiefs, but he was allowed by Ensign Gaylord (of the train-band) to stay and enjoy his apple-trees, the "Old Siacus orchard."   It is related by one of the Gaylords that being grateful he attached himself as a follower of the family, and, on an Indian uprising, "carried

Château Gaillard in Normandy) came on the *Mary and John* and signed the first land grants in Dorchester.   He then went to Windsor with the Rev. John Warham, and Widow Gaylord devised twenty acres of land to the church of Windsor forever.   There exists to-day a town, Gaylord by name, in Kansas, Michigan, Minnesota, Montana, and Virginia.

my grandmother and her child on his back to safety in the woods."

Through the Gaylord home-lot ripples *Naromiyock-nowhusunkatankschunk*, otherwise Deep or Big Brook; this name has been handed down by the Gaylords of the "Old Red Abbey" homestead. "Grandfather Gaylord" at the Cross-Roads jotted down the aboriginal names in his note-book. Red Plum Plains, that is the whole valley here, is *Whemenuck;* Cat Rocks is *Motompquasuc;* Long Mountain, *Quanictuck;* Cedar Hill, entered through the horse-shoe bars, is *Pawquiak.* In the Gaylordsville home-stead, Charles Seelye Gaylord, the artist, was born. The Gaylord grant included Town Hill, New Milford, where the Ingleside School and Christ Church now stand. In the earlier Milford deeds, the Housatonic is always "The Great River" until 1744, when in a deed by William Sherman, father of Roger Sherman, to William Gaylord, the Houssatunnick River is mentioned.[1]

The Hon. Orange Merwin, whose house stood at "Merry-all," New Milford, travelled on horseback to Washington City, when a member of Congress. He writes home to Mr. Daniel H. Gaylord at the Cross-Roads (now Gaylordsville):

Washington, Feb. 20, 1826.

"My dear Friend.—

"The state of society here, is easy and pleasant, a person can associate with such as he chooses—the most stylish and extravagant can find others like themselves, whilst the more plain, sensible, and prudent, are respected and easily assimilate. . . . The utmost ease of manners and equality of deportment is shown . . . and no notice

---

[1] This, "in the Seventeenth year of the Reign of our Sovereign Lord George the Second over Great Brittain, King Defender of the Faith," etc., is signed in the presence of Abel Wright, Jr., William Gaylord, Roger Sherman. The Gaylord deeds are possessed by Mrs. Henry E. Bostwick.

is taken of any peculiarity of appearance or character.
Mr. Adams himself is a plain man with simple Republican
manners.   Mrs. Gaylord may perhaps inquire—how is Mrs.
Adams?—At the Levees her usual dress is white silk
flounced with rows of [blurred] a long mantle shawl, hand
wrought, a head dress of flowrets and hair in ringlets—she

*The Hon. Elijah Boardman House, of 1793, New Milford on the Housatonic.
Residence of Mrs. George Wm. Wright.*

is elegant, easy and graceful, a very interesting woman—
here you may find beauty and fashion with all their charms.
. . . You talk and chat with anyone, sip a cup of tea, partake
of viands   .   .   .   carried through the crowd by servants,
and finding yourself at length weary, quite pleased,—if
small talk, fine bows and pretty faces are calculated to
please you,—sentiment here has nothing to do; if you are
well dressed and can say some simple thing in an easy way,
you pass off for a Gentleman, the Ladies smiling upon you
at every step—"

Again Mr. Merwin writes:

"Our Mess consists of Mallary, Waters and Swift of Vermont, Wright, Vinton and Woods of Ohio, Wing of Michigan and Barker and myself of Conn. . . . The house was engaged about ten days in deciding whether the damage done by a negro in the line before New Orleans should be paid for or not; in the debate Genl. Jackson was represented a tyrant, a monster, whilst the next man would describe him as a hero, a patriot, a benefactor—Cuffe in the meantime would be forgotten for hours together—this was no matter however as the speeches were designed for the good people at home and not for Cuffe. . . ." [1]

On leaving New Milford, where was built the first bridge across the Housatonic, one may see the remaining lakes of the Lake Country by taking the road to Litchfield, which skirts Lake Waramaug set in steep wooded heights, such as remind one of the beautiful Highlands of the Hudson. Lake Bantam at Litchfield, of some 900 acres, is the largest in the State.

---

[1] Hitherto unpublished. By the courtesy of Miss Jeannette Gaylord.

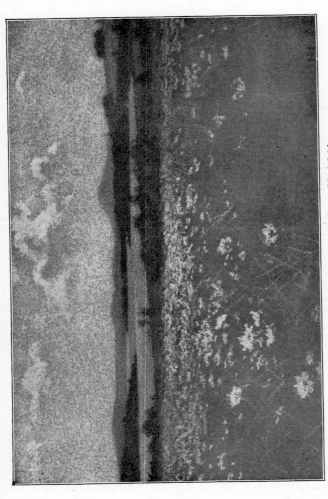

Bantam Lake and Mount Tom, Litchfield.

"*I want, I want the field's unbounded space.*
Where throbbing germs spring up and flowers blow;
I want, I want as a young colt to race
Through meadows, lithe and free;
I want the rainbow's colors all aglow, the fathoms of the sea!"

ADA NEGRI (One shut-in-doors).

366

LITCHFIELD, 1720–1724

*"There were a good many cogs in the mighty wheel which turned the machinery of the American Revolution. The swords of Washington, Greene and Lafayette—the eloquence of Adams, Henry and Lee—the pens of Franklin, Jefferson and Jay—were equally necessary, the good work was achieved not by an individual but by a multitude. Peyton Randolph was not the only eminent Crown officer who forced a bill of attainder—Putnam was not the only farmer who left one horse in the furrow, and mounted the other in his farmer's frock to speed the battle muster, . . . the mechanic who gave his all—his labor, and sat up night and day to forge the pike-peak . . . and the maiden who stopped not to weep over her slain lover, but handed up cartridges and carried water to the dying soldiers . . . were each but one among a thousand."—*RANDALL'S *Life of Jefferson.*

The Beecher Elm.

ANY a New England mile lies between Old Portsmouth and Salem by the sea and Litchfield on the west border, yet the stranger is conscious of a kinship between the stately town among the hills and the seaports. There is a certain grace of architecture and dignity common to the homes of colonial days, a kinship of motive and action which speak, although the setting may sharply differ; on the coast the merchant houses stood often at the head of a lane leading up from the owner's wharf, or even on a cow-path; in Connecticut the lay of the land chosen by the settlers is generally high, and

367

Litchfield's two old-fashioned, lovable, livable grass-rib-boned streets are of double width, and cross at right angles on a lofty plateau, crowned by many an elm, "the most beautiful vegetable of the Temperate Zone." At neighborly distances, in strong simplicity the homesteads stand flanked by luxuriant apple-blooms; the wayside is

Deming Homestead, "The Lindens," North Street.
Erected 1790–3. William Sprats, Architect (London) for Captain Julius Deming A. A. C. G., "Eastern Division," Continental Army. Residence of the Hon. J. Deming Perkins.

yellow with buttercups and butterflies, and the wind blows fresh from Mount Tom and his brother hills, across the pasture-lands, ruffling Bantam Lake and the gentle river.

One of several unusually fine houses of the Georgian period on lower North Street is architecturally correct in every part. It was built for the merchant Julius Deming

"*Town Hill Street*" (*South St.*) *Litchfield.*
*The Elihu Harrison house, residence of Mr. James Parsons Woodruff;
and the residence of the Hon. George M. Woodruff.*

24

(formerly of Lyme) by William Sprats, a London architect acting with the King's forces; he had chosen to remain in America, and the first house of his design was that of General Champion at East Haddam.   Certain houses on the North River are known as "Sprats" houses.

There is a striking analogy between the reflections of a "yellow haired little rascal" in Portsmouth and young Oliver Wolcott of Litchfield (Judge Oliver Wolcott, Secretary of the Treasury and Governor of Connecticut) on the strange gloom of a New England Sunday, "when people who were prosperous, natural and happy on Saturday became the most rueful of human beings in the brief space of twelve hours. . . . It was merely old Puritan austerity cropping out once a week."   You remember the description of the "Bad Boy"—Tom Bailey (Aldrich):

"It is Sunday morning . . . the deep gloom which has settled over everything set in like a heavy fog on Saturday evening.   At seven o'clock my grandfather comes smilelessly down stairs.   He is dressed in black, and looks as if he had lost all his friends during the night.   Miss Abigail, likewise in black, looks as if she were prepared to bury them and not indisposed to enjoy the ceremony: . . . My grandfather looks up and inquires in a sepulchral voice if I am ready for Sabbath school—I like the Sabbath school; there are bright young faces there at all events.   When I get out in the sunshine alone, I draw a long breath; I would turn a somersault up against Neighbor Penhallow's newly painted fence if I had n't my best trousers on, so glad am I to escape from the oppressive atmosphere of the Nutter House."

Oliver Wolcott, Jr., says:

"Sunday was to me the most uncomfortable day of the week, from the confinement in dress and locomotion which it imposed on me after Prayers and Breakfast.   I was taken by my mother to a Wash Tub and thoroughly scrubbed with Soap and Water from head to foot. I was then dressed in my Sunday Habit which, as I was growing fast, was almost constantly too small. My usual dress at other times was a thin pair of Trousers and a Jacket of linsey-woolsey; and I wore no shoes except in frosty weather. On Sunday morning I was robed in Scarlet Cloth Coat with Silver Buttons, a white Silk Vest, white Cotton Stockings, tight Shoes, Scarlet Cloth Breeches with silver buttons to match my Coat, a close Stock, Ruffles at the Breast of my Jacket, and a cocked Beaver Hat with gold laced Band. In this attire I was marched to the Meeting House with orders not to soil my clothes, and to sit still, and by no means to play during meeting time. . . . Mr. Champion[1] not infrequently exchanged Sunday services with the neighboring Parson, whose performances were most uncomfortable . . . in the afternoon they frequently exceeded two hours. As I was not allowed to sleep during meeting time, my sufferings were frequently extreme.

" After service new toils awaited me. Our Sunday was in fact the old Jewish Sabbath, continued from sunset to sunset. In the interval from the end of services in the Meeting House until sunset, my father read to the family from the Bible or some printed sermon, and when he was done, I was examined by my mother in the Assembly's Shorter Catechism. I learned to recite this in self-defense; and I comprehended it then as well as at any time afterwards. When this task was ended, I was allowed to resume my ordinary Habit. It exhilarates my spirits, even at present, to think of the ecstacies I enjoyed when I put on my Jacket and Trousers and quit my Stockings and Shoes.

---

[1] An historic event in the old Litchfield meeting house was the remarkable prayer of Parson Champion on the going out of the Revolutionary troops. One of the greatest of American orations, *The Age of Homespun*, was delivered by Horace Bushnell at the Centennial of Litchfield County; the poem was also by a native of Litchfield, the Rev. John Pierpont, and the address by Judge Samuel Church.

I used to run to the Garden Lawn or into the orchard;
I would leap, run, lie down and roll on the grass, in
short play all the gambols of a fat calf when loosened from
confinement." [1]

Litchfield, as the frontier village of Bantam (so-called
from the Bantam Indians), had five palisaded houses. A
pioneer, Captain Jacob Griswold, at work alone in the fields
west of the present Court-house in 1772, was pinioned by
two Indians, carried into the Canaan wilderness, and bound
hand and foot. Griswold cleverly disengaged his feet while
his captors slept and, seizing their guns in spite of pinioned
arms, took the home trail. The Indians overtook him after
a time; he pointed one of his pieces and they fell back: thus
he travelled until sunset brought him near Bantam, when he
fired and called the villagers to the rescue.

Litchfield was at the crossing of many post-roads and at
the opening of the Revolution became an important depot
of supplies; soon after the new County of Litchfield was
established in 1751, Oliver Wolcott was elected High
Sheriff. He came to reside in Litchfield, building a house
on South Street, on land bequeathed him by his father,
Major-General Roger Wolcott, poet and Governor, and
first on the seating roll of the church at East Windsor.
From this house (the oldest standing in Litchfield) he
went out to the Continental Congress; a signer of the Declaration of Independence, he was also Major-General, Brigadier-General, and Commissioner of Indian Affairs, and
took part in the battle of Saratoga. Governor Oliver
Wolcott held more offices than any other of the famous
Wolcotts, whose ancestral seat in the "Old Home" is
Galdon Manor, and the unsullied motto on their knightly
arms—*accustomed to swear in the words of no master.*

---

[1] *Litchfield Book of Days*, edited by George C. Boswell. Alex. B.
Shumway, Litchfield.

At the Door of the Wolcott Mansion, Litchfield, Conn.

Elizabeth Wolcott Merchant and Livingston Tallmadge Merchant, great-great-great-grandchildren of Oliver Wolcott and great-great-great-great-grandchildren of William Floyd, each a Signer of the Declaration of Independence. The house was erected in 1753 on "Town Hill Street" by Oliver Wolcott. Birthplace of Oliver Wolcott, Jr., Secretary of the Treasury, and of Frederick Wolcott. The home of Miss Alice Wolcott.

Ursula Wolcott, a sister of Oliver, holds a unique position in American annals as the daughter, sister, wife, mother, and aunt of Governors of Connecticut: she became the wife of Governor Matthew Griswold of Blackhall, Lyme. When the young and retiring Matthew Griswold was Governor Roger Wolcott's private secretary, he fell desperately in love with his daughter, sweet Mistress Ursula, which she divined. One day as he met her on the stairs, scarcely daring to lift his eyes to the beautiful creature of his dreams, she remarked mischievously, "What did you say, Mr. Griswold?"—"Noth—nothing, Miss Wolcott,"—"Well, it is time you did."

Revolutionary days were most exciting in Litchfield and particularly at the Wolcott house: soon after the Sons of Liberty tore down the statue of George III., Oliver Wolcott transported it to Litchfield, and Madam Wolcott, her daughters, the Marvins, and other neighbors moulded it into bullets in the Wolcott orchard; Oliver Wolcott, Jr., at nineteen was quartermaster and had the difficult task of collecting supplies and forwarding them to the army; when the infamous Tryon descended on Danbury and Norwalk, young Oliver and the veteran hunter Paul Peck went out with the last few men capable of bearing arms in Litchfield. Colonel Elisha Sheldon of North Street was in the heat of battle with his famous Second Light Dragoons in which Major Tallmadge commanded a troop. Yet in spite of the depletion of Litchfield of able-bodied men, the crops were gathered in by patriot women and boys. At the crucial moment of need, when General Washington asked more supplies of "Brother Jonathan" Trumbull, he was not disappointed, and watched with joy the wagon-trains from Hartford and Litchfield wind up the hill at Newburgh, at the appointed moment promised by Governor Trumbull.

One of the Kilbourn[1] family, Appleton Kilbourn (admitted a freeman of Litchfield in 1762), was a methodical farmer and probably had never been ten miles from home.

The home of Judge James Gould, North Street, built by Colonel Elisha Sheldon in 1760; in a small building which stood in the garden, sessions of the Law School were held. When Samuel Sheldon kept tavern here, General Washington spent a night in the northeast room. For many years the summer home of Professor James Mason Hoppin of New Haven. Now owned by Mrs. James Mason Hoppin, Jr.

To church to mill was the extent of his travels. One pleasant September morning in 1780, "Uncle App." mounted Dobbin and set out for East Mill with a load of grain. On reaching the old tavern at County House corner, a friend

---

[1] *The Kilbourn Genealogy*, by Payne Kenyon Kilbourne.

called out: " Hi! Uncle App.—you 're a *leetle* too late again as usual."—"Why—what has happened now?"—"General Washington and his suite have just left for the westward, there they go"; in an instant Dobbin was seen dashing off at full speed down West Hill—the bags bounding with every jump, and the rider's long skirts streaming, till the front of the procession was gained. Suddenly wheeling his horse Uncle App. confronted the chieftain face to face. "Are you General Washington?"—"I am, Sir."—"God Almighty bless you!" waving his hat in the air, and next moment he quietly pursued his way to the mill.

LANDMARKS: South St.: East side— The Noyes Memorial Building containing the Litchfield and Wolcott Memorial Libraries and Collection of the Litchfield Historical Society; a Memorial to Mrs. William Curtis Noyes by Mr. John A. Vanderpoel; D. A. R. Memorial Window to the Litchfield County Patriots of the Revolution, designed by Frederic Crowninshield; unveiled and presented by the Mary Floyd Tallmadge Chapter to the Litchfield Historical Society, on its semi-centennial celebration, July 5, 1907. This building stands on the site of the Ebenezer Marsh house (1759). Ancient elm used for sign post to present date. St. Michael's Episcopal Church. Phineas Minor house (1819) Benjamin Hanks-Abraham C. Smith house (1780) Dr. Alanson Abbey house, residence William H. Sanford, Esq. Gov. Oliver Wolcott homestead (1753). Reynold Marvin house (1773); King's attorney in the reign of George III.; enlarged by Phineas Bradley, and occupied by Gideon H. Hollister, historian and Minister to Hayti; Belden residence. On the southeast corner of Gallows Lane and Lake St. is a well, marking the home of Nathaniel Woodruff (conveyed to him by John French in 1721), whose property was largely at South Farms, now Morris. Site of the supposed birthplace of Ethan Allen now occupied by Thomas

Washington passed through Litchfield on his road between West Point and Hartford more than once. The conferences between Washington and the French officers were held inland, as it was unsafe on the coast. In Washington's first visit to Litchfield, accompanied by Hamilton, they stayed at the home of Oliver Wolcott; on another occasion, stopping at the Sheldon Tavern on North Street, Washington entered through one of the most beautiful doorways in the land, to which he was attended by his horse-guards. This house, built by Colonel Elisha Sheldon, is best known as the Judge Gould or Professor James Hoppin house; for a time the residence of General Uriah Tracy, United States Senator, it was long the home of

Jewelled Trees, " Town Hill Street," Litchfield.

" The elm boughs bend, like a searching thought,
With their silvery weight of beauty caught." —BARRY STRATON. *The Silver Frost.*

The Seymour Homestead of 1784, built by Samuel Seymour, Captain of Militia. Now "The Rectory," a gift to St. Michael's
Parish by Mrs. Truman, a niece of Captain Seymour. Birthplace of Horatio Seymour; and for a few years the home of the
Rt. Rev. William S. Perry, Bishop of Iowa, Residence of Dr. Origen Storrs Seymour.

377

Aylmar house; others say he was born in a house on the West Goshen road. Abner Baldwin-John Phelps house (1794). On South Street, west side, is a strikingly handsome house built by Gen. Elijah Wadsworth (1799), enlarged by Governor Oliver Wolcott the second; residence of Colonel George B. Sanford. The Chief Justice Charles B. Andrews place. Lyman J. Smith - Gen. Woodruff house, residence of Mrs. John H. Hubbard. Judge Tapping Reeve-Ogden house (1773), residence of Charles H. Woodruff, Esq. George C. Woodruff house, on site of the Major Moses Seymour house (1735), residence Judge George M. Woodruff; additions made by Major Seymour during the Revolution to contain supplies. Ozias Seymour homestead (1807), residence Hon. Morris Seymour; birthplace Chief-Justice Origen Storrs Seymour and Judge E. W. Seymour. Moses Seymour, Jr.-Josiah G. Beckwith house. Phelps Opera House on site of Catlin's Tavern; famous gatherings held in the Assembly room; in 1807, Jerome Bonaparte and his wife drew up with coach and four. Martin Van Buren and Adams lodged here. West Park or Training Green. *North Street:* Phœnix Bank building (1815). Old Whipping-post elm, at County Jail. Thomas Sheldon-Tallmadge house (1775), residence of Mrs. Emily Noyes Vanderpoel; birthplace of Frederick A. Tallmadge. Sheldon-Gould house (1760). Allen Butler house, residence of Frederick Deming, Esq. Dr. Daniel Sheldon – Theron Beach homestead (1783), long the home of Mrs. N. Rochester Child, property of Captain Edgar Beach Van Winkle. Perkins house, "The Glebe," on site of Parson Champion house, property of Mrs. William Woodville Rockwell. Congregational Parsonage on site of James Brace place. Old Beecher well on the estate of Henry

the eminent jurist, Judge James Gould; he was associated with Judge Tapping Reeve in Litchfield's celebrated Law-School.

On his ride between Litchfield and Hartford, doubtless many impending questions were settled by Washington. The time of Washington's absence at Hartford in September, 1780, was that chosen by Benedict Arnold to betray West Point into the hands of the enemy. This very journey of Washington was also the indirect means of the capture of Major André, first aid-de-camp of Clinton; as, in the disguise of a countryman, while hastening on with the fatal plans in his stockings, he was arrested by a small band of patriot farmers belonging to the strict patrol corps formed to insure Washington's safe journey to Hartford.

Count Jean Axel de Fersen,[1] aid-de-camp of Rochambeau, gives an interesting description of Washington on the occasion of this conference at Hartford, in a letter to his father from Newport.

" About fifteen days ago I went to Hartford with Mon-

[1] The same Count Axel de Fersen who played an interesting part in the French Revolution and assisted the King in his flight to Varennes.

The Colonel Benjamin Tallmadge–William Curtis Noyes House.
Built by Thomas Sheldon in 1775. Residence of a Great-Granddaughter of
Mary Floyd Tallmadge—Mrs. Emily Noyes Vanderpoel. Colonel
Tallmadge, the friend of Washington and Lafayette, the first treasurer
of the Connecticut Society of the Cincinnati was one of the picturesque
figures of his time; in the southeast room—the Colonel's office—every
morning his wife used to powder his queue.

R. Jones, Esq. Lynde Lord-William Deming house (1771); summer residence of Mrs. E. Le R. Ferry. Alexander Catlin-Dr. Henry W. Buel house. Dr. Buel founded the Spring Hill Sanatorium. Reuben Webster house (1786), summer residence of Mrs. W. H. Maxwell. Deming-Perkins house. Smith-Asa Bacon house, Coit residence. West Street' formerly "Old Meeting-House St.", Eli Smith house (1780), Kenney residence; here about 1800, Toby Cleaves curled the wigs of Litchfield "notables." Luke Lewis house (1781), property of Miss Phelps, built by John Collins, son of Rev. Timothy Collins, first minister. David Buel house (1787), now sieur de Rochambeau. There were only six of us; the general, the admiral, Viscount Rochambeau (the general's son), a superior officer of the engineering corps, and two aid-de-camps. An interview was arranged between Washington and Rochambeau. I was sent on slightly in advance, to announce Rochambeau's approach, and thus had an opportunity to study this most illustrious man

United States Hotel; ball given to Lafayette, 1824. Gen. Timothy Skinner-Hon. Seth P. Beers house. (1787), Webster-Candee house Milestone (1787) at Elm Ridge placed by Jedediah Strong. Birthplace of Horace Bushnell, son of Ensign Bushnell, at Bantam, on site of residence of Mrs. L. S. Kilbourn.

References: Woodruff's *Litchfield*. Kilbourne's *Litchfield*. *The Chronicles of a Pioneer School*. Compiled by Emily Noyes Vanderpoel. *Litchfield Book of Days*. Dwight's *Travels*. Barber's *Connecticut*. "Mary Floyd Tallmadge," by Elizabeth C. Buel in *Chapter Sketches of Connecticut D. A. R.* "Poganuc People," by Harriet Beecher Stowe. *Statistical Account of the Towns of Litchfield County*, by James Morris, Jr., founder of Morris Academy, 1790. *A Record of Inscriptions upon the Tombstones of Litchfield and Morris, Ct.*, by Dwight C. Kilbourne; *The Champion Genealogy* by Francis Bacon Trowbridge.

of our century. His majestic, handsome countenance is stamped with an honesty and a gentleness which correspond well with his moral qualities. He looks like a hero; . . . he is very cold, speaks little, but is frank and courteous in manner; a tinge of melancholy affects his whole bearing which renders him, if possible, more interesting. His suite outnumbered ours ; the Marquis de Lafayette ; General Knox of the artillery; Monsieur de Gauvion, a French officer of engineers: and six aid-de-camps besides an escort of twenty-two dragoons—indispensable, as he had to cross a country bristling with enemies. During our stay in Hartford the two generals and admirals were closeted together all day. The Marquis de Lafayette assisted as interpreter, as General Washington does not speak French, nor understand it. They separated, quite charmed with one another, at least they said so. It was on leaving Hartford that General Washington discovered Arnold's treachery. He was one of their most heroic generals, had been twice wounded, and always conducted himself bravely."

In the meantime André was carried a prisoner to North Castle, where Major Benjamin Tallmadge penetrated his disguise, for he saw by his manner of turning his heel as he restlessly paced the room that he was a military man. Eventually Major Tallmadge was appointed to attend André on the last fateful day at Tappan. Tallmadge writes: "I became so deeply attached to Major André, that I can remember no instance where my affections were so fully absorbed in any man."

After the war, Colonel Tallmadge brought his bride, Mary Floyd, daughter of General William Floyd, a Signer, to Litchfield. His devotion to the memory of Washington is shown even by the additions to the house he purchased, which resemble the wings at Mt. Vernon, and differ distinctly from the general architecture of Litchfield. The miniature of Mary Floyd Tallmadge, the patron saint of the Litchfield Daughters of the American Revolution, is in the possession of Mrs. Neely (Mary Floyd Delafield), wife of the Bishop of Maine. In the painting[1] by Earl, she is of a stately appearance with a head-dress of ostrich feathers and pearls. Her hand was sought by James Madison. The Tallmadge house is now the home of her great-granddaughter Mrs. Emily Noyes Vanderpoel, who compiled the history of the celebrated girls' school of Litchfield, conducted by Miss Sarah Pierce.

A letter to Colonel Tallmadge from Washington is in the unusually interesting collection of the Litchfield Historical Society; a chair from Mt. Vernon given to Governor Wolcott by Washington, also a chair from the Bradley Tavern in which Washington sat; the *MS.* of the first law reports of the U. S. by Ephraim Kirby; acorns from the oak at Fort Jedediah Huntington, Valley Forge; a silk bonnet sent from Paris by Margaret Fuller to Mrs. Gabriel Greeley (née Cheney); Colonial money, etc., collection of W. L. Ransom —silhouettes, egg-shell china, etc., endowed with traditions of Connecticut families.

The incident of several famous Tories being sent here

---

[1] The paintings by Ralph Earl of Mary Floyd Tallmadge and children, and of Colonel Benjamin Tallmadge, and son are in the possession of Mrs. Edward W. Seymour of Litchfield and New York. There is also an animated pencil sketch by Colonel Trumbull of Colonel Tallmadge.

for safe-keeping is recalled by a genuine Franklin stove, in possession of Judge George M. Woodruff, and brought to Litchfield soon after the Revolution. One of these royalists was William Franklin, estranged from his father by a determined loyalty to the crown; he was the last royal Governor of New Jersey being appointed by Lord Fairfax. It is said that Litchfield did not know what to do with this distinguished prisoner and allowed him to escape. Another was David Matthews, royalist Mayor of New York, who imported the first pleasure carriage to Litchfield.

Chief-Justice Tapping Reeve also served in the Revolution; Lafayette paid him a visit in his Litchfield house, which is of an hospitable architecture; above the stairs hangs the fire-bucket marked "T. Reeve 1." which in Colonial towns is the hall-mark of the country gentry, who composed the fire-brigade. Judge Reeve's brasses were all made in Litchfield, and like many country Squires his law-office adjoined his house. He started his law-school in 1784 and was principal for forty years. Nearly all the professional men[1] of prominence of that day were modelled under his eye. He married the sister of Aaron Burr, who lived with them for some time. The garden has many blossoms of the old garden planted by Miss Ogden; a deep red rose bush by the well has a famous rose similar to the American Beauty.

Aaron Burr was a handsome youth of twenty when he came hither to study law under Judge Reeve, his brother-in-law. He arrived direct from Fairfield, where he had

---

[1] A few of the graduates of Judge Reeve's law-school were John M. Clayton of Delaware, Colonel Theophilus Ransom of Lyme, Benjamin H. Rutledge, Chief Justice Richard Skinner, Governor of Vermont, Levi Woodbury, Marcus Morton. When John C. Calhoun attended the law-school it is said that he helped set out the elm trees on Prospect Street in front of the Reuben Webster house; "Calhoun held the trees and Webster threw in the dirt."

The dining-room at "Ardley," the residence of Miss Mary Perkins Quincy, Litchfield. Built after the colonial style. Howells, architect. The portrait is of Miss Quincy's grandfather, John Williams Quincy of Boston (from a painting by "the elder Sargent" in 1788), a great-grandson of Judge Edmund Quincy, whose portrait hangs in the adjoining hall; the original by Smybert is in the Copley room of the Boston Museum of Fine Arts. The sideboard (Chippendale), an heirloom, was owned by General Champion of Colchester, Conn.

met the beautiful Dorothy Quincy of Boston, at the house of his favorite cousin Thaddeus Burr. She was passing the summer at the home of Mr. Burr, her father's friend, under the chaperonage of Mistress Lydia Hancock, an aunt of her betrothed; the "rebel" John Hancock had contrived

The Old Bradleyville Tavern, Bantam, Litchfield.

Stages from Poughkeepsie stopped on their way to New Haven. In Dr. Beecher's day, weekly prayer-meetings were held here, and here he conceived the idea of his "Six Temperance Sermons." Now owned by Mrs. Mary Sedgwick Coe, a cousin of the distinguished General John Sedgwick of the Army of the Potomac, who was born not far away at "Cornwall Hollow."

to elude the red-coats and escort sweet Dorothy in his coach and four, far from war-turmoil at Boston, to serene Fairfield on the Sound. When "Cousin Aaron," the gay cavalier was presented to the stately and coquettish Miss Quincy, the pleasure was mutual, and "consequences disastrous to Hancock's peace of mind might have ensued had not the safe counsels of elders prevailed over youthful passion and folly."[1] In a letter to a friend, Miss Dorothy complains that Aunt Lydia would not allow them to pass a moment alone in each other's society; she finds Aaron Burr "a handsome young man with a pretty fortune." That he never refused a flirtation has been said, yet his conduct on this occasion was exemplary; he fled temptation, and made his adieux leaving shortly for Litchfield. The last festivity in the hospitable Burr mansion was the wedding of John Hancock, President of the Continental Congress, for in 1779, the house was burned to the ground by command of the relentless General Tryon.

Dr. Lyman Beecher lived on the corner of North and Prospect streets, and many are the stories of his remarkable family; "the world is made up of saints, sinners, and Beechers," is an old saying. In a letter to Mrs. Ensign H. Kellogg of Pittsfield, Dr. Holmes refers to Mrs. Stowe:

"BOSTON, Oct. 27, 1872.

" My dear Mrs. Kellogg:—

"   . . . I was not a little pleased that you and Mrs. Stowe agreed in a charitable opinion about such a heretic as I am—The real truth is, those Beechers are so chock-full of good, sound, square-stepping, strong-hearted humanity that they can't shut the door of their sympathy against Jew and Gentile—I find everywhere except among the older sort of people (you and I must be old too in time, but even I am not old)—and the smaller kind of human potatoes, —there is much more real 'Catholicism'—much more feeling that we are all in the same boat in a fog, than there was when I was studying Calvin's Essence of Christianity

---

[1] From the charming monograph of Miss Quincy of Litchfield, a great grand-niece of Madame Hancock—*Two Colonial Dames*, "*Dorothy Q.*" *and Dorothy Quincy Hancock.* Read by the author before the " Colonial Dames of America.".

25

in the Assembly Catechism. So I can understand that a couple of good-hearted and large-souled women manage to tolerate the existence of such a person as I am,—but to be spoken of so very kindly as you say Mrs. Stowe spoke of me, made me color up so, that I thought at first you had written on pink paper—it was the reflection of my blushes."

The life at the Beecher parsonage was typical of a New England country town. Miss Catherine Beecher describes that remarkable occasion, the minister's wood-spell.

"On some bright winter day, every person in the parish who chooses to do so sends in a sled load of wood as a present. . . . For nearly a week our kitchen was busy as an ant-hill . . . the cake was placed in large stone pots and earthenware jars and set around the kitchen fire and duly turned until the proper lightness was detected . . . and the bushels of doughnuts I boiled over the kitchen fire! . . . When the auspicious day arrived, the snow was thick, smooth and well packed for the occasion . . . and the whole town was astir . . . runners arrived with the news of gathering squadrons—Mount Tom was coming with all the farmers, Bradleyville also, Chestnut Hill and the North and South Settlements. . . . The boys heated the flip-irons, and passed around the cider and flip, while Aunt Esther and the daughters were as busy in serving the doughnuts, cake and cheese. And such a mountainous wood-pile as arose in our Yard never before was seen in ministerial donation!"

The Beecher house has been moved but the old well is still in its place and the Beecher elm.

Beecher Corner is still shaded by the elm with the ring to which Dr. Beecher hitched his horse. After meeting, he generally forgot his horse with proverbial absent-mindedness, of which many a tale has been handed down by

Bantam River, Litchfield, Conn.

387

his contemporaries.   Often when fishing o' week-days, a
mile away, at the Little Pond, in his boat, the "Yellow
Perch," the bell would summon him ashore to a forgotten
service, and he would make a hasty dash up-town behind
his pastoral nag.   At one unlooked for summons it is related that a fish dropped from his coat-tails as he mounted
the pulpit-stairs.   One of his Deacons on a fine spring day
found the Doctor trout-fishing.   "Dr. Beecher, how can
you, a minister of the Gospel, enjoy fishing! it is n't even
respectable."   "Then I 'll make it respectable, Sir," replied
the Doctor as he made another cast of the line.[1]

Another absent-minded man, much admired by Dr.
Beecher, was Judge Tapping Reeve:[2] a valuable legal document for which his family searched all night was discovered
stuffed into the bung of the vinegar barrel.

The era when flourished Miss Pierce's school for young
ladies (some three thousand were educated by her between
1792 and 1833) was the most picturesque in the history of
old Town Street.   Red coaches came and went, swinging
through Litchfield with cracking of whips and rattling
wheels from Hartford, Poughkeepsie, Boston, or New York.
Or, one might see a private coach and pair setting off with
some Litchfield Honorables to Philadelphia or Washington
in powdered queues and wrist ruffles, whenever sessions of
any consequence in legal or political crises were held.

It was a pretty sight on a spring morning to witness the
flutter at Miss Pierce's school as, at the sound of flute and
flageolet, young ladies, in ringlets and wide hoop-petti-
coats, started out on their promenade.   One had just
dropped her music practice, others had been studying the
graces of deportment or designing elaborate colored his-

---

[1] *Anecdotes of Two Beechers*, by Clarence Deming, a native of Litchfield.

[2] Dr. Lyman Beecher once said: "Oh, Judge Reeve, what a man he was!
When I get to heaven and meet him there what a shaking of hands there
will be."

torical charts for which the school was noted. And doubtless one might discover under glass in almost every State
of the Union, one of the exquisite samplers embroidered by
a scholar of Miss Pierce's school.

After a half mile the ranks of the procession would break
and the walk change to a stroll in the company of the young
gentlemen of Judge Reeve's law-school, the picturesque
effect being enhanced by the pink jackets of the students
from the South.   Whenever the young ladies went rowing

*The Summer Residence of Frank L. Underwood, Esq., of New York, on the
site of Miss Pierce's School, North Street, Litchfield.*

on Bantam River, or acted the plays written by their
preceptress in good Johnsonese, it was also with the assist-
ance of the law-school.

"My mother told me," said Mrs. B. of Litchfield, "that
when she came here to live there were six young ladies
in the Wolcott family; the law-school was just opposite
and the students would watch to catch a glimpse of the
beautiful Miss Wolcotts."   It is said that when one of the

Wolcott family was shining at Washington, the British
Ambassador remarked to General Uriah Tracy, "Your
countrywoman would be admired at St. James"; to which
General Tracy replied, "Why, sir, she is admired even on
Litchfield Hill." An aged French gentleman, Count S——,
who was a student at the law school at the time his family
was exiled in the First Revolution, called upon Mrs. Stowe
at Paris; he was most enthusiastic over society in Litchfield,
which he declared "the most charming in the world."

After all Litchfield is but little changed comparatively.
The modern homestead blends with the mellow charms of
elderly roofs in the happiest manner, especially in the case
of such Colonial houses as those of Miss Quincy, or the
Underwood summer home on North Street.

One discovers a simplicity and stateliness in the hospi-
talities of Litchfield carried down from the past, an aroma
of the period of leisurely grace, when the minuet and archery
were in favor. Even in the age when we had little leisure
for the social graces, and log-huts and homespun were the
chief products of the New England border, Colonel Francis
Lovelace wrote in a private letter to King Charles: "I
find some of these people have the breeding of courts, and
I cannot conceive how it is acquired."

INDEX

A

Abbey, Dr. Alanson, 376
Abbot, Archbishop, 106
Abbott, Rev. Abiel, 191
Abenakis, the, 177, 188
Adam, Mary Geikie, 354
Adam, William, 354
Adams, Mass., 330
Adams, John Coleman, 351
Adams, John Quincy, 364
Adams, Dr. Lucius, 223
Addison, Joseph, 226
Agassiz, 164
Albany, 10, 158, 177, 178, 203, 204, 264, 293, 294, 338, 340, 343
Albany Road, the (Deerfield), 59, 173, 191–193
Albany Road, the (Lenox), 288
Aldrich, T. B., 123, 267, 277 282, 284
Alford, 217
Algonquins, the, 181
Allen, Colonel, 340
Allen, Edward, 170
Allen, Ethan, 188, 302, 357, 376
Allen, Heman, 33
Allen, Samuel, 170
Allen, Rev. Thomas, 301, 304
Allen, Judge William A., 212
Allyn, Rev. John, 166
Allyn, Matthew, 49
Ames, Oakes, 29
Amherst, 192, 194, 196, 198, 199
Amsterdam, 3, 10
André, Major John, 86, 135, 378, 381
Andrew, Governor, 308
Andrews, Judge Charles B., 378
Andrews, Mrs. Emma, 258
Andrews family, 229
Andros, Sir Edmund, 34, 37, 98, 117, 167
Anne, Queen, 117, 118, 226, 227
Anthony family, 330
Appleton, Captain, 171
Appleton, Rev. Jesse, 191
Appleton, Nathan, 239, 246, 317, 320

Arms Corner, 162, 163
Arms, John, 186
Armstrong, Gen. S. C., 247
Arnold, Benedict, 65, 68, 90, 134, 136, 160, 231, 378
Arnold, Matthew, 215, 252, 253, 341, 342
Arthur, Chester Alan, 290
Ashburner, Luke, 223
Ashfield, Mass., 160, 215
Ashley, Capt. John, 218, 243
Ashpelon's raid, 172, 173
Aspinwall estate, 285
Atwater homestead, 131
Atwater, Jeremiah, 260
Atwater, Ward, 138
Auchmuty, Richard T., 275, 278, 290
Aupaumet, Capt. Hendrick, 225
Austen, Jane, 44, 190
Austin, Rev. James, 127
Avery, Christopher, 68
Avery, James, 67
Avery's Island, 68
Avila, Admiral, 2
Ayres (Ayer) homestead, 32
Ayscourt, Dr., 225

B

Bacon, Asa, 379
Bacon, Judge Ezekiel, 223
Bacon, Dr. Leonard, 1, 146
Baker, C. Alice, 160, 186, 187
Baldwin, Rev. A., 109
Baldwin, Abner, 378
Baldwin, Judge Henry, 127
Baldwin, Michael, 120
Baldwin, Ruth, 120–123
Ball, Thomas, 357
Ballard, Prof. Harlan H., 288, 319
Bancroft, George, 22, 213, 304
Barker, Judge James M., 310, 324
Barlow, Joel, 101, 120–122
Barnard, Daniel Denwy, 351
Barnard, Dr. Frederick, 351
Barnard house, 162
Barnard, Joseph, 162
Barnard, Dr. Lemuel, 228

Index 399

Hellegat (East River), 4, 5
Hempstead, Joshua, 71, 72
Hempstead, Robert, 71, 72
Henshaw, Judge Samuel, 212
Higginson, Francis, 103
Higginson, Rev. John, 102, 103, 106
Hill, George, 109
Hillhouse family, 97
Hillhouse, James, 127, 145
Hillhouse, James A., 129, 145
Hillhouse, William, 145
Hillhouse, Maj. William, 72
Hinsdale, Mass., 322
Hinsdale, Ebenezer, 162, 193
Hinsdale, Mehuman, 162, 167, 186
Hinsdell, Samuel, 161
Hoadley, John, 104, 109
Hoadley, Samuel, 108
Hockanum, Mass., 194–198
Hoffman, Mrs. Bernard, 244
Holland, 3, 18, 19, 158, 312
Holland, J. G., 214–216, 319
Holland, Lord, 7
Hollanders, 3, 4, 9
Holley, Gov. Alexander H., 358
Hollister, Gideon, 376
Holloway, Charlotte M., 73
Holmes, Oliver Wendell, 123, 171,
247, 275, 293, 294, 307, 316
Holmes, Rev. Stephen, 31
Holms, Rev. Abiel, 190
Holyoke, Elizur, 202
Holyoke, Mass., 199, 205
Hooker, Rev. John, 210
Hooker, Gen. Joseph, 196
Hooker, Thomas, 19, 29, 49, 159,
238, 298
Hoosac, 203, 233, 332
Hoosac Mountain, 159, 163, 234,
293, 296
Hoosac River, 234, 330–332
Hoosac Tunnel, 296, 332
Hopkins, Admiral, 71
Hopkins, Gov. Edward, 22
Hopkins, Mark, 222, 223, 226, 228,
242, 288, 313
Hopkins, Col. Mark, 344
Hopkins Memorial Manse, 344, 349
Hopkinson, Francis, 148
Hoppin, Prof. James Mason, 375,
376
Horsford, Eben Norton, 95, 97
Hotchkin, Rev. John, 278, 288
Hotchkiss, Parson, 32, 38
Hotchkiss, Russell, 138

Hotchkiss School, 358
Housatonic River, 3, 6, 152, 220–
351, 360–365
Howe, Judge Samuel, 213
Howe, William, 50
Howells, W. D., 163
Hoyt, David, 178
Hoyt, Gen. Epaphras, 191-192
Hoyt house, 162
Hoyt, Jonathan, 192
Hoyt Tavern, 162, 189
Hubbard, Amos, 79
Hubbard, Daniel, 107
Hubbard, Gardiner G., 87
Hubbard, Mrs. John H., 378
Hubbard, Samuel, 104
Hubbell, Matthew, 327, 328
Hubbell, Wolcott, 327, 328
Hudson River, 4, 5, 12, 84, 94,
365
Huguenots, 5
Hull, Commodore Isaac, 33, 138
Hull, Commodore Joseph, 33
Hunt, William M., 161
Huntington, Judge Andrew, 79
Huntington, Arriah, 198
Huntington, Cornelia, 87
Huntington, Rt. Rev. F. D., 194
198, 212.
Huntington, Gen. Jabez, 79
Huntington, Gen. Jedediah, 66,
79, 148, 381
Huntington, Capt. Joshua, 79
Huntington, Lydia, 79
Huntington, Gen. Samuel, 79, 149
152
Huntington, W. H., 53
Hurd, Ebenezer, 124
Hurlburt, Thomas, 26
Hurons, the, 181, 187
Hurst family, 164
Hutchinson, Ann, 5, 132
Hutchinson, Capt. Edward, 166
Hyde, Dr. Caleb, 250
Hyde, Major Caleb, 285
Hyde, homestead, 79

I

Ice Glen, Stockbridge, 220, 250, 292
Ingersoll, David, 342
Ingersoll, Peter, 345, 349
Ingleside School, 363
Ingraham, James, 31, 36
Iroquois, the, 27, 177

Index

2   113